SLOW BALL CARTOONIST

Slow Ball Cartoonist

*The Extraordinary Life of Indiana Native
and Pulitzer Prize Winner John T. McCutcheon
of the* Chicago Tribune

By Tony Garel-Frantzen

Purdue University Press
West Lafayette, Indiana

Cataloging-in-Publication data on file at the Library of Congress.

Cover image courtesy of the Virginia Kelly Karnes Archives and Special
Collections Research Center, Purdue University Libraries.

Paperback ISBN: 978-1-55753-730-0
ePub ISBN: 978-1-61249-433-3
ePDF ISBN: 978-1-61249-432-6

CONTENTS

FOREWORD

My GREAT-GREAT GRANDFATHER, Andrew McNally, was among the industry leaders in the late 1800s who helped transform Chicago into a world-class business center. He cofounded Rand McNally & Co., which would become famous for maps and other travel-related products. Another giant from that era who shared a passion for travel was *Chicago Tribune* cartoonist John T. McCutcheon—the plainspoken Indiana native and Purdue University graduate whose charming and delightful cartoons graced the pages of the newspaper from 1903 until his retirement in 1946. I am pleased to introduce readers to the story of his fascinating life.

More than a cartoonist, McCutcheon was a veteran world traveler, combat artist, and foreign correspondent whose drawings and illustrations provided readers with commentary and reflections about the day's scientific, political, commercial, and human progress at a time before television, Internet, and e-mail.

The gentle soul from rural Indiana quickly became a favorite among *Tribune* readers. His longtime friend, George Ade (a noted humorist and playwright), summed up why readers were so fond of McCutcheon in a 1903 book titled *Cartoons by McCutcheon* that was published by Chicago-based A. C. McClurg & Co.:

> Those who have studied and admired John McCutcheon's cartoons in the daily press have been favorably impressed by the two eminent characteristics of his intent: First, he cartoons public men without grossly insulting them. Second, he recognizes the very large and important fact that political events do not entirely fill the entire horizon of the American people.

When McCutcheon did cover politics, it was with gentle humor, clever artistic execution, and considerate treatment of the public figures he targeted with his pen. His style was in marked contrast to contemporary cartoonists who attacked public figures with a vicious wickedness. Noted his friend Ade: "McCutcheon tried to avoid hackneyed political subjects and give his readers pictures of their *real interest*—everyday life."

At the beginning of McCutcheon's career, the process for reproducing photographs in newspapers was not yet widely adopted. So, papers relied on a cartoonist to be a sort of graphic reporter, illustrating major news events by making sketches on scene. In the beginning, sporting events, courtroom trials, fires, and crime scenes were all part of McCutcheon's typical day's work. Eventually, however, he settled into cartoons exclusively.

McCutcheon may have had the soul of a poet, but his heart was all adventurer. He sketched General Pancho Villa as the Mexican Revolution leader sat menacingly holding a pistol. He was aboard Commodore George Dewey's flagship at the start of the Spanish-American War. He was likely the first civilian to fly in a warplane over a World War I battlefield. He hunted big game in Africa with Theodore Roosevelt. He rode horseback through Persia and Chinese Turkestan, explored the jungles of New Guinea, traveled the Gobi Desert in a motor car, and made two airplane trips to South America. The list goes on. All this before commercial airlines, ATMs, and cell phones.

John T. McCutcheon also likely crossed paths with Andrew McNally.

In 1889, an executive committee was formed to secure a location in Chicago for the World's Columbian Exposition. In addition to McNally, the committee included such famous members as industrialist George Pullman, steel magnate Charles H. Schwab, publisher Joseph Medill, and Chicago's thirty-third Mayor DeWitt C. Cregier. McCutcheon was assigned to provide sketches of the construction, opening, and ongoing events. The *Chicago Daily News* prominently featured his work. Thus, it seems likely that McNally and McCutcheon at least knew *of* each other.

In *Slow Ball Cartoonist*, Tony Garel-Frantzen chronicles all of McCutcheon's adventures, from his birth on a small rural farm near Lafayette in 1870, to his rise as the "Dean of American Cartoonists" and winner of the first-ever Pulitzer Prize awarded to the *Tribune* for McCutcheon's cartoon about bank failures in the Great Depression. I hope you enjoy reading the story of this great Indiana native, Purdue University graduate, and iconic Chicago figure.

Andrew McNally IV
Former Chairman and CEO
Rand McNally & Co.

December 2015

Author's Note

A FEW WORDS ABOUT how this book came to be. Early in my career I worked as a newspaper reporter and editorial cartoonist. On the reporting side, one of the beats was a high school district in the suburbs of Chicago. Shortly before I arrived at the newspaper, that high school district endured a bruising teacher's strike. In my view, several colleagues in the newsroom had deliberately, and perhaps unfairly, painted the administration in a poor light. So when I took over the beat, I tried instead to find positive stories to tell. The beleaguered high school officials were grateful. One day, after I no longer covered the high school, a box arrived with a copy of *Drawn From Memory*, by John T. McCutcheon (hereafter, "JTM"), the *Chicago Tribune's* longtime cartoonist. A handwritten note was inside:

> To Tony Garel-Frantzen, a promising cartoonist:
> From my collection of books by Hoosier authors
> —a cartoonist worthy of emulation.
> Best wishes from Gilbert R. Weldy, March 8, 1982

Gil Weldy was an assistant superintendent in that high school district I covered. A lifelong educator, he also was a Hoosier. Dr. Weldy was born in Indiana and earned his PhD in education from Indiana University. I did try to read JTM's book in 1982, but life (marriage, three kids, career, and all the etc. that goes with it) got in the way. So, Dr. Weldy's gift was placed on a bookshelf. I moved on from the newspaper business to a career in public relations and corporate communications. Then, thirty years later, itching to write my own book, I was searching for a topic close to my heart when I rediscovered JTM's volume. I would have liked to personally thank Dr. Weldy for his long-ago gift, but I learned in the course of working on *Slow Ball Cartoonist* that he passed away in 2008.[1]

After a few pages of reading, I realized why I never completed *Drawn From Memory*. To borrow a phrase from JTM himself, the autobiography can best be described as "rambling memoirs."[2] But by applying a little patience and imagining that JTM was personally telling me the story of his life, I came to realize what an extraordinary, kind, and gifted man he was. I became fascinated with how a boy born in 1870 on a farm in rural Indiana could end up as a war correspondent, cartoonist, and author. A graduate of Purdue University, he worked at the *Chicago Daily News* from 1889–1901 and at the *Chicago Record-Herald* from 1901–1903, before joining the *Chicago Tribune* in 1903, where he drew cartoons until his retirement in 1946. Along the way, he married Evelyn Shaw in 1917 and they had four children: John T., Evelyn, Shaw, and Barr.

JTM traveled the world extensively, hunting wild game, crossing deserts, riding in zeppelins across the Atlantic, and serving as a war correspondent. The list of famous (and notorious) people that he personally knew or met includes Theodore Roosevelt and his two sons, Franklin D. Roosevelt, Kenesaw Mountain Landis, Booth Tarkington, Pancho Villa, Ring Lardner, Billy Mitchell, Winston Churchill, and Carl Sandburg, to name a few. His 1931 cartoon, "A Wise Economist Asks a Question," won the *Chicago Tribune* its first-ever Pulitzer Prize. His cartoon, "Injun Summer," originally published in 1907, was reprinted each fall for decades by the *Tribune* (I remembered seeing it as a child). JTM authored eleven books.

He died June 10, 1949, and was inducted posthumously into the Indiana Journalism Hall of Fame in 1981.[3] Cartoonist Carey Orr followed JTM at the *Tribune*. Orr, lifting a phrase from his days playing semi-professional baseball with the Seattle Seals as a young man, wrote that "McCutcheon brought change of pace. He was the first to throw the slow ball in cartooning, to draw the human interest picture that was not produced to change votes or, to amend morals, but solely to amuse or to sympathize."[4]

What follows is the story of how one man drew delight from adventure and enjoyed an incredibly well-lived life pitching his slow ball cartoons.

NOTES

1 "Gilbert Ray Weldy (1923–2008)," *North Manchester Historical Society*, accessed November 11, 2013, http://www.nmanchesterhistory.org/obituary-gilbert-weldy.html.

2 John T. McCutcheon, *Drawn From Memory* (Indianapolis and New York: Bobbs-Merrill, Inc., 1949), 456.

3 "John T. McCutcheon-1981," *Indiana Journalism Hall of Fame*, accessed November 11, 2013, http://indianajournalismhof.org/1981/01/john-t-mccutcheon/.

4 "John T. McCutcheon," *Chicago Daily Tribune* (1923–1963), June 11, 1949, ProQuest Historical Newspapers.

1

A Sleepy Setting
of Uneventfulness

MANY IMPORTANT DEVELOPMENTS in US history that are taken for
granted today trace their beginnings to the year 1870. Americans
witnessed a step forward for women's rights on campus with the found-
ing of the first sorority—*Kappa Alpha Theta* at DePauw University in Gre-
encastle, Indiana.[1] New York City's first subway line opened for service.[2]
Groundbreaking began for construction of the Brooklyn Bridge.[3] John D.
Rockefeller incorporated the Standard Oil Company.[4] Congress created
the Department of Justice.[5]

But for the purposes of this story, a jackass and a particular birth
trumps all of these.

The first recorded instance of the use of a donkey to symbolize the
Democratic Party appeared on January 14, 1870, in a political cartoon
titled, *"A Live Jackass Kicking a Dead Lion,"* published in *Harper's Weekly*.[6]
Surely German-born American caricaturist and pioneering editorial

cartoonist Thomas Nast could not have known when he penned his piece for *Harper's* what a profound impact that unassuming ass would have on legions of political cartoonists and pundits who followed in his footsteps. Nor could the artist considered by many to be the "Father of the American Cartoon" have anticipated how the elephant that he would ink four years later as the symbol for the Republican Party also would become universally accepted and influence the next crop of cartoonists.

Including, it can be argued, the greatest cartoonist of his generation—John Tinney McCutcheon.

JTM was born on May 6, 1870, to Captain John Barr McCutcheon and Clara Glick McCutcheon in a farmhouse perched on a gentle hilltop near South Raub a few miles from Lafayette in rural Tippecanoe County, Indiana. John Barr McCutcheon was the son of Suzanna Caldwell and another John McCutcheon whose ancestors emigrated from Scotland. Together they had five children: John Barr, Margaret, Martha, Joseph, and George. John Barr, the eldest, was born in 1828 in Ohio. When John Barr was about five, his father moved the family to Indiana where he built the first brick house in Tippecanoe County. JTM described it as "located up the cross-road beyond the tollgate at our corner."[7] To JTM's boyish fancy, the house "seemed vast and impressive with its queer gables and diamond-shaped windowpanes surrounded by somber cedar trees."[8] JTM's grandfather went on to develop "a fine stock farm and accumulated considerable land." He died when JTM was one. Being his namesake, the family gave JTM his grandfather's gold watch, a gold-headed cane, and an oil painting portrait that depicted "a clean-shaven, clearcut face of strength and intelligence."

His mother's ancestors emigrated from Germany around 1749 and originally settled in Pennsylvania. JTM's maternal grandmother married Benjamin Glick. Like other pioneers at the time, the Glicks had a large family that included three daughters and five sons: Sarah, Clarissa, Mary, Elias, Daniel, Rufus, and Monroe. One child, Richard, died young. The family moved to Ohio, where JTM's mother, Clarissa, was born in 1841. Shortly thereafter, they moved west to the rich farming land of Tippecanoe County and settled several miles from JTM's other grandfather.

The Glick farmland fronted nearly a mile on the main route leading from Crawfordsville to Lafayette, a road that in 1850 had been improved by paving it with lumber planks two inches wide and twelve feet long to make the surface true and level. The improvement made it all that much easier to reach the Glick farm, which the poor and destitute new to the county were encouraged to do because the Glicks were a very hospitable family, to say the least. In addition, "the Glick homestead was headquarters for meetings of young people for miles about, and nearly always there was excitement of some kind"[9] at their place. Rare was the week that on a least one evening, twenty or more people did not gather to eat at the Glick table—and the number often swelled beyond that.

In anticipation of such crowds, "seining parties" were formed to gather fish. The men headed to the river with their reels and poles and bait and after a day's labor returned with a wagonload of fish. The Glicks also raised and kept several hounds for hunting, as the countryside was flush with wild geese, duck, turkey, pigeons, and quail. Fruit foraging parties also were organized by the older children to pick plums, grapes, berries, and nuts that grew wild in the prairie. It is fair to say the preparation, cooking, and cleanup of these feasts was an enormous task for the women of the Glick household, but the meals were always served promptly and cheerfully, and the food was well-prepared and abundant.

Around this time, Clarissa was blossoming into a woman and "was possessed of a beautiful face and form," JTM wrote. She was regarded as an expert in all types of house chores, a "fine horsewoman," and sang in a beautiful alto voice. "She was charitable and friendly to everybody," JTM recalled, "and was universally loved." When her mother died in 1855, it was only natural, given her upbringing and her temperament, that the management—and the bulk of the backbreaking daily work of the Glick family homestead—fell upon her young shoulders. As was her way, Clarissa graciously and eagerly accepted both.

When JTM's father was nineteen, he became a drover and wrangled hogs over the mountains to sell them in Pennsylvania. He gradually built up his business until he was "shipping very large droves." Then a depression began in 1857 after a series of bank collapses and his father's hog business failed. Rumors of war began circulating and in 1861, JTM's father helped recruit neighbors and friends in Tippecanoe County to fight in the Civil War; he was commissioned as captain of Company K, 15th Indiana Volunteers. While serving in Virginia, he was wounded at the battle of Greenbrier River in West Virginia. During the action, a shell fragment hit him, lodging behind his right ear and creating an injury that would never heal. He went on to fight battles at Shiloh, Inka Springs, Perryville, and Stone [sic] River; after the war, he resumed his cattle business. "My father was always known by his middle name of Barr," JTM wrote. Everyone regarded him as "a gay citizen, with a military beard, a broad-brimmed campaign hat and a jovial sense of humor. I have talked to many old ladies—belles of an earlier day—whose eyes have lighted up at the mention of 'Captain Barr.' Evidently he made love to all the girls in and around Lafayette until he met Clara Glick and his affliction ceased to wander."

A family friend, Will Wilgus, described JTM's father as follows:

> Captain Barr returned to peaceful pursuits followed by the love and devotion of his whole command. He returned (from the war) unmarried and heartwhole. Clarissa Glick, or Clara as she was called by her friends, had many suitors, but the man had not yet appeared who could win her away from her duty to her father and her home. The dashing Captain Barr soon became an active and persistent suitor. Her family unselfishly advised her to accept him, and their advice and the ardor of the captain's wooing gained the day. [10]

Captain Barr and Clara were married in October 1856. Clara's father gave her two farms as a wedding present, one of which was north of the Glick homestead on Romney Road. It was there that JTM's brother, George, was born in 1866. "Not long afterward," according to JTM, "the family moved to the less pretentious (farm) across from the Yellow Barn, where I came along on May 6, 1870." [11]

From the front porch during the day, the brothers could see the Yellow Barn—a weather-beaten notorious local icon. At ninety feet long and nearly fifty feet wide, it was more of a familiar landmark than the town of

Lafayette itself to the steady stream of travelers trudging westbound on Romney Road to seek their fortune in the government land grants being offered to points west and beyond. It was while playing one day in the Yellow Barn that JTM suffered an early disaster as a boy:

> My brother George's legs had the advantage of four years' growth over mine. In following him across some open joists, I failed to bridge a gap by a couple of inches. I fell and broke my nose, thereby distracting still further from an already minus quantity of pulchritude (i.e., beauty), which had previously occasioned some concern in the family.[12]

Although it is said that all babies are beautiful in the eyes of their mothers, JTM must have been an exception. Family legend has it that shortly after he was born, JTM's Uncle George (his father's brother) attempted to console Clara: "Don't worry," Uncle George assured her. "He'll look all right after a while."

The McCutcheon family land was surrounded by unending fields of corn on the Wea Plains (pronounced *we-aw* and named after an Indian tribe) not far from the mighty Wabash River—the longest free-flowing river east of the Mississippi. To the north lay the Tippecanoe battlefield where General William Henry Harrison (who would later become the ninth president of the United States and the first to die in office) defeated Indian warriors led by Tecumseh and his brother, the Shawnee "Prophet" Tenskwatawa. Naturally, conversations among adults at the time regularly concerned campaigns still being waged against Indians in the West and included news about the latest uprisings. One story in particular had a telling impact on the young John: the massacre of Lieutenant Colonel George Armstrong Custer at the Battle of the Little Bighorn in the eastern part of the Montana Territory. Custer, two of his brothers, a nephew, a brother-in-law, and 268 soldiers of the 7th Cavalry were killed.

The year was 1876. JTM was six years old:

> I must have listened popeyed to reports of the Custer massacre, for soon afterward I rushed into the kitchen screaming, "Ma! The Indians chased me!" as I retired to new line of defense where I knew I was always safe.

"To arms! To arms!" was my slogan in times of danger. I claimed to have escaped the onslaught of a presumably superior force unscathed except for a slight crisis of the nerves [he joked it was probably his first experience as a war correspondent]. In any event, there was little on my young horizon in the middle seventies beyond corn and Indian traditions.[13]

With Indian activity the all-consuming subject of daily discussion, it is no wonder that in 1800, Congress coined the name for the land "Indiana," meaning land of Indians. Amusements of any kind were few and far between for young boys growing up in rural Indiana in the 1870s, where the view of one's prospects for the future typically held as much excitement as the view of the endless rows of corn stretching mind-numbingly to the horizon. From today's perspective it sounds like a stifling existence, but JTM's felt differently: "I suppose I was much like any other small boy growing up on a farm, unless down there in Indiana we wore more freckles and less shoes. Even dressing in our little bare cold room was not a hardship, because we knew nothing different."[14] Besides, distractions included cornhuskings, barn raisings, spelling bees, weddings, and funerals—not to mention the sure-to-thrill option of venturing *beyond* the Yellow Barn. That's where one would find:

Jean La Pelle's house, silent and deserted and believed to be haunted. Something had happened there—another mystery! It bore a gruesome brand and was avoided by everyone. Up that same road plodded the local bogeyman, Thorntown Cyrus. He had become harmlessly demented at the death of his wife and now traveled through the country dragging a little wagon and a large doll. Thorntown Cyrus exercised such a hold on my imagination that whenever his name was invoked, I was always careful to behave. At night, I would lie in bed with nothing to do except listen to the kildeer [*sic*] birds calling across the misty bottom lands down by the creek. Later in the darkness, if the wind were right, the sound of an accordion came up from a neighbor's farm playing "The Year of Jubilo" or "Listen to the Mockingbird."[15]

One break in the monotony of farm life was the ride to town.

JTM's parents often took him and his brother George with them in the family surrey when they drove to Lafayette for supplies, banking, and other business errands. Captain Barr would soothe their boredom on the slow eight-mile ride with lyrical recitations that included geography jingles, commentary from current political pundits, and literary quotes from such ancient scribes as Sir Walter Scott. The surrey rides left a lasting impression on JTM, who gives credit to his father, whom he said:

> thrilled us then as I have seldom been thrilled since. Sometimes he would stop the horses, get out and be gone for a few mysterious moments. Upon his return, our eager voices arose, clamorous for information: "What's the matter, Pa? What d'you get out for, Pa? Where'd you go, Pa?" This rapid-fire quiz always brought the same answer: "I thought I saw a prairie chicken." Further cross-examination always disclosed his failure to catch the prairie chicken.[16]

Years later during long car trips, JTM would delight in using this handy euphemism for bathroom breaks on his own small sons who, once they caught on, also were similarly entertained.

Meanwhile, Captain Barr's career as a drover continued to boom and be profitable. When JTM was six years old, a prolonged depression in the country that began in 1873 continued to afflict the United States. Despite the downturn, "our family life," JTM wrote, "was always cheerful" and in 1875, family life got more interesting as Captain Barr and Clarissa gave birth to a third boy, Ben. No doubt the McCutcheon home was happy in part because Captain Barr's cattle herds could be encountered on almost every road and his beef was sold in markets as far east as Baltimore and as far north as Chicago. He kept a positive outlook when the markets went against him and often paid a bonus to farmers for their stock when the markets were on his side. Farmers would turn away other buyers, retaining their stock year after year for Captain Barr. But his business continued to have its ups and downs, in part because he was generous to a fault:

he was too kindhearted. He would give whenever he had. [His personal philosophy] was not the code of a money-maker. Friends and neighbors soon discovered this convenient weakness. His generosity was greatly admired but often abused. His [business] failure in the panic of 1857 resulted in the loss of $60,000—a lot of money even today. After the war, there was never an end of old soldiers coming to him. By the early 1870's he had regained considerable fortune, which he once more lost.[17]

Market conditions continued to worsen and in 1876, at the age of forty-eight, Captain Barr left his life as a drover. For all practical purposes, he had never been a farmer and had no intention or desire to become one, so he made career decision that would have a dramatic effect on JTM's future: Captain Barr became associated with Purdue University. JTM's horizon suddenly broadened beyond the green and yellow cornfields.

Exactly one year to the day before John was born, on May 6, 1869, the Indiana General Assembly accepted a gift of $150,000 from John Purdue, as well as $50,000 from Tippecanoe County and 100 acres of land near Lafayette from various residents to establish a college of science, technology, and agriculture in Purdue's name. Purdue, a successful industrialist and businessman from Lafayette, profited greatly during the Civil War by providing clothing, textiles, and other dry goods to the Union Army. Purdue would only enjoy watching his namesake develop for a short time because as fate would have it, he died in September 1876 on the first day of classes during the third year of the university's existence. The fledgling university was not much to speak of in those days:

> Purdue was only a little older than I. Its fame had hardly crossed the state line. The few buildings were crudely new; trees and vines had not yet started to soften a general baldness of the campus. Less than 100 students were in attendance. The list of alumni numbered one—an imposing uniqueness.[18]

Captain Barr took a job managing the university's commissariat and the family moved into the west end of Ladies' Hall on campus where they lived for about a year. JTM related that running the commissariat "is a euphemistic way of saying [my father] ran the place where the students ate, an occupation for which he was conspicuously unfitted." Not surprisingly, after a year at Purdue, Captain Barr "was in a frame of mind distinctly receptive to any change." Then in the summer of 1877, Captain Barr's friend James Baird was elected sheriff of Tippecanoe County. Baird offered the position of deputy sheriff to Captain Barr on the condition that he would live in the sheriff's residence adjoining the jail and oversee care of the prisoners.

The McCutcheons moved into the sheriff's residence where for two years JTM "lived in close and friendly relations with various criminals and malefactors, male and female, who were domiciled behind the sturdy walls and bars of the county calaboose. It was not perhaps a refining influence for a boy from seven to nine, yet, I found many likable qualities among the inmates."[19] During this period, a sister, Jessie, was born to the family. When JTM was ten years old, a new sheriff was elected thanks to "the vicissitudes of local politics." The family relocated to the tiny village of Elston, about two miles from Lafayette, and Captain Barr resumed his life as a drover. The family occupied a two-story brick house that belonged to a cousin. To the young JTM, it was not much of place:

> Go south from Lafayette, then with the Wabash River on your right, climb the hill past the old Lafayette Junction and go two miles farther. You will now arrive at the outskirts of Elston. If you are in a car, you will slide through it so quickly you are hardly aware it is a settlement. But in that day in 1880 there were no cars or even bicycles. Your horse-drawn vehicle would plod along, pass an occasional house, reach a tollgate no longer in use, and then perhaps draw up at a watering trough in front of a two-story brick store flanked by a one-story frame saloon. From this simple nucleus which constituted the business district, 20 to 30 unpretentious dwellings were strung out for a mile or so. In the blazing sun of a summer day, you could not find a sleepier setting of uneventfulness in all the land, yet it was the glamorous background for absorbing activities. A belief I've had for a long time is that it doesn't matter where one

is, it's wholly a matter of what one does while there that makes life inter-esting. Imagination is the handmaiden of adventure, and when aided by enterprise, no life can be wholly dull.[20]

During the summer, JTM accompanied Captain Barr to help him with the hog drives. The experience helped him acquire "a lot of information about [hog] habits that was later to be useful in my cartoon work." Driv-ing hogs is dirty work and after a long summer day of riding in the wake of a drove of hogs, "it was difficult to distinguish between the driver and the driven." But the trips offered JTM an opportunity to get to know his father better and Captain Barr proved to be quite the entertaining com-panion on the long drives:

> He talked and hummed a lot. He had a vast fund of reminiscences cov-ering the war and his life as a drover, which he told with keen humor. Nearly always, in the corner of his mouth was a much-chewed cigar, usu-ally unlighted. His beard and longish hair still had much of the jaunti-ness that made him such a romantic figure in Lafayette society. As the pair led their hogs down the road, men and women in wagons or those working in the farm fields would call out, "Hello, Barr!" Captain Barr would gesture with his whip, call out and sometimes stop and talk. He was never greeted as "Mr. McCutcheon" and the rank of "captain" was rarely used.[21]

He was arguably one of the most popular men in Tippecanoe County and knew more of its citizens than just about anyone else (this and his gre-garious personality probably accounted a few years later for his victory—despite his Democratic affiliation—in the sheriff's election in Republican-dominated Tippecanoe County, and his later election to the position of Lafayette treasurer).

In Elston, JTM attended Red Eye School—a country school about half a mile from where the family lived. Approximately fifty children of all grade levels attended the school. Although JTM never mentions in his autobiography how and when he first started drawing, a single sentence in the obituary published by the *New York Times* decades later offered a hint: "He began displaying his artistic genius as a schoolboy when he drew caricatures of his teacher on the blackboard during recess."[22]

When JTM advanced beyond Red Eye's curriculum, Clara and Captain Barr transferred him to Ford High School in Lafayette, which didn't sit well with him:

> Of all the wretched unhappy days of my life, those at the Ford were the most poignant. Torn from the easy yoke of the Red Eye, dropped among strangers, I was so acutely miserable that my parents, taking pity, withdrew me and arranged with the teacher at Red Eye, Pierce Arnold, a patient elderly man of scholarly attainments, to provide an additional class to fit me and a very fat and pleasant young lady named Jennie Geyer.[23]

To keep busy and earn spending money, JTM established a Sunday newspaper route that included about forty widely scattered farmhouses and residences. He awoke at 4 a.m. each Sunday—including the below-zero cold and predawn darkness-shrouded days of winter—and jogged two miles to Lafayette to get his papers. Driving the family buckboard (an open horse-drawn carriage), he delivered the papers on his ten-mile route and returned home for breakfast by 8 a.m. In what may have been his first artistic undertaking, he and a friend also formed a house and sign painting company and soon cornered the Elston sign painting market—although how skilled they were was another question. "Regardless of the quality of our work," he wrote, "I feel that the people were amused by our serious efforts and good-naturedly wanted to help us out, even though art suffered in the attempt."[24]

JTM began reading an eclectic assortment of periodicals, magazines, and books. On the one hand, he was an enthusiastic fan of *The Boys and Girls of New York* and *New York Weekly*—both of which were adventure publications full of exciting sea stories, pirate tales, tomes about trappers, Indian fights, and an ample supply of detective yarns. On the other hand, in his book pile also sat some strange neighbors to the cheap adventure yarns, including *A Boy's Version of Iliad*—Alfred John Church's adaptation of Homer's epic poem of the Trojan War and the ten-year siege of the city of Troy with its bloody battles between King Agamemnon and the warrior Achilles. It was written for young boys to get them interested in the Greek classics. Yet, for JTM, everything paled in comparison to the delight he took in reading Harry Castlemon's *Frank on a Gun Boat*—and all the other *Frank* stories. Harry Castlemon was the *nom de plume* of Charles Austin Fosdick, a prolific author whose adventure stories were targeted at boys. He was the most-read author among boys in the post-Civil War era, of which JTM was one. All of these provided the beginning influences on his creative abilities:

> This type of reading undoubtedly quickened my imagination and stirred an intense desire to do things. If a boy's family life is normal, and his parents are not unkind or unjust, the books he reads in the formative period of his boyhood are likely to be important character-makers.[25]

In an undertaking that mirrored his later career activities, JTM published a hand-printed and hand-illustrated newspaper called the *Elston News*, featuring advertisements, editorials, news items, and roughly drawn cartoons promoting the candidacy of Grover Cleveland in the 1884 US presidential election. He also dabbled as a playwright and actor, producing a play titled *The Blunders of a Bashful Dude*. Using "yards and yards of unbleached muslin" sewn together and stretched tightly on frames, JTM painted two backdrops and a curtain. The show had a two-night run at the Red Eye schoolhouse. He and some friends played the various roles and JTM's brother Ben served as usher and candy salesman. The schoolhouse was packed both nights because "there were no movies or radio or any other attractions in the community" in those days.

About this time, JTM began to dabble at drawing. He also began writing a weekly column for the *Lafayette Call* that "more or less contained poetry as well as a strong ingredient of public works propaganda," such as a campaign against local gunsmiths:

The gunsmiths of Lafayette kept their explosives in three little square brick powder magazines in Elston. I began an intensive campaign to have these removed, and pictured them a deadly menace to the safety of the community. The Lafayette readers of the Call must have thought, after several weeks of this crusade, that the good people of Elston were lying awake nights with indignation. As a matter of fact, I never heard any Elstonite express the slightest concern about the "deadly menace."[26]

In the back of JTM's various books and novels about pirates, distressed damsels, and sea-faring heroes of old, there was an odd collection of illustrations, mostly of schooners and calla lilies. He regarded the latter as a curious inclusion because his beloved adventure stories had as much to do with plant life as the pirates in those stories had to do with being law-fearing citizens. But there *was* a reason for the sailing ships. In the typical pirate and sea story of the day, the "low, rakish craft in the offing" invariably was a schooner. In fact, no good sea story "could get along without one," and JTM was fascinated by their majestic masts, fully deployed sails, and sleek but simple lines from bow to stern. Taken by this "seafaring mood," JTM did "one of the characteristically foolish things that lie plentifully sprinkled throughout my life": he bought a skiff from an acquaintance for $5—the profits of many weeks of delivering newspapers. He stored it in barn, "paying frequent visits to it." He even named it *Fanchon* (the Teutonic word for free), but he never took it on the water; it gradually disintegrated and one day it was "no more."

As if all this was not keeping him plenty busy, JTM enrolled in the Elston "Cleveland and Hendricks Drum Corps" where he learned to "beat a long [drum] roll and do fancy alterations on the rim of the snare drum." All in all, it was a full life for the young lad:

With my drum corps, my Elston News, my weekly column for the Lafayette Call, my painting business, the Sunday newspaper route, my school-work, and one thing and another, I was the busiest thing you ever saw.

Yet all this went on in a tiny village which the casual traveler, on passing through, would consider the dullest, most unstimulating spot in the country, if indeed he noticed it at all.[27]

In 1885, Captain Barr was elected sheriff of Tippecanoe County and the family moved back to the now-familiar sheriff's residence where they had lived from 1877–1879, opening "a new and fascinating phase of life" for JTM. JTM describes the facility's interior:

It was an imposing house with four huge rooms on each of two floors. Wide hallways separated the rooms. In the basement were the kitchen, laundry and service quarters, and backed up against this residence was the jail surrounded by a high brick wall. Adjoining our house was the office, reached by stone steps leading from the street. A large, cheerful prisoners' dining room came next, flanked by the women's cell. The women prisoners were permitted the use of this room when the men were not at meals; at those times the women were locked in their quarters behind a steel slab door. Beyond the dining room, and separated from it by another solid steel slab door and also a circular barred door which locked and unlocked by a lever operated from the outside, was the men's cell house. Half were for the "State" cases, the more serious crimes; the other half for milder offenses—vags, drunks and drunk-and-disorderlies.[28]

Meanwhile, JTM, now fifteen, entered the preparatory program at Purdue University—a supplementary year offered at the time in addition to the university's standard four-year curriculum. About three hundred students total were registered at Purdue when JTM enrolled—up from a mere total of six in 1874—the school's first official academic year. Purdue consisted of a three-story main building, a three-story men's dormitory, a chemistry lab, an engine house, a gymnasium, and the Ladies' Hall—where students ate—the same building the McCutcheon family lived in when JTM was a small boy. He was acutely aware that most of the students were "country boys like me," but a few carried an unmistakable mark of city savvy—the first he had ever seen. He was intimidated by the surroundings and his own self-esteem was in short supply:

I was shy and scared and appeared to myself in comparison hopelessly green and awkward, like a puppy who has been taken into a family and doesn't yet know if he is to be kept, ready to like everybody but too timid to make friends. The fact that I was the next-to-youngest in my class did not help. My abysmal shyness, my hero worship, my crushing sense of youthful greenness are etched in my memory. I remember my feeling of not being in the current of college life and my long rides to and from the campus from Elston.[29]

Life at the jailhouse would help change all that in short order. According to county rules, a jailer was supposed to sleep in an enclosed corner of the jail office and be ready to respond at a moment's notice any hour of the night when prisoners were brought into the building. Since JTM's father was the sheriff, when the jailer was absent for illness or other reasons, he convinced his dad to let him sleep in the jailer's bed at night where "many and exciting were the interruptions to my repose":

> One night I was aroused by what seemed to be a national uprising. I unbarred the door and a whirling mass of struggling figures surged in, made up mostly of police clubs and violent curses. Finally the huge, well-dressed form of Dan Scribner, the notorious confidence man, emerged panting and exhausted. I had to search him, place all his possessions, properly listed, in the jail safe; then take him—this time with police help—to a cell.[30]

His most noteworthy adventure at the jail involved a horse thief named Douglass Kramer. One morning, JTM was supervising the transfer of twenty prisoners from the dining room to their cells. Kramer, hiding behind the heavy steel door, surprised him when he returned, escaping to the street and slamming the door behind him. JTM grabbed a revolver from a desk drawer and ran outside in pursuit. Shouting "Halt!" he fired the gun several times as he chased Kramer. One bullet grazed Kramer and he fled across a street into a brewery yard. JTM finally cornered him and marched him back to jail at gunpoint. It got a "fine write-up" in the

Lafayette newspapers. "He Ran But Johnny McCutcheon Outlimbed and Outwinded Him" was the headline in the March 27, 1886, edition of the *Evening Call*, which included this account:

> Douglass Kramer, one of the Cass County thieves, made a bold attempt for liberty this morning, which would have proved successful had it not been for the bravery and intrepidity of a 15-year-old boy.[31]

Despite these occasional adventures, the daily household life in the jail for the McCutcheons basically was quiet but was "always busy and entertaining," thanks to Captain Barr's boundless generosity—and Clara's limitless patience:

> We never knew how many there would be for dinner. Old soldiers—my father couldn't turn them down—neighbors, everybody apparently felt welcome to drop in. My mother had a couple of [hired] girls to help her at this period and nothing seemed to ruffle her. She had a most gentle, patient disposition, calm and philosophical, with a delightful sense of humor and a character of gold.[32]

Meanwhile, back at Purdue, one day JTM noticed an upperclassman sitting down near the front of the hall at one of his lectures. He had a "delicately modeled face, strangely clean-cut and refined among its more rugged and corn-fed neighbors." His name was George Ade. In those painfully bashful and self-conscious days, JTM only could muster the courage to observe him from afar. He did not yet have an inkling that one day the phrase "Ade and McCutcheon" would be as common as "ham and eggs."

"FOR SOME REASON which I have now forgotten," JTM did not enter Purdue until three weeks after the rest of his class. In later years, he joked that from that day on he never caught up. He also frequently noted that he was always three weeks behind in algebra, a subject that for him was a sort of a perpetual guessing contest that always began the same way with the professor asserting "Let *x* equal so-and-so and let something else equal *y*." The mystery of what drove the professor's choice of *what equaled what* never revealed itself to him. This was unfortunate, for at Purdue, he had set out to study mechanical engineering, a course "beset with mathematics of a most virulent type." He struggled with the mathematics from the get-go and partway through his freshman year, he began showing acute signs of stress, including a loss of appetite and trouble sleeping.

One day, a friend asked, "Your heart isn't set on being a mechanical engineer, is it?" "No," he answered quickly. "I'd prefer to *graduate*." The friend then advised him to "switch to a course less infested with math," the industrial arts, which was "much more humane." He and a classmate named Bruce Rogers (who would go on to be one of the world's leading typographers and book designers) were the only males majoring in Purdue's industrial arts program—the rest were women; however, that "was not the reason I took it," JTM said. He was quite sure at the time that he had no serious intention toward pursuing art as a career. He recalled, "If the agricultural course had had still less math, I might have taken that." But the transfer to industrial arts not only enabled JTM to eventually graduate, but also changed his destiny from one road to another, altering the rest of his life's journey, and as far as he knew, the mechanical engineering field never "suffered any sense of loss" from his decision.

Following the advice that "learning to draw is learning to see"—one of the keystone teachings of an industrial arts professor who taught art—JTM's portrait drawings began to garner notice, as evidenced by a review in 1887 in a local newspaper:

> Young John T. McCutcheon, son of the Sheriff, a student at Purdue University, is developing a wonderful talent in portrait making. With an ordinary lead pencil or pen he has a faculty of making a correct likeness of anyone who chances to come within his vision. In the Sheriff's office is a portrait of President [James Henry] Smart of Purdue and of Deputy Sheriff John Kennedy. They are as clean and clear as though made by a first-class crayon artist.[33]

One of the first fraternities on the Purdue campus was Sigma Chi. In JTM's sophomore year, the Sigma Chi chapter delegated a member to "look [him] over" for the purposes of recruiting his membership. The assignment went to George Ade, the upperclassman whose profile JTM had been admiring in the lecture hall. "Evidently George's report . . . was favorable" because JTM was invited to join the Sigs. His membership in Sigma Chi and the numerous lifelong relationships he would enjoy as a result had a power-ful influence on his career, but "the greatest asset Sigma Chi gave" him . . . "was the friendship of George Ade." From the time they met and for more than ten years, through their college days at Purdue and through all of their early Chicago newspaper work, their paths "lay intimately together." Early on, he saw great things ahead for his friend:

> It is customary when a man becomes great for friends who knew him early on to claim they knew away back when that he was bound to suc-ceed. In this case, even my undeveloped instinct told me that here was an exceptional person . . . [who] gravitated to leadership with easy inevi-tability. When he first showed signs of embarking in literary work, his father, who was a prosperous banker in [their] old home town of Kent-land, and his brothers, who were well-to-do landowners, predicted a future for [George] that would contain very little money. When his Fables in Slang were syndicated [years later] and the royalties began rolling in in huge streams to his father's bank, the home folks were mystified and amazed. His brother began buying choice land for him until he owned 2,000 acres in the rich heart of the corn belt.[34]

Ade graduated two years before JTM in Purdue University's 1887 class, which consisted of eight students. He obtained a job at a Lafayette news-paper, which paid a miserly $6 a week. The pay was considered cheap even for the times and "another economy of the editor was to use old envelopes, split open, as copy paper."

When the deadline demands eased each afternoon for Ade, he and JTM went calling on young ladies who, at various times, wore the boys' Sigma Chi fraternity pins. To enhance their social skills with their "pinned" ladies, JTM wrote the titles of all the songs he and Ade knew—in whole or part—in a little book and numbered them, one to 165. They memorized which song went with which number. To entertain their girlfriends, they gave them the book and asked them to select any musical number. Then the boys would sing it. Despite their best effort, their acquaintances with the girls proved to be short-lived. Perhaps that is how Ade came upon the idea for a book, titled *"The Fable of the Two Mandolin Players"*:

A very attractive Debutante knew two Young Men who called on her every Thursday Evening, and brought their Mandolins along. They were Conventional Young Men, of the Kind that you see wearing Spring Over-coats in the Clothing Advertisements. One was named Fred, and the other was Eustace. The Mothers of the Neighborhood often remarked, "What Perfect Manners Fred and Eustace have!" Merely as an aside it may be added that Fred and Eustace were more Popular with the Mothers than they were with the Younger Set, although no one could say a Word against either of them.[35]

Summers typically were dull times but on occasion included some wild adventures, like the time JTM, Ade, and a friend names Jasper "Jap" Dresser decided to do some boating even though the Wabash River was "in high flood (and) spread far out over the bottoms, its angry, sullen current carrying branches, logs and other flotsam":

I don't know why we thought this would be a good time to go boat-ing, but (the boys) rowed up the old Erie Canal and then, some miles up, portaged the boat over into the Wabash and started down with the current, a mad rush homeward. Darkness came on. We shot under the Brown Street Bridge and then through the gloom we saw we were headed for one of the stone piers of the Main Street Bridge. Frantically, we used our oars and barely cleared it, but unfortunately we did not see the tree that jutted out from the tangled mass lodged against the pier and overhanging the swirling waters by only a couple feet. We ducked and tried to ward it off with our hands, but the swift current yanked the boat out from under us. We were left dangling from the tree, our legs in the rushing water. We yelled and yelled. Jap said he couldn't hang on any longer, but we begged him to because we couldn't help him. Finally, somebody heard us and just as Jap's hands were slipping, old Joker Hill came and rescued us. Joker Hill was the boatman at the end of the bridge, and we had chartered our craft from him. Later it transpired that he had first rescued his boat, thus distracting somewhat from the nobility of his heroic deed.[36]

In 1888, John traveled to Chicago for the first time—in fact the first time he had been outside of the state of Indiana—to see President Grover Cleveland as he appeared on a balcony at the Palmer House. He had never been near so many people in one place and "the crowd in the street was so dense I thought I would be suffocated."

During the summer of 1888, Captain Barr died after a short illness. The shell that had lodged behind his right ear during the Civil War had been removed decades earlier, but the entrance wound never fully healed. For more than twenty-two years, the dressing on the wound had to be changed daily. When a doctor in Lafayette finally succeeded in healing it "with some powerful drug," Captain Barr succumbed to blood poisoning immediately and died. The funeral procession was reported by local newspapers to be one of the largest ever witnessed in Lafayette. Obituaries in the local papers variously praised his honesty, affability, and generosity. His passing gave JTM pause to reflect on Captain Barr's life:

> As I think back about my father, he seems by force of economic unkindness to have been out of place in his daily activities. You thought of him as riding up on a spirited horse, sweeping his broad-brimmed hat in salutation to ladies of the old school. I don't remember ever seeing him fixing anything about the place. He seemed too elegant for anything like that. There always seemed to be other hands around even when the depression hung heaviest. He was never really a farmer, and even in his days as a drover his only chore was the care of a horse or two.[37]

Captain Barr died in the middle of his term as Lafayette treasurer and a portion of his annual salary of $3,600 was paid out to Clara; JTM's brother, George, was appointed to serve as acting deputy treasurer. The rest of the summer hung heavily over JTM except for the time when he and a friend decided to go "tramping" to "find out how far we could get on our wits." The trip began on the old wooden Brown Street Bridge where earlier that day two other young men murdered a man. For a time, JTM and his friend were chased by police who mistook them for the real suspects, who eventually were apprehended.

⸙⸙⸙⸙⸙⸙⸙⸙⸙⸙

IN HIS SENIOR YEAR, JTM served as coeditor of Purdue University's first yearbook, the *Debris*. The senior class "got it out as a memorial" and the name "was my suggestion." JTM did not speak French but thought the word *debris* meant a "mess of stuff." Although JTM graduated from Purdue in 1889 with a bachelor of science degree in industrial arts, he continued to provide art and other contributions to succeeding editions of the *Debris*. Another would-be artist by the name of Booth Tarkington also contributed to the yearbook. JTM wrote, "Had he continued in this promising field, [Tarkington] would have made a great name for himself, but he got sidetracked and took to writing."[38]

No doubt a wise decision as Booth Tarkington went on to become one of only three authors to win the Pulitzer Prize for fiction more than once.[39]

NOTES

1   "Leading Women," *Kappa Alpha Theta*, accessed November 11, 2013, http://www.kappaalphatheta.org.

2   Marc Santora, "When the New York City Subway Ran Without Rails," *New York Times*, August 14, 2013, http://www.nytimes.com.

3   "The Great Caisson: Foundations Laid for the Bridge from Brooklyn to New York," *San Francisco Chronicle* (1869–Current File), May 15, 1870, ProQuest Historical Newspapers.

4   "About Us," *ExxonMobil,* accessed November 11, 2013, http://www.exxonmobil.com /Corporate/history/about.

5   "The Department of Justice," *New York Times* (1851–2009) with Index (1851–1993), July 10, 1870, ProQuest Historical Newspapers.

6   "The Historic Elephant and Donkey: It Was Thomas Nast 'Father of the American Cartoon,' Who Brought Them Into Politics," *New York Times* (1857–1922), August 2, 1908, ProQuest Historical Newspapers.

7   John T. McCutcheon, *Drawn From Memory* (Indianapolis and New York: Bobbs-Merrill, Inc., 1949), 17.

8   Ibid.

9   Ibid., 21.

10   Ibid., 22.

11   Ibid.

12   Ibid., 16.

13   Ibid., 15.

14   Ibid., 17.

15   Ibid., 18.

16   Ibid.

17   Ibid., 23.

18   Ibid.

19   Ibid., 25.

20   Ibid., 26.

21   Ibid., 28.

22   "John McCutcheon, Noted Cartoonist," *New York Times* (1923–Current File), June 11, 1949. ProQuest Historical Newspapers.

23   McCutcheon, *Drawn From Memory*, 28.

24   Ibid., 29.

25   Ibid., 30.

26   Ibid., 34.

27   Ibid., 36.

28   Ibid., 38.

29   Ibid.

30   Ibid., 39.

31   Ibid., 40.

32   Ibid., 41.

33   Ibid., 43.

34   Ibid., 44.

35   George Ade, *Fables in Slang* (Chicago and New York: Herbert S. Stone and Company, 1899), 84.

36   McCutcheon, *Drawn From Memory*, 46.

37 Ibid., 47.

38 Ibid., 56.

39 "The Pulitzer Prizzes-Fiction," *The Pulitzer Prizes,* accessed November 12, 2013, www .pulitzer.org. Tarkington won for *The Magnificent Ambersons* in 1919 and *Alice Adams* in 1922. The other two authors were William Faulkner and John Updike.

2

YOUNG, GREEN, AND NOT A FRIEND IN THE CITY

A FEW MONTHS BEFORE JTM graduated from Purdue University, he received two job offers. The *Lafayette Journal* offered him a position editing news stories delivered by telegraph. The *Lafayette Courier* offered him a job as city editor. Both positions would start immediately, which would mean JTM would have to put his college career on hold. "Preferring to get my degree," JTM declined the offers and by the time he graduated, both positions had been filled. Although he had always intended to be "a writer of sorts," he was told by someone that "art paid better than writing." In 1889, newspaper artists were the source for all illustrations and drawings published in papers of the day. Artists drew pictures of everything because the process for reproducing photographs for halftone printing on large rotary presses was not adapted until 1897. They served as graphic reporters covering all the events that photographers would cover later. JTM spent a couple months after graduation "sizing up the drawings in

Chicago newspapers and sketching a number of samples that he could show." He asked Bob Jaques, owner of a Lafayette bookstore, for a letter of introduction to Horace Taylor—a fellow Sigma Chi brother and an artist employed at the *Chicago Herald.*

In the late summer of 1889, with $17 in his pocket and "not a friend in the city," JTM departed for Chicago and upon arrival checked in at the Windsor Hotel, near the corner of Dearborn and Madison streets. He met Taylor, who reviewed his samples and then offered the following advice: practice some more. Taylor also suggested JTM check out of the pricey Windsor and find a boardinghouse, which would be considerably cheaper and help conserve his limited capital. JTM rented a room for $6 a week, including board and lodging, "in a fairly decent place down on South Wabash Avenue." His stay didn't last long:

> All day I practiced drawing in that room and only went up for meals. One of the young lady boarders, a Miss Martin, was sympathetic, knowing— as who didn't?—that I was young and green. Then there was a shooting scrape upstairs and a police raid, and it dawned on me that all was not well, so I departed.[1]

After about a month in the city, JTM returned to Lafayette where he continued to work on his drawings for three weeks. In October, he returned to Chicago with a more robust portfolio. This time Taylor at the *Chicago Herald* took him across the street to the offices of the *Chicago Daily News,* where he "was taken on at once on two weeks' probation." His new boss was William "Schmetty" Schmedtgen, chief artist and head of the *Daily News* art department, and Schmedtgen spent much of his time at the courthouse covering a murder trial so "perhaps for this reason a helper was required." Whatever the reason, it proved to be a key factor in helping JTM successfully settle into his new life in Chicago:

> If I ever became an artist, it was largely due to the kindness of this gentleman, whose wise counsel guided me through those early years. Either he took a liking to me or took pity on me, because from the very start he

did everything to help me along. With endless patience, he drilled me in the rudiments of the profession. After only college publication experience, I doubt if I would have weathered the first few weeks had it not been for his unfailing help.[2]

After the two weeks of probation were concluded, Schmedtgen introduced JTM to Victor Lawson, the publisher of the *Chicago Daily News*. Lawson ended his probation and increased JTM's salary to $16 a week. He also promised to raise it to $20 if "I improved by the end of the month. Tremendous excitement! I was bursting with pride. Friends at home were getting $9 at most!"

Under Schmedtgen's direction, JTM drew all day long and the list of subject matter was virtually endless. For the first five years, most of his work centered on illustrating all types of major news events, working from sketches made on the scene. A typical day might include a courtroom trial in the morning, a sporting event, crime scene, local fire, or other catastrophe in the afternoon, and a show opening or charity event in the evening. When not scurrying from news event to news event, he developed numerous portraits of politicians, municipal officials, and dignitaries, which were used to accompany stories and columns. For one assignment in December 1889, he was sent to illustrate the interior architecture and other details of the newly constructed Auditorium Theater—Adler and Sullivan's 11-story, 4,200-seat structure that was considered an architectural wonder of the world with its massive edifice and modern new technology such as electric lighting and air conditioning.

JTM also wrote various features on his own initiative, showing "industry and ingenuity in getting up feature stuff, and the editors were pleased." These included a column called Artistic Doorways with his own illustrations, drawings of the Pullman Tower against the moon, and scenes from the stockyards. He also developed a series called "Scraps of Conversation in Different Hotels," which was "snatches to illustrate the types of people who frequented each hotel." This included the commercial and business travelers at the Palmer House, the stylish and well-to-do from high society at the Richelieu Hotel and the various clientele of a kind altogether unique unto themselves who frequented the lower-scale Grand Pacific Hotel and the Sherman House.

Meanwhile, in an unusual twist of fate, JTM graduated from life in the boardinghouse and upgraded his living quarters—thanks to arrangements made by, of all people, his mother Clara—and an early romantic interest.

As a child growing up on the farm, JTM was enamored with a Miss Lydia Jones, a pretty young schoolteacher whose parents were old friends of Clara and Captain Barr. Although he was only six at the time, the image of Jones was love at first sight. To the surprise of all, JTM's infatuation continued to persist for several years until it became a matter of family concern. Eventually, JTM mostly outgrew his attraction to Jones. Years later, this tendency of "little boys to fall in love with older young ladies provided cartoon material of the human-interest sort." Time passed and Lydia married a man named Charles Lang, settling in a house at 3113 South Michigan Avenue. Clara learned about this and helped arrange for JTM to be a boarder at the Lang house, which he shared not only with Lydia, but also her husband and their children. JTM recalled, "As there were six children, the atmosphere was homelike and nice, if somewhat crowded, and dampening to the last remnants of those early embers."[3]

In 1889, Schmedtgen produced a five-column cartoon featured on the front page of the *Chicago Daily News*, "but it so happened that Dr. [Frank W.] Reilly was not overly friendly to the chief artist, or to his cartoon style, and wanted to work me into his place." One day when Schmedtgen was away, JTM was ordered to draw a half-page cartoon. This was in December 1889, "long before I had given up realism," the name given to a drawing style that produced realistic newspaper art. It would be JTM's first political cartoon. The *Chicago Daily News* was supporting an attorney named Hempstead Washburne for mayor. Washburne was regarded as a highly reputable businessman, but something of an amateur in politics. For JTM the artist, it meant "I had to be made over into something requiring whimsy and, if possible, humor." He continued, "The next day they wanted another [cartoon] and they were drawn and printed—by far the largest drawings ever seen in a Chicago paper up to that time. What was my astonishment when on top of such unusual prominence, I was called in and detailed to draw a full-page one!" So impressed with his responsibility for the full-page cartoon, JTM worked all night on the assignment:

> The caption was to be "We Are the People," and it was to represent a great horde of aroused voters of all classes pouring through a triumphal arch on the way to the polls to elect the reform candidate. It was the first as well as the last of this size I ever did, although in later years several of my cartoons were reprinted on a full-page and in color.[4]

The cartoon ended up creating "something of a sensation." The publisher of the *Daily News*, Victor Lawson, ordered copies of it to be printed and presented to every employee of the paper. The original was framed and hung in Lawson's office, where it remained for many years.

JTM took a philosophical view of the turn of events:

> Perhaps in being selected to draw these conspicuous campaign cartoons, I was the unintentional beneficiary of the feud between the managing editor and the chief artist, who was at that time my very best friend. It might be called a piece of luck which was the outgrowth of conditions I had no part in forming.[5]

⸙⸙⸙⸙⸙⸙⸙⸙⸙⸙⸙

G EORGE ADE WAS STILL BACK IN INDIANA, suffering through a career launch that was languishing like a field of corn seed shriveling in a drought. In reality, his career had lurched, or more precisely, bumbled forward dubiously with an oddly eclectic series of jobs. At first, he worked for a Lafayette newspaper at a paltry $6 a week, then for $10 a week on another paper; the latter ended up plunging into bankruptcy shortly after he started. To make ends meet, Ade took a job generating publicity for a company selling a short-lived antismoking product, which was guaranteed to cure even the most persistent tobacco habit—if only the patient followed a *which-came-first—chicken-or-egg* requirement. The direction was: "Discontinue the use of tobacco." Therein lay the product's ultimate undoing.

Harry L. Kramer owned the company that made the antismoking cure. He also operated Mudlavia, a health resort located near Attica, Indiana. On the side, Kramer also pedaled Cascaret brand laxative tablets ("The things that work while you sleep") and published the *Lafayette City Directory*—a less-than-thriving directory and listing of local businesses. Kramer employed Ade to collect fees from the advertisers. Ade found such work less than a desirable outlet for his budding literary genius, so he was ripe for change when a letter from JTM arrived touting the glamorous life up north in Chicago.

JTM's seeds of propaganda fell on fertile soil.

Less than a year after JTM's arrival in the city of Chicago, Ade followed him northward to the bright lights. Based on the strength of a personal reference from JTM, Ade landed a job at the *Chicago Daily News*, which gave him "a try-out doing the weather at $12 a week." Of course, the chances of "holding him down to this humble niche were absolutely nil," as JTM could have told them, "Only somehow they always like to make such a discovery themselves." Although JTM certainly influenced Ade's decision to take his chances in Chicago, he was reluctant to take credit:

> Perhaps I played a role in getting George to Chicago. I should be proud to think I contributed even so little to his start along the brilliant trail he subsequently followed. But as a cold matter of fact, I know perfectly well that he would have succeeded no matter where or how handicapped the start.[6]

And succeed is exactly what Ade did, in a most propitious manner. His chance came one night when he was alone in the *Daily News* editorial offices. Much to the trepidation of the editor on duty that night, cub reporter Ade was going to get his chance as JTM had imagined. He was assigned to cover one of the worst river accidents in the city's history. After several hours on the scene at Randolph Street and the Chicago River talking to police, eyewitnesses, survivors, and medical personnel, Ade wrote and filed the story that ran in the *Chicago Daily News* and eventually was wired worldwide:

> This was the moment the steamer *Tioga* chose to blow up in the [Chicago] river. In despair, the editor had to send the cub weather reporter [Ade] to do the best he could with this whale of a story. The rest is history. It was a gem of reporting. His star had risen—or rather shot up. From that moment he became not *a*, but *the* star reporter. Thereafter he covered assignments of nationwide interest like the famous Homestead Strike and the John L. Sullivan vs. "Gentleman Jim" Corbett boxing fight when the invincible John L. was dethroned.[7]

Ade and JTM picked up the fellowship of their college days. Ade's "advent in Chicago, pleasantly trivial as it may have seemed at the time," proved to be a major influence on JTM's ultimate destiny. When he first arrived, Ade shared JTM's living arrangements at the Lang household on south Michigan Avenue. But since the pair often left the newspaper office late at night, the Lang residence was too far away to depend on the "owl cars"—the slow and unreliable Chicago Night Owl Bus Service. So they moved out and rented a room in a three-story annex south of the Bucklin Building at the corner of Michigan Avenue and Peck Court. It was there, in humble surroundings, that the two first established their life in the city:

> The room, a little back-hall bedroom, extended in sweeping perspective 12 feet in one direction and 10 in the other. You had to take careful aim to walk between the bed and sofa. There was no closet, and no bathroom on that floor. Across the corner hung a curtain behind which we draped our wardrobe on a row of hooks—a row of two hooks. The single window looked out over a back area filled with discarded packing cases, bottles and other rubbish. In the distance was the magnificent uplift of the Polk Street Station [a hub of Chicago's intercity rail system at the time].[8]

The furnishings included one double bed (which JTM and Ade shared) and a rickety sofa with a ridge down the middle when opened. There was a washbasin, a plush-covered armchair, and two paintings. One painting had a "forest of asparagus" in the foreground, a lake in the middle, "and a range of the Himalayas shooting violently upward from its edge." The other painting portrayed a large pink watermelon. The rent was $5 a week and they christened it "The Oaks" in honor of a "couple of stunted, half-dead trees in the yard below." They added their own decorating touches, including scattering newspapers on the floor to "give the place a literary aspect" and tossed the remains of cigars all over "to impart a jolly Bohemian atmosphere." They stayed for three years, not because they liked it so much, but for a charitable reason; they "couldn't bear to tell the landlady we were going. She had a tubercular daughter and we knew how much she depended on our rent."

Ade and JTM thought of themselves as men-about-town, and in fact they were:

> We were about town much more than we were about our little radiator. We never went home as long as there was anything more interesting to see or any place more inviting to go. We saw nearly everything and every place in Chicago.[9]

Full of the joy of life and in love with their work, they experienced little or no drudgery and regarded each day as an adventure. Money was tight and "in consequence of a contracted currency system and the high cost of living, [they] lived on a high moral plane." They were both "hard up all the time." Each week, JTM pawned an opal ring set with thirteen little diamond chips—a gift from a cousin. Ade pawned a watch he owned. On payday, they redeemed their items from the pawn shop until the next week. They regarded the watch and the ring set as their "gold reserve." The city of Chicago was "still a novelty," particularly because it was a "tough town with a good deal of crime." Like any mother, Clarissa would not have been pleased to learn how close they lived to a bad part of the city:

> Peck Court led from the old levee district—cheap lodging houses and cheaper saloons. The riffraff drifted back and forth from sleeping in the park. One night George stepped on a fellow asleep in the hall; one

morning there was a crowd in what is now Grant Park where a fellow had been murdered. There was often shooting in the alley and police-men chasing someone. We used to walk home in the middle of the cob-bled streets [afraid to use the sidewalks away from the street lamps].[10]

Such precautions were not unwarranted as JTM would learn while he was out one evening:

One night I stopped in the Auditorium drugstore. It had huge plate-glass windows down to the sidewalk. I bought something and, in doing so, displayed a very modest roll [of cash]. It was late. Congress Street was silent and deserted. Of course, there were no automobiles then. Even the street-walker traffic indigenous to Wabash Avenue had called it a day. I turned south on Michigan. That was empty too. Presently I heard a man's footsteps behind me. I slowed to let him pass and noted with definite concern that he also slowed down. I scanned the street ahead for some reassuring signs of life. There was not a soul in sight. I walked faster, and the footsteps quickened their pace. There was no doubt I was being followed. Suddenly the steps quickened to catch up with me. A cold chill went down my back. It looked like a holdup, and I felt the moment had arrived. So, just as suddenly, I stepped off the sidewalk and turned to face him.[11]

The man approached JTM and asked for "something to help him out," explaining he was broke and hungry with no place to sleep. JTM stepped back from him to get out of range before reaching into his pocket to give him something. He took out "not enough to show how nervous I was, but still enough to get him a meal and a bed for the night." They stood and talked for a while and then JTM said good night. The man thanked him and started west on Peck Court toward South State Street, "the haven of the derelicts and criminals." JTM was "sure [the man] was desperate" and "might have reached a point where he was ready to do anything." But his instincts led him to believe the man "was not a real crook" but instead "a country boy up against a run of hard luck."

In 1892, JTM was assigned by the *Chicago Daily News* to produce sketches of the construction site for the World's Columbian Exposition, which was scheduled to open the following year to mark the 400th anniversary of Christopher Columbus landing in America. The site was Jackson Park, a marshy bog seven miles south of downtown. The site included 630 acres bounded on the north by 56th street, on the east by Lake Michigan, on the west by Stony Island Avenue, and on the south by 67th Street. The World's Fair, as it became known, created "feverish activity" in Chicago, which had been dubbed the "Windy City" by Charles A. Dana, an editor at the *New York Sun*. Most of JTM's drawings were done on the spot, but some were made from photographs that included "involved and intricate detail." Dozens of noted sculptors were modeling the clay into the tremendous sculptural designs "which later were to contribute so greatly to the beauty of the fair. Everything was in a chaotic state and it was hard to realize that completion would come within a year." Being awarded the World's Fair was a tremendous honor for Chicago, which had competed against New York City, St. Louis, and Washington, DC. Keen interest in the construction placed a sense of urgency on JTM to produce sketches quickly. He employed a state-of-the-art method that helped speed up the printing process:

> I used what was called a silver print [to create the drawings]. You inked
> in the picture on the print and then bleached out the print in a chemi-
> cal bath, and there was your completed drawing ready for the engraver.
> It was a tremendous timesaver.[12]

His drawings of the World's Fair construction attracted the attention of Charles Higgins, an assistant passenger traffic manager for Santa Fe Railroad. Higgins asked JTM to illustrate a small advertising booklet for the railroad called "The Land of Sunshine." JTM was "delighted" by the request and "soon completed the drawings." The success of the booklet led to a proposal for a "more elaborate one" covering the entire Santa Fe system. It would be called "To California and Back." Production of the booklet would require Higgins and JTM to make the cross-country trip—"he to write, [JTM] to draw." JTM had mixed feelings about the assignment:

I had never been outside of Indiana and Illinois. California seemed as far as India, and in my opinion, the opportunity seemed gigantic. I was almost prepared to resign from the paper if necessary, but they let me go. Even now I can feel something of the heart-stirring thrill of the prospect of my first real trip.[13]

The train departed westward and somewhere near Manitou Springs at the base of Pike's Peak, JTM was standing on the back platform of the "pokey little three-car train admiring the scenery" when the train suddenly stopped roughly and abruptly. Curious about the delay, JTM looked forward down the track and saw "the engine was overturned in a ditch." A baggage car also had derailed and the train car just ahead of his had partially left the tracks. No one was injured, nobody was "apparently, much scared," and it was the only "railway wreck in which [he] ever took part."

The trip continued by stagecoach and JTM sat with the driver. When he learned the driver had been operating coaches in all parts of the western United States for many years—including the Black Hills—he "licked [his] chops":

> Now for some firsthand stories of redskins, road agents and runaways! I worked hopefully [conversing with him] for several hours, but as nearly as I could discover by painstaking cross-examination, nothing in the world had ever happened to him—not even a busted trace [straps attaching a horse to the vehicle it is pulling] or surcingle [a blanket strap for a horse]. And that was in the bad old days. Cripple Creek [a former gold mining camp in Colorado] was wide open day and night, with saloons, gambling and ladies of doubtful virtue, although I don't think there was any reasonable doubt about it.[14]

As JTM sketched on the back platform of the train, "a pretty girl used to look over my shoulder." He made no pass at her because "the art of picking up was not so prevalent then." The girl departed the train at Flagstaff where they bid each other farewell; however, "For several years [JTM] kept her in my mind's eye and wove a sort of dream romance about her, always looking for her face wherever [he] went—especially at the World's Fair." Years later he was visiting the Chicago Press Club when he ran into a newspaper acquaintance, Herbert Jones, who was writing a letter to a girl in Coronado, California. Jones took out her picture and showed it to JTM; it was the same girl—"a Miss Babcock from Indiana whose father ran the great hotel at Coronado Beach." Jones ended up marrying the girl, whom JTM ran into at party in Chicago years later. Babcock said she remembered the "exchanged look and wave" when they said good-bye in Flagstaff years earlier—"or at least politely said she did."

Upon returning to Chicago, JTM went right back to "my *News* job." But at night, in the room on Peck Court, he produced for the railroad project what "would easily have been $10,000 worth of work on [100] most elaborate drawings"—for which he received no actual compensation. Of course he was provided "the trip itself, a fine time, the companionship of a fine man, a tremendous lot of practice and a certain measure of fame." All that at a mere twenty-two years old made him feel "amply repaid." Years later he "still [thought] he was." In 1893, a representative collection of the drawings JTM produced for Santa Fe was placed on exhibit at the Art Institute. The pleasure and pride he took in the accompanying publicity was dampened by the fact that the museum materials announcing the exhibit listed his middle initial incorrectly.

JTM's first official cartoon for the *Chicago Daily News*—as opposed to sketches and illustrations—was a two-column drawing that appeared a few weeks after he returned to his job at the paper from the train trip out west. The drawing "emphasized Chicago's claim to be the site of the fair scheduled for 1893." Once the World's Fair opened on May 1, 1893, he spent a full year working exclusively on it, including "six months during the construction period before the opening, watching it grow from wasteland of scrub and brushwood into a vision of loveliness, and six months during the operation of the fair." His entire focus was everything and anything about the fair. Rather than tire of the subject, "his wonder grew steadily" at the "incomparable spectacle." He invited his brother, Ben, now eighteen, to visit Chicago and accompany him on a tour of the fairgrounds. Ben "had never traveled anywhere" and JTM "could think of no greater pleasure than showing [the] breath-taking wonders to Ben." JTM expected his younger brother to react with "openmouthed and popeyed amazement," but Ben "never showed it by the flicker of an eye." JTM could not see "how he held it in" because he personally was "slinging adjectives around and gaping till my hat nearly fell off."

During his coverage of the World's Fair, JTM witnessed a tragic fire at the cold storage warehouse on the grounds:

> The building had a tower 90 feet high above its flat roof, and while some of the firemen were up there, fire broke out between them and the roof below. They slid down the hose till it burst. Then they jumped the 90 feet to the roof [below], their bodies turning over and over in the fall. [JTM] saw 19 of those trapped firemen plunge to certain death. In the bright sunlight of a lovely day 100,000 spectators looked on, helpless and hor-rified. As each man jumped, a groan welled up from the crowd. The last poor fellow hung by his hands till the tower crashed down with him. This most agonizing experience haunted me for months.[15]

To honor the work covering the fair, Harlow N. Higinbotham, head of the World's Columbian Exposition corporation, presented JTM with a medal for "distinguished service." The medal was stolen several years later from JTM's room while he was staying at the Granada Hotel. The medal had his name on it and "was absolutely no value to anyone else." About twenty years later, "a man returned it with the story about a friend who found it in the snow. He did not explain why it took so long to find [JTM's] name on the back."

The World's Fair helped introduce JTM to a number of people who would be influential in his life, including a chance encounter with "a chubby-faced young reporter from Kansas working for *The Chicago Tri-bune* [whose] name was Ed Harden." When the World's Fair ended in 1894, Harden was commissioned to write about a new rail line extending service on the Burlington Railway. The new line cut across from Sheridan, Wyoming, to the Northern Pacific, and Ed invited JTM to come along. JTM accepted; he "seemed always ready to go somewhere." During the trip, Harden and JTM had an opportunity to visit the site of Custer's Last Stand and toured the Crow Indian Agency. Then they "ran out of money and had the humiliation of having to borrow $30 from a rancher we met, oddly enough named 'Hardin.'" In Montana, they hired a handcar to take them to Billings, where they arrived at 4 a.m. Despite the early hour, "every saloon [was] wide open and the life of the town running at high tide."

Their trip culminated in a three-day tour of Yellowstone Park, where they drove in a "surrey piloted by a tobacco-chewing gentleman who wore whiskers." Their driver's name was Dave Johnson and "he swore all the time," although "not unpleasantly. It just rolled out naturally without the slightest effort." One day while driving the surrey up a steep incline, "the horses were languidly turning their heads from side to side and showing a noticeable lack of interest in their work."

Johnson rebuked them, saying, "Giddap there, you goddam, ornery, pisellum, scenery-lovin' sons o' bitches!" The phrasing Johnson used struck JTM and Harden as "quite an artistic bit of word painting." Later when they were back in Chicago, the two had a silver medal made. On one side was engraved "To Dave Johnson, Champion Cusser of the Pacific Slope." On the other side were their two names under the signature: "From his admiring friends." The medal hung by a ribbon from a silver bar. Inscribed on it—in stenographer shorthand—was the "salty expression" Johnson had directed at his horses. They sent the medal to Johnson but received no response. About fifteen years later, a Union Pacific official named E. O. McCormick looked up JTM and stopped by one day.

"Our driver in the Yellowstone wore a medal with your name on it," McCormick said. "I asked him what the shorthand meant. He said, 'Oh, jest ornyment, I reckon.'" Not satisfied, McCormick said he took the medal to several [female] stenographers who "professed to be unable to read it," but McCormick found a male clerk who read it off "without hesitation, but not without considerable surprise."

That was JTM's "first trip with Ed Harden." Harden may not have spawned JTM's love of travel, but he was certainly responsible for many of JTM's most interesting experiences. In 1897, Harden suggested another trip, this time to New Orleans and JTM "couldn't seem to refuse [because] in those days, everything presented itself as an opportunity which shouldn't be let slip." So they boarded a steam ship—the *Aransas*—to Tampa, Florida, where Harden visited his mother. JTM continued on to Havana, Cuba. He was the only human passenger on the ship, which also carried 165 mules for General Valeriano Weyler of the Spanish Army. The Spanish-American War was about a year away and "relations were already rather tense," so JTM was allowed to land in Cuba "only for the day."

Prior to sunset, JTM sailed home on the *Aransas*. A "bad storm came up" and the ship "being absolutely empty, practically rolled over." This was the first of "several terrifying nights at sea" that JTM would endure in his life. At Key West, he changed to a side-wheel steamer, the *City of Richmond*, and proceeded over to Miami and then on to Palm Beach. He enjoyed "feeling rather important dallying thus idly at a winter resort, sketching a pretty girl—until [his] money ran out." Now broke, he resumed his trip and arrived at Waycross, Georgia, where he was to rejoin Harden who, "to [his] consternation, turned up also stone-broke." They managed to get a train berth to Washington, D.C., where they connected with the train to Chicago and returned home.

⤙⸿⸿⸿⸿⸿⸿⸿⸿⸿⸿⤙

WHEN THE WORLD'S FAIR ENDED, the *Chicago Daily News*—as well as the city in general—"seemed dull and dead." To help infuse energy into the newspaper's daily offerings, editor Charles H. Dennis "joyfully received George's [Ade] suggestion of a story department [featuring] atmospheric bits about the Chicago of those days—'Stories of the Streets and of the Town.'" The first installment appeared on November 20, 1893, and from that day forward, "the space was George's to do with it as he liked." JTM held the view that in subsequent years, Ade could have "sold the stories for a couple thousand each, instead of the small

$25 weekly salary he was getting for six of them." JTM did not hold any bitterness about it, however, because "those were very happy days and money meant little to us except as a medium of barter for food and lodging." When the *Stories of the Streets* had been running for less than a year, some of them were published in a book, with additional books appearing "every few months."

From the inception of the column, JTM provided the illustrations—"several drawings each day" in varying sizes and dimensions. The column provided an opportunity for JTM and Ade to learn "more about Chicago" by going "all over, writing up people and neighborhoods, events" and more:

> We got to know the police stations, the jails, the hospitals, schools and universities; in fact nearly every department of human life and activity in Chicago during the [1890s] was material for us. We didn't suspect that we were painting the portrait of a special decade that was to go down through history as "the Gay Nineties." But certainly the collection of these stories and pictures published by the Caxton Club [of Chicago] would give a future historian useful information on that period, its life and customs.[16]

In January 1894, a group of Chicago-based journalists—including JTM and Ade—were invited to participate in an all-expenses-paid trip to attend the California Midwinter International Exposition in San Francisco "as an advertising stunt" to promote the city and the state. Both Ade and JTM "felt flattered to be included on [the] junket. In addition to attending the fair, they were provided a tour of Chinatown and its off-shoot, the Barbary Coast [a nine-block red light district]. They "saw everything the police permitted, and that was just about everything." In fact, "for a couple of boys from the farmland, [they] had [their] eyes well opened."

With the San Francisco trip behind them, Ade and JTM finally decided to move out of their place on Peck Court. Their sympathy toward the consumptive girl and her mother was finally outweighed by their dislike of the "dangerous and undesirable part of town in which they lived." They moved several times to better quarters as they "became still more affluent," progressing to living arrangements on LaSalle Avenue, Chestnut Street, and, for a couple of years, a place at the "old Granada Hotel" on Ohio Street where they had a room on the seventh floor.

Around dawn on the morning of Halloween in 1895 while living at the Granada, Ade and JTM were awakened by their beds shaking; they noticed the gas fixture on the ceiling was swinging and jingling. "Full of excitement, [they] dressed hastily and went down to the main floor" where they awakened the night clerk who was sleeping over his paper and "was surprised to see [them] at that hour."

"What's the matter?" the clerk asked. "The earthquake. Didn't you feel it?" Ade and JTM both said at once. The clerk gave them an annoyed look. "Oh, now you boys better get back to bed," he said sharply. "But everything in our room jiggled," they assured him. "You must have been dreaming," the clerk continued. "It's all right now. You boys go on back to bed and get a good rest." He waved them away and went back to his reading. Puzzled, Ade and JTM returned to their room upstairs.

Later that morning, the two "had a lot of fun over [the clerk's] astonishment when he saw the bold headlines in the newspapers: 'Earthquake Shakes City.'" The earthquake was centered near Charleston, Missouri, and registered 6.6 on the Richter scale.[17]

The ability to improve their standard of living "depended entirely on [their] employer, Victor Lawson." Lawson had a reputation for paying poorly, but as a boss he let it be known to his employees that "a man who did his work conscientiously was certain of his job as long as he wanted to stay, and also was certain of excellent treatment in case of illness or misfortune." As a result, many stayed at the *Chicago Daily News* even though they could have accepted jobs elsewhere at high salaries.

Although he paid his employees poorly, it was clear Lawson had money. Sporting a carefully trimmed pointed beard, Lawson dressed "unlike anybody else," wearing "a long gray Prince Albert suit" with a "flat-topped derby, doubtless made from an individual mold because only in early pictures of J. Pierpont Morgan, Sr., and Winston Churchill did you ever see its prototype." He was known to have only a "few social contacts," which JTM attributed to the need to "retain his journalistic independence by avoiding too friendly relations with powerful citizens who might have favors to ask."

Lawson left a rather modest home on LaSalle Avenue to build a "magnificent house on the Lake Shore Drive," which was famous for "many stories of the beauty of its interior." *Stories*, because as far as JTM was aware, only three or four people he knew had ever been inside. Eventually, his social activities did expand and improve. In 1899, as Ade was crossing the Atlantic Ocean to England on an assignment for another newspaper that would take him to Turkey and the Near East to "engage foreign correspondents for [a] new foreign service," he happened to discover Lawson was on the same steamer. Although their relationship as employer and employee at the *Chicago Daily News* had been "friendly but formal," when they arrived in London, Ade took Lawson on a tour of the city's music halls and Lawson "enjoyed himself enormously." Years later after JTM himself had left the *Chicago Daily News*, he joined a monthly dinner club to which Lawson happened to belong. Lawson attended regularly and it was clear to JTM that Lawson "relished the contacts." Once the two of them sat together and the discussion turned to the topic of retiring from the business world:

> "I know of only one man who retired successfully," Lawson said. "A. M. Day. He was senior partner of his firm. He retired at 50." "But," [JTM] said, "Mr. Day took over the presidency of the Presbyterian Hospital and worked harder than ever." Lawson smiled. "Perhaps that is why his retirement was successful."[18]

After Ade arrived in Chicago, each time he or JTM asked Lawson for a raise "the other did too." Lawson finally decided to pay them the same salary and when he issued a raise, he "raised [them] together." By 1894, they were being paid $25 a week; it had "necessitated six or eight personal calls to Lawson" asking for a raise because he "didn't believe in spoiling young men by raising their wages too fast." It was a good thing Lawson paid them better because after *"Stories of the Street"* became established, other job offers appeared. The *Chicago Times* offered them $60 a week to leave. Hearst Publications offered $80 a week to come work in New York City. Some thirty years later both Ade and JTM would write stories and provide illustrations for Hearst-owned magazines, but in 1895, though the offers dazzled them, they "never thought of accepting any." They had "lofty ideals of what a newspaper should be, and [they] were very loyal to" Lawson and the *Daily News*.

They also had an itching desire to visit Europe. When they received a $10 raise, bringing their salaries to $35 a week, Ade proposed a financial strategy for coming up with the fare: "Let's pretend we didn't get that raise. Let's put away $10 a week, and when we get $500, we'll go abroad." For the next fifty weeks, they never missed putting away $10 each and by spring 1895, they had their $500. Now the question was, what to say to their employer:

> We were determined to go, and we had no intention of asking favors of the paper. We decided we'd have to tell the editor we were resigning in order to travel. It never occurred to us we could go away and still connect with the weekly pay roll! So we simply walked up and told Mr. Lawson we were going to Europe for four months, and waited with bated breath. "Well, that'll be a nice trip," he said. "Send home two illustrated stories a week, and I'll keep on with your salaries."[19]

The stories were called *"What a Man Sees Who Goes Away from Home,"* and the friends sailed to Europe in April on an old Cunard ship, the *Etruria*. Coincidentally, Carroll Kent, an old friend from Kentland, Indiana, whose father had founded the town, accompanied them. They were pleased to secure the minimum round-trip rate of $110 apiece with the help of a peer from the *Chicago Tribune*, but shocked in New York where they "ran into [their] first high prices—$5 a day rent for two and no food! [They] nearly came home."

But they didn't and after crossing the Atlantic they landed at Liverpool, where they were relieved to be able to take a train to London. After all those unstimulating days at sea, "rural England with its hedges and stone walls and big luscious trees, its clean, neatly built villages and its damp haze seemed a close approximation to Heaven." It was JTM's twenty-fifth birthday and to mark the occasion, he bought himself a walking stick, which would become one of his lifelong trademarks. Later they attended a prize fight and traveled to Whitechapel [a district in East London] where the infamous Jack the Ripper was still at large. JTM regarded Jack the Ripper as an "engaging personality [who] spent much of his time murdering women, and always left his victim ripped wide open." The squalor and poverty had an impact on the young JTM:

> The people I saw and the places in Whitechapel were so unbelievably awful that I went back and got my old-fashioned box camera and returned alone to get some good effects. I went into narrow alleys of the most noisome [i.e., disagreeable] slums. I picked out the most vicious and villainous-looking characters and snapped them as they glowered with blazing eyes at the impertinence. I felt I might be risking my life getting those shots. At last when I got back to the safety of Trafalgar Square and went to leave the films to be developed, the man took the camera, looked at it a moment, and then remarked mildly, "But you haven't pulled out the slide [i.e., a glass plate coated with photosensitive emulsion]."[20]

Ade and JTM traveled to Holland, Belgium, up the Rhine River to Switzerland, Italy, France, and finally back to England and Ireland. Being as they were conscientious employees, they "sent back two stories a week to the paper, and it was just as well [they] did." Otherwise, they would never have gotten home. Their $500 ran out in Paris where JTM cabled Schmetty for an advance. The total cost of the trip added up to $800 for each of them, but it was an investment of a lifetime. JTM and Ade "may have each spent at least as much in a single week in New York in later years, but never had so much for [their] money again."

Ade and JTM set sail for the return trip on the *Lucania*—"then queen of the seas"—but even the queen could not smooth the very rough water they encountered, which made "nearly everyone ill." Unbeknownst to JTM, the queen would offer him a chance encounter with a princess:

> One day a woman, frowsily [i.e., unkempt] dressed, collapsed on a bench beside [JTM]. "Isn't it dreadful!" she moaned, and told [JTM] it was her first voyage, and that she was going to Newport for a few weeks. She

had reddish hair and looked terrible. Like a jay of jay, [JTM] feared [his] position might be compromised, and [he] shied away assiduously on all subsequent occasions lest she might try to resume the acquaintance.[21]

One evening, the ship's entertainment included a concert, "and the name of a princess appeared on the program." When the show started, "out she came, red hair and all, beautifully gowned and blazing with jewels. She sang wonderfully, and showed absolutely no sign of remembering a certain young man."

JTM and Ade arrived home safe and sound, but "dead-broke and owing $100."

⟿⟿⟿⟿⟿⟿⟿⟿

B Y 1896, THE *CHICAGO DAILY NEWS* had gone through several changes, first becoming the *News-Record* and then the *Chicago Record*. Ade's fame was growing and his first serial, *Artie: A Story of the Streets and Town,* appeared much as [Charles] Dickens' first stories were run in London newspapers and magazines. It made an instant hit. *Pink Marsh,* a series of stories featuring a black shoeshine boy, followed "to equal popularity . . . as different as possible from 'Artie,' but alike in humor and charm." William Dean Howells, an author and literary critic, introduced the *Pink Marsh* series to none other than Mark Twain, who thanked him in a letter, which later came to JTM's attention and included "the most gratifying bit of praise [JTM] had ever received about [his] illustrations."

George Ade would go on to become a noted humorist and playwright, but not before drafting a line or two of cartooning history himself.

In addition to illustrating George's stuff—five or six pictures a day—and doing a news picture, [JTM] began drawing a regular five-column front-page cartoon. And [he] leaned heavily on George Ade for ideas. Up to that time [JTM] had been a [realistic newspaper artist]. Now [he] had to be made over into something requiring whimsy and, if possible, humor. In this transition George helped materially. He provided excellent suggestions that gave [JTM's] early cartoons whatever distinction they had.[22]

When the presidential campaign of 1896 began, Lawson assigned JTM to cover the Republican National Convention in St. Louis. William McKinley received the party's nomination and at the conclusion of the convention, JTM took a train to McKinley's home in Canton, Ohio, where McKinley "had the time and graciously gave it while [JTM] made [his] first sketch of him." Several weeks later, 20,000 people "sweltered in the stifling heat of the old [Chicago] Coliseum . . . and spent days trying to nominate a Democrat to run against McKinley." JTM was in the hall and at first, things did not go well:

> Nobody could hear the speakers, and as time went on, nobody wanted to hear them. [Illinois] Governor [John] Altgeld, [New York Senator David] Hill, [Wisconsin] Senator [William] Vilas all tried without success. The voice of [former] Governor [William] Russell of Massachusetts, who ordinarily would have been granted a courteous hearing, was lost in the steadily rising din of inattention and boredom. [JTM] was sitting on the platform, the better to draw the various speakers. The last one was announced. Then a miracle happened.[23]

A "clarion voice stilled the crowd" and thirty seconds later former US Representative William Jennings Bryan began to speak, hushing the coliseum. To JTM, "it was so silent it seemed as if everyone was holding his breath." Delivering what would become his famous "Cross of Gold" speech, Bryan's "voice of uncommon beauty" swelled throughout the hall as "each sentence rang out to a crash of thunderous applause. When he sat down, the convention went wild, the huge building rocked and rocked again with the storms of cheers. The name of Bryan was taken up by the stamping processions which surged to a frenzied crescendo."

Those in attendance at the 1896 Democratic National Convention "watched a man march relatively unknown to the platform, and march down again the leader of a national party." JTM returned to the newspaper office "still under the spell of the voice." JTM's cartoons favored McKinley, but even though he took a position against Bryan in his work, "he apparently bore [JTM] no ill will. Many times [Bryan] sent him cartoon ideas which [JTM] was able to use, with due credit."[24] Bryan always looked up JTM whenever he passed through Chicago. "Often in after years," [JTM] and his wife would visit Bryan and his wife when they were near Bryan's home in the Miami area.

The McKinley-Jennings Bryan presidential race was particularly bitter and was "rich in material for George Ade's keenness and wit, and he kept strengthening [JTM] with ideas . . . until [JTM] was able to stand alone." JTM felt he "could not have effected the change from realistic newspaper artist to cartoonist by himself." With Ade's continued help, JTM "gradually acquired the knack of looking at things with the eye and technique of a cartoonist." Ade was the "pillar" he leaned on until 1897, when JTM was granted a leave of absence from his newspaper job to embark on an around-the-world trip scheduled to last six months; in fact, the trip would last three years. When he returned, he would resume his cartooning without Ade's help, because his dear friend had "originated his first *Fable in Slang* and had stepped from $60 a week into big money." No matter, because by then, JTM "got the hang of it—at least sufficiently to hold [his] job [now] at the *Chicago Tribune* for more than 40 years."

DURING THE MIDPOINT of the 1896 presidential campaign, one day JTM prepared a cartoon for the newspaper that had "some space left untouched in a lower corner." He "might have put in a bush or a fence post, but without any purpose except to fill the space," JTM drew a little dog— "not a valuable one, just a harmless-looking little dog." The next day, a similar situation presented itself and again he drew a small dog as the solution. By chance, the second dog "bore a faint family resemblance to the first one."

It did not go unnoticed among readers: "Four people wrote in, demanding to know the significance of the dog." On the third day, JTM intentionally drew the same dog again. The paper received thirteen letters from readers. Thereafter, the dog appeared every day, "sometimes with McKinley, sometimes with Bryan, so you couldn't tell whether he was a Democratic dog or a Republican." As days passed, the numbers of letters to the paper increased; everybody wanted to know what the odd-looking dog in the political cartoons meant—"there were guesses, suggestions, and poems." One letter writer demanded that the newspaper "kindly state in your columns what the cheerful little square-nose pup represents."

JTM's newspaper colleagues were amazed by the interest in the dog. By election time, the *Record's* reporters had to reconcile the fact that in the minds of their readers, the campaign issues appeared to have been superseded by the meaning of the dog. Even JTM became inextricably linked to the dog. Whenever he was introduced to someone, the first question asked of him was: "You aren't the fellow who draws the dog, are you?" At first, JTM was amused but "by and by [he] resolved to get rid of him." So he drew a cartoon in which "a tail was shown disappearing off the side with a little banner saying, 'Farewell forever.'" Thousands of letters poured in with the same inquiry: "'What has become of the flop-eared dough-faced hound?' readers asked because 'we feel real lonesome without him.'"

Later, on his three-year world tour, he sat down next to an American soldier in the Philippines and struck up a conversation. When they exchanged names, the soldier's eyes lit up. "You're not the fellow that draws the dog, are you?" he asked.[25]

NOTES

1   John T. McCutcheon, *Drawn From Memory* (Indianapolis and New York: Bobbs-Merrill, Inc., 1949), 61.
2   Ibid., 62.
3   Ibid., 65.
4   Ibid., 66.
5   Ibid.

6   Ibid., 67.

7   Ibid.

8   Ibid.

9   Ibid., 68.

10 Ibid., 69.

11 Ibid.

12 Ibid., 70.

13 Ibid.

14 Ibid., 71.

15 Ibid., 75.

16 Ibid., 79.

17 "Earth in a Quiver: Chicago Visited by Two Pronounced Seismic Shocks," *Chicago Daily Tribune* (1872–1922), November 1, 1895. ProQuest Historical Newspapers. See also "Historic Earthquake Near Charleston, Missouri," *US Geological Society*, accessed November 12, 2013, www.usgs.gov.

18 McCutcheon, *Drawn From Memory*, 82.

19 Ibid., 83.

20 Ibid., 84.

21 Ibid., 85.

22 Ibid., 87.

23 Ibid., 88.

24 Ibid., 89.

25 Ibid., 92.

3

INTO THE JAWS OF A DRAGON

McCUTCHEON'S TRIP TO EUROPE with George Ade in 1895 helped temporarily quiet a growing urge to travel, but when another opportunity arose to satisfy his wanderlust, he seized it and achieved national fame in the process. In late 1897, his friend Ed Harden invited him to go on a round-the-world shakedown cruise of a new revenue cutter, the *McCulloch* [a ship of the US Revenue Cutter Service, a precursor of the US Coast Guard] as guest of Frank Vanderlip, a financial editor at the *Chicago Tribune* who had been appointed assistant secretary of the treasury in President McKinley's cabinet. JTM later learned that Vanderlip and Harden were on a ship together when the subject of the *McCulloch's* cruise came up. Vanderlip invited Harden to go and asked, "Is there anyone you'd like to have with you?" "John McCutcheon," Harden replied. When Harden extended the invitation to JTM, he had mixed feelings:

At first I was frantic with joy—but of course the thing was impossible! I sat down and composed eight closely written pages explaining how I had no money, how I had just returned from a self-elected vacation, how it was quite inconceivable the paper would let me go again so soon, and how I most certainly could not think of it—and ended by saying that I would do everything in my power to arrange it![1]

JTM sent a written request to his boss, Victor Lawson, who was in Switzerland. Lawson "proved as usual most obliging. 'It is too great an opportunity for you to miss,' Lawson wrote. 'By all means go. But remember we have a mortgage on you. You must come back to us when you return.'"

Numerous issues delayed the departure. One question was whether the *McCulloch* should sail around Cape Horn or around the world [it was ten years before the Panama Canal was built] and the cost of coal was a factor. JTM and Harden "expressed a preference for circling the globe, and through Vanderlip's influence, it was so arranged." After numerous delays, the *McCulloch* set sail for Madeira [a Portuguese archipelago] with a crew of one hundred on January 8, 1898, from Baltimore. The *McCulloch* was "narrow and built for speed" but there was "no bilge keel or other device to prevent rolling." It had a "new type of construction and nobody knew how she was going to act." The first evening everyone had a "jolly dinner, all unsuspecting what lay ahead." JTM wrote:

> During the afternoon we ran into an unusually heavy sea and the ship turned on her side. A lot of coal fell off and the cabins were flooded. She didn't right! Another great sea came on board, and tons and tons of water rolled into the wardroom. A third wave like that probably would have sunk the ship. Slowly, slowly, the *McCulloch* came up to position. Everyone was scared stiff. Then her steering jammed and there was more genuine terror. From that time on nobody had any confidence in the ship.[2]

After fourteen days of "constant storm," the *McCulloch* reached Ponta Delgada in the Azores. JTM recounted, "Not enough coal had been saved [some fell overboard during the storm] to reach Madeira." The ship stayed

six days to make improvements and then headed on to Gibraltar, crossing the border into Spain and then on to Tangier and Morocco where "by
night [they] toured the underworld of dancing girls and sensual music."
Next stop was Malta, where the *McCulloch* was notified about the sinking of the US battleship *Maine* in the Havana harbor; 265 lives were lost.
The incident "seemed a very remote occurrence" and JTM "did not even
record it in [his] diary." It was not clear from the dispatch whether the
sinking was an accident or an act of war by the Spaniards. Nevertheless,
"from then on the thought of war hovered in the offing."

The *McCulloch* left Malta for Port Said, where JTM and others "went
to the Heliopolis, the Pyramids, Cairo and the famous fish market." The
journey continued down the Suez Canal to the Red Sea and on to Aden [a
seaport in Yemen]. Although it was officially monsoon season, the *McCulloch's* Indian Ocean crossing "was unbelievably smooth, even glassy at times
so that a pencil set on end would not fall over." On those quiet nights, JTM
"climbed up to the foreyard, far above the deck, and [rode] for hours in
the comfortable perch, whence [he] had the exquisite pleasure of watching a full-rigged ship cross the rising moon." At Colombo [the largest city
in the former British colony of Ceylon in the Indian Ocean], JTM "came
to a crossroads in [his] life":

> Harden and I were eager to see more of India, it was so tantalizingly
> near. The French ship *Dupleix* was about to sail for Bombay. We could
> take her, see a lot of India and catch up with the *McCulloch* in Japan.
> Not to do so seemed to us a terrific loss of opportunity. On the other
> hand, what if war with Spain should be declared? Perhaps there would
> be time for the one before the other broke. The debate seemed endless.
> Finally we tossed a coin—a momentous coin! As it was, the coin said no.
> We sailed for Singapore with the *McCulloch*, and that night the *Dupleix*
> burned at her dock![3]

Six days later, a message came in to the *McCulloch's* captain. The *McCulloch* was being transferred from the US Revenue Cutter Service to the US
Navy Department "with orders to proceed at once to Hong Kong where

Commodore George Dewey was assembling elements of the U.S. Pacific Fleet." Enroute the *McCulloch* was "to avoid Spanish ports and Spanish ships. War was not yet, but was inevitable."

—ιιιιιιιιιιιιιιι—

T HE CREW AND PASSENGERS of the *McCulloch* did not know at what moment the ship might be recalled to America because there was no ship-to-shore or ship-to-ship radio. They proceeded from port to port on their way to Singapore, but no recall came. Yet at each succeeding port, "the news dispatches grew graver and more inflamed. It was like reading a suspenseful weekly serial." At Singapore, the *McCulloch* received its orders to report to Commodore George Dewey in Hong Kong. The "peaceful round-the-world cruise supposed to take five months was to be interrupted" and JTM would find himself in the "throes of war experiences for the better part of three years." For JTM, the "many unusual experiences, by-products of war, made life interesting" and "the uncertainty of it all was thrilling."[4]

The *McCulloch* added coal in Singapore and then steamed for five days up the China Sea, where they found the commodore. It was unclear whether Dewey would allow Harden and JTM to continue on the trip under the circumstances, and they "nervously awaited an opportunity to speak to Dewey." When they finally got to meet with him, Dewey told them that "in any other circumstances he would have to say no, but inasmuch as [they] were guests of the Treasury Department, [they] could proceed. Of course [JTM and Harden] were jubilant." They turned their attention to working out their duties going forward:

> Harden made arrangements to act as a New York World correspondent. Joseph Stickney, who had been naval editor of the *New York Herald*, also was a passenger on the ship. [JTM] cabled the *Record* for instructions

and was told to send all the stuff [he] could. [JTM] wrote three long letters describing the Navy's preparations. Great numbers of Spanish and
foreign residents were leaving the islands and it was doubtful if any but
natives and the Spanish fighting forces would be there when the fleet
arrived. It was thought that the land batteries would open up on [the
fleet], and that the Spanish vessels would remain inside the harbor behind
the protection of a torpedo-filled strip of water and the highlands flanking the bay. Supplies and coal were a consideration in a long siege. It was
prophesied that while [the] naval conflict was going on in the bay the
rebels would attack the city.[5]

To the newspapermen, "it appeared a good deal like going into the jaws
of a dragon. No one had ever heard of a naval battle in which less than a
quarter of the participants were killed." As a result, everyone wrote farewell letters to relatives back home. The *McCulloch*, the *Boston*, the *Concord*, and the *Petrel* met the *Olympia*, *Baltimore*, and *Raleigh* to form the
Asiatic Squadron at Mirs Bay, a "sheltered cove 35 miles north of Hong
Kong," which was a neutral state and could not allow the US ships in its
harbor. On their first evening, a ship drew along the armored cruiser
USS Olympia to deliver a dispatch to Dewey: "In 15 minutes the signal
was flashed through the night from ardoise lights on the foremast . . .
war had been declared."

Dewey's orders were to sail to the Philippines to capture or destroy
the Spanish fleet. The squadron formed up and sailed on the afternoon
of April 27, 1898. The *McCulloch's* crew were assembled to hear a lieutenant read the Spanish proclamation of war that had been issued in Manila:

> It was an inflammatory cry to the people of the Philippines to unite
> against the sacrilegious vandals who were coming to loot their churches
> and insult their women. It was an appeal to the ignorant passions of an
> unlettered people. At the conclusion of the reading, which contained a
> number of other uncomplimentary things about American seamen as
> well as Uncle Sam, there was a second of silence. Then the crew broke
> into three ringing cheers for the American flag.[6]

The Asiatic Squadron crossed the China Sea in three days, which "were filled with signal drills, musket drills, cutlass drills." As the crew of the *McCulloch* was relatively small in numbers, "even the three civilians, including [JTM], were assigned positions with the gun and ammunition squads." At night, the ship moved in "absolute darkness except for the masthead lights ahead." For JTM, "it was the lonesomest trip in the world—with the conviction in everyone's mind that in a very few days a lot of us would be killed."

On April 30, the ships formed into a single column with "every light extinguished. There was to be not talking, not even a whisper." The column slowly steamed south to reach the entrance of Manila Bay. The plan was to sneak past the bay's forts and attack the Spanish fleet inside the bay in the morning. The night weather cooperated as "masses of cloud hid the half-moon." The fleet moved forward noiselessly, "separated from one another by 400 yards." Then a surprise:

> Just at that moment, the soot in the *McCulloch's* funnel caught fire and flamed up like a rolling mill! A faint light flashed up and down, up and down, on shore. A rocket leaped from Corregidor. Discovered! But nothing further came, so [they] kept on. And then the funnel flared again! The *McCulloch* was almost directly between two forts. We heard the scream of a cannon ball from a near-by rock called El Fraile! Just a single pinnacle nobody had realized was large enough for a battery. The shell seemed to go between the masts of the *McCulloch*. The *Boston* sent an eight-inch shell like a crash of thunder. This was the first shot fired by the Americans. The *McCulloch* fired the next three. The column of ships continued, the Spanish still firing into the darkness.[7]

During the exchange of gunfire, the chief engineer of the *McCulloch* died of heart failure. He was "a stout, thick-necked man who had been pretty excited and obviously nervous. The others had joked him about it a good deal and he had been drinking rather heavily in consequence." He had stood by JTM for a moment on the deck when the ship started into the bay. JTM "was the last to see him alive." After his body was discovered, the *McCulloch* signaled to the flagship it needed a doctor, but the "*Olympia* signaled back: 'Impossible.'"

Manila was now twenty miles ahead. The column slowed to four knots an hour "not wishing to arrive before daybreak." The surface of Manila Bay "was like glass" as dawn broke the morning of May 1. As "the sky showed the first faint tint of gray, the domes and spires of Manila were silhouetted spectrally. To each side was revealed the position of the enemy." The Spaniards started firing when the Asiatic Squadron was "still four miles distant." Dewey responded quickly:

> At the sound the *Olympia* wheeled and started straight for them, grim and determined, without answering fire. From every mast and peak of the American squadron floated a flag, which aroused tremendous enthusiasm. The captain [of the *McCulloch*] appointed Harden and [JTM] in charge of the first ammunition magazine to keep the guns supplied in case the *McCulloch* went into action.[8]

JTM, Harden, and Stickney were the only journalists in the world to serve as eyewitnesses for Dewey's historic assault on Spain's colonial fortress in Manila Bay and the only reporters who could have heard Dewey's infamous command. JTM recalled, "The Spaniards had started firing at 5:10 a.m. Thirteen minutes later Dewey gave the historic order [to Captain Charles Gridley of the *Olympia*]: 'You may fire when ready, Gridley.'"[9] The battle lasted two and a half hours until "only masts and battered funnels and parts of shattered decks were above water." As night fell, the shoreline was "bright with burning ships." From Manila came the sound of cathedral bells. Years later, JTM would reflect on what he had witnessed:

> The Battle of Manila was, of course, the peak of my war experiences. In its historic significance, it was the greatest single event of my life. I passed the time of battle trying to sketch and to photograph, but it was too early and too far, although from our position we could see the whole panorama of the battle better than anyone else. The next afternoon, I

took a dinghy and went among the wrecks. The only living thing was a chicken perched on a bow stanchion of the *Reina Cristina,* once the proudest [Spanish ship] of them all.[10]

Meanwhile, the newspapermen were "very anxious to get ashore as soon as possible" to send their stories. The *McCulloch* was sent to Cavite, where JTM "landed with a party." The Filipinos greeted them enthusiastically, and JTM visited the arsenals and hospitals "and were offered all sorts of souvenirs." He took a flag from the Spanish gunboat *Isla de Luzon* and one of its smaller guns. The *Isla de Luzon* was seized and salvaged by the US government and later "ended its career, curiously enough, in Lake Michigan." On May 5, the *McCulloch* was ordered to Hong Kong where, it was agreed, Dewey's dispatch was to be filed first:

> After that it was a free race to the cable office. Each of us had his dispatch ready. I sent mine of 600 words at press rates, 60 cents a word. I noticed that Harden was sending a brief 30-word message. "What's the short one?" I inquired. "Just a bulletin for the *World,*" he answered. So I filed a 60-word bulletin for the *Record* at the regular commercial rate of $1.80 which took precedence over press dispatches. But Harden [who was more experienced] had failed to mention that he was sending his bulletin "Urgent." It took precedence over everything else but cost $9.90 a word! Harden's message got to the *New York World* at about 5:30 a.m. Saturday morning, too late for the regular edition. There were no plans for an extra, so it was sent to the *Chicago Tribune,* which used the *World's* news. Jim Keeley, then editor of the *Tribune,* had kept his office open for several nights with everyone on hand for just this news. It was five days since the battle; nobody knew anything and there was intense anxiety. The *Tribune,* then, receiving it in Chicago at 4:30 a.m. Central Time, was able to use it and scored a tremendous "beat" [i.e., scoop]—one of the most conspicuous in American journalism.[11]

Jim Keeley wrote JTM about it in a letter:

> Murphy was our correspondent in New York in the *World* office. The last edition of the *World* had gone to press and a few of the dogwatch men were staying around playing poker. Murphy, who didn't get "30" [his night's

dismissal] until about half past four Chicago time, was in the [poker] game. The telephone rang. Every guy around the table had what he thought was a good hand except Murphy who chucked his in, and somebody said: "Murphy, you're out. Answer that damned telephone!" He did. It was the cable operator announcing the receipt of Harden's "Urgent" message. Murphy took it over the telephone, then hopped to our open wire with it. When he had done that little trick, he turned it over to the *World* people. Then a *World* row started as to whether the *Morning World,* which had gone to press, was entitled to it, or the *Evening World,* which was getting its first edition ready. Bob Peattie, who was Hearst correspondent in the *Chicago Tribune* office, shot it back to New York before the *World* squabble was settled.[12]

Keeley, "always an enterprising fellow," telephoned the news to the White House. A night watchman patrolling the corridor outside the bedrooms heard the telephone ring. The phone was down the hall, an "old-fashioned wall phone." The guard answered it.

"The *Chicago Tribune* speaking. I have news for the President. May I speak with him?" Keeley asked. "The President is asleep. I can't disturb him," the guard replied. "You'll lose your job if you don't call him. I've got news from Manila," Keeley said. The watchman debated and finally knocked on the president's door. JTM recounted, "It was a warm night, so, barefoot and in his nightshirt, [President William] McKinley ambled down the hall to hear from Jim Keeley the news of the Battle of Manila in the words of Ed Harden's dispatch." Months later when Ed Harden returned to the United States, President McKinley sent for him because "doubtless he wanted to find out about Admiral Dewey, who was being spoken of as his opponent at the next election."[13]

As for JTM, his "inexperience in handling cable material" was responsible for putting him at a disadvantage in the race to file the biggest news scoop of the day. Years later he looked back at it philosophically:

At the time, of course, I was sorry, but I'm really glad poetic justice was served. If it hadn't been for Harden, I wouldn't have been there at all. I had a job. My career, except for the acclaim, would hardly have been altered.

[Harden] had no definite job and needed a boost. To have scooped him in addition would have been a pretty serious blow. At the same time, I didn't know about "Urgent" dispatches![14]

JTM regarded the fate of his own news dispatch, on the other hand, as one of the big disappointments in his career. The *Chicago Record's* editor was "not so alert as Mr. Keeley" and in fact was asleep [in his home in the Buena Park neighborhood on Irving Park Road] when JTM's news was coming over the wire: "There was no one on hand [at the office] except a night police reporter and he didn't know what to do with it." The *Record's* editor did not own a telephone—"they were scarce in those days"—and it would have taken hours to drive up to his home and back to the newspaper in a horse-drawn carriage. Even so, they could have had an extra edition out on the street only an hour later than the *Tribune*—with their own correspondent's story in it.

JTM's lengthier dispatch began arriving at the *Record* on late Saturday morning. To add injury to insult, because there was no Sunday *Record*, the story could not be used until Monday. Further, the paper had "an ironclad rule that the *Evening News* could not use the *Morning Record's* material." With Victor Lawson out of the country on a journey up the Nile River, "there was nobody at home with authority to break the rule." The paper cabled Lawson, but for reasons that were unclear, he refused to break the rule.

Meanwhile, the *New York Journal* telegraphed the *Record* asking if they could use JTM's dispatch. They obtained permission, rewrote it, and published it on Sunday, and the *Chicago Tribune* published it too. JTM's "own paper was the very last to make use of the tremendous opportunity—with only three correspondents in all the world on hand."

I never asked [the *Record's* editor] for the details of this miserable business. I was afraid it might imply dissatisfaction on my part. The *Record* was always generous and considerate about our mistakes, but it was doubtless touchy about its own. I felt, too, a little bitter over not receiving special word from my paper about my 60-word message and wondered what happened to it. It was many months before I learned, and then I was disappointed. However, [the *Record*] cabled me in Hong Kong, "file without limit" and "details in full." I sat up all night to write another full dispatch from my very complete diary. Cutting out all the unnecessary words, I skeletonized it down to 4,500 words and sent it press rates at a cost of $2,700. George Ade received this one and filled it out to 6,000 words. It was printed along with my two other dispatches on a Monday morning. So the *Record* did, after all, get the first long complete story, which was reprinted all over the country.[15]

On May 10, the *McCulloch* returned to Manila. Six weeks later, newspapers from home began arriving. JTM "found [his] story horribly garbled, especially in the Hearst newspaper versions," and "it made me ashamed to talk to the Navy officers. This, coming on top of Harden's scoop, was very depressing."

JTM stayed in the Far East living in Manila and from the middle of August 1898 until after Christmas "was one of the most delightful periods of [his] life." He lived with other journalists in a place called Calle San Luis No. 21, a double house, each side featuring its own spacious courtyard. JTM and the other journalists had their own room, eleven servants, a laundress, and a florist at their disposal. Wealthy Spaniards were selling their possessions and returning to Spain, so JTM and his colleagues "procured horses and carriages." JTM "had a *carromata* [i.e., a two-wheeled covered vehicle] and a stunning horse and [his] own driver." They called the place "*Casa de Todas*—The House Where Everything Goes." He wrote:

> It was perpetually interesting. Against a background of insurgent fighting in the hills, and an ever-increasing friction between the Americans and the Filipinos, we carried on in super style. Everything was cheap. There were constant luncheons and parties. Women correspondents had begun arriving. There were many nurses. The Filipino girls were friendly. And in the other half of our double house lived two beautiful Spanish girls. [Later] at a Manila Day dinner in Chicago in 1928, to [his astonishment, JTM] met one of them again. She had married an American and lived in Indiana![16]

Near the end of 1898, JTM received a new assignment. The *Record* was in the process of creating a global network of cable correspondents and asked JTM to recruit candidates from various countries in the Far East. Coincidentally, George Ade was asked to do the same thing and was sent to southern Europe and the Balkans. JTM recruited correspondents in Hong Kong, Saigon, Singapore, and Ceylon. Then he set sail for Bombay. When he reached Colombo, he cabled the *Record* for money, expecting to get it at a bank in Bombay in a day or two. Unfortunately, the bubonic plague "was raging [and] deaths amounted to some 600 a day." The money did not arrive and JTM was becoming desperate:

> By this time I was getting worried and cabled the *Record* that the money had not come. It answered that a draft had been sent on a certain date. I cabled again to say the money could not be traced. The *Record* answered that it was sending a duplicate amount. But there was no sign of that! It took practically my last cent to cable, "Please investigate." I was in despair. My hotel bill had grown to 119 rupees. Each day . . . I tried to borrow some money to send one final message. The American consul was sympathetic. He gave me 50 rupees, 37 seven of which I spent at once in a last despairing cry: "Am broke. Money unarrived. Cannot explain. Investigate immediately. Shall cable no more."[17]

JTM stayed in his room with 13 rupees left to his name, because "The plague-infested streets were too hot for walking." A servant JTM had hired "got nervous and resolved to test [JTM]. His pay was not due, but he said he wanted to leave some money with his wife. [JTM] casually drew a 10-rupee note from [his] pocket and handed it to him. This satisfied him but left [JTM] with three rupees." They were valued at approximately 33 cents each.

> After that I couldn't even buy magazines! I became unbelievably depressed. It seemed incredible that both remittances could have gone wrong. I feared I would have to take any sort of work I could get there in Bombay. The chances were not too good. In all my life, I was never so low in my mind.[18]

Then a bank messenger, "very imposing-looking in a red sash and fez," arrived and handed [JTM] a note saying they had just received to [JTM's] credit 5,900 rupees, the equivalent of £400. JTM "dashed to the bank. They said it had been sent over to them from the very small French Comptoir Bank where it had been all the time!"

While in Bombay, JTM visited numerous exotic places including Afghanistan by way of the fabled Khyber Pass. He was also enamored with the notion that he was in Rudyard Kipling's India and must visit the city of Lahore, where Kipling first earned his reputation as a writer. He went to the office of the *Civil and Military Gazette* where Kipling worked and mentioned to the editor "the wide renown Kipling had achieved in America." The editor "seemed vastly surprised. To him, Rudyard Kipling was still merely a former associate who had made some success as a writer." JTM was taken to a room where Kipling had "written many of his early stories" and the staff showed JTM Kipling's old files before entering an adjacent building:

> [It] had been part of the background for *The Man Who Would Be King* [Kipling's 1888 novella about British adventurers in British India]. An Oxfordshire soldier showed me through the old fort mentioned in *Soldiers Three* [Kipling's collection of short stories about three privates—Terence Mulvaney, Stanley Ortheris, and John Learoyd]. "So this is where Mulvaney and Ortheris and Learoyd used to live," I said. He said nothing, so I tried again. "Kipling has written a lot of his stories about this place." He said, "Oh, there's lots of writers that comes 'ere." "You know about Kipling, of course?" "I don't know the names o' them old Johnnies as lived 'ere." It struck me with crushing force that this British Tommy had never even heard of the man who had practically put him on the map, although living right here amid the scenes rendered famous by the stories hardly a dozen years before.[19]

When US forces took over the Philippines, two batteries of the 23rd Infantry were sent to occupy Jolo, a volcanic island in the Sulu Archipelago in the southwest Philippines populated by Moros, a group of Muslims indigenous to the area. The word was that General John C. Bates was intent on making a treaty with the Moros and their leader, the Sultan of Sulu, who "had bitterly opposed white men." Stories of how "a sultan and his retinue had once come to pay a visit to a Spanish governor" were well-known to the troops. As the story went, once "when all were assembled, the sultan presented to the governor a valuable gift, and as the governor bent over to admire it, the sultan whipped out his barong [i.e., a large cleaver] and sunk it from the top of the governor's head clear down to his chest." It was a signal for the Moros to slaughter the Spanish garrison. While it made for a good story, it was never verified. It did, however, "serve to prepare our soldiers for any such diverting eventuality."

JTM thought that Bates' trip "promised great interest," so he secured permission to go along, and "things went on more or less comfortably for a time." But not for long:

> Then the sultan began to get a little worried about whether the Americans were going to continue his yearly allowance according to the terms of his agreement with the Spaniards. Nothing had been said about it and he felt himself face-to-face with the prospect of having to cut down his harem and smoke several less pipes of opium each day. The sultan noticed that the Americans were making no effort to occupy the enchanting little island of Siasi. He hurried down there with an army of 12 men, assumed formal possession, collected $8,000 [M]exican in cash and hoisted his flag over the whitewashed ramparts of the island's mud fort.[20]

It was this very kind of situation Bates' trip was intended to prevent. JTM, Bates, and his staff member, John Bass, set sail in July 1899 and cruised for three days "among most exquisite islands. Many of them were uninhabited." Bass and [JTM] used to "sit with our feet on the rail looking out across the smooth sea, and pick out islands on which we might reign as neighboring kings." At Jolo, "the streets were as clean as brooms could make them, for there were no vehicles and horses were allowed in the village only by special permission." Fifteen minutes was all the time required to "walk through every street in town" in the tiny island's walled city. JTM,

Bates, and Bass took up quarters ashore and the general sent word to the Sultan inviting him to a conference. The sultan ignored the invitation and after some time had passed, "more than the usual Oriental delay," JTM and Bass approached Bates and asked permission to go see the sultan. The general was horrified:

> He considered it much too dangerous and was not disposed to grant permission. "If you go, you go at your own risk. We can do nothing to help you!" [he told them]. We decided to try it. Of course . . . we had to have an interpreter. A renegade Nubian [Nubia is a region along the Nile River] from Busbus [*sic*], [the name of a fishing village] just outside Jolo, was found who could speak a little English. [We] got all ready to start. Then we couldn't find the interpreter. We combed the town and finally located him cowering in hiding. He refused to go, saying the sultan would murder him, so we had to compel him at the point of our revolvers.[21]

No American had ever crossed the island before, and as they left the town and entered the hills, [JTM] "began to remember all the tales that had been told of Moro treachery. The Moros might jump from behind the tall waving grass flanking the single trail and attack with krises, barongs and campilans—an assortment of curved or double-headed knives and swords" (a selection of souvenirs of those kind of weapons would later "adorn [JTM's] studio in a much less harmful manner").

After three hours of "slow riding . . . we had seen not a single soul on the way. Now it became necessary to leave our horses and proceed on foot." Finally, the group emerged on the far side of the hills and came to a long causeway that led into town of Malibun; the narrow causeway was the only way into or out of the town—"Once in Malibun, we knew that a hasty retreat would be impossible."

Shortly after they entered the narrow causeway, "swarms of half-naked savages with krises [a dagger whose blade has a wavy shape] surrounded us, their teeth black from betel nut. Such a vicious-looking mob there never was!" The natives seemed more surprised by their discovery of the white men, whose "attitude remained cool" and who "showed no signs of force or hostility . . . they remained curious rather than suspicious." The group continued into town where they waited in the marketplace and "were relieved when we were taken to a little shack where a man named Hadji Butu, the sultan's chief official, came to see us." JTM wrote:

> We told him our desire to confer with the sultan, but he was unimpressed . . . until we showed him a five-dollar gold piece. This, he indicated, he would like to show to the sultan. He took it away and we never saw it again. After another interminable and nervous wait, with the hum of hostility rising from the marketplace, we were at last led to where the sultan was living, a better type of native house with a galvanized iron roof, evidently the mark of royalty. His regular palace, it was explained, was farther out of town.[22]

Butu motioned to the group to enter and "any anticipation of glamour or regality hastily evaporated." The sultan, who was sitting in a plain chair, "was a small man about 30 with a pock-marked face and a little fringe of a mustache. He wore a turban and a long, white, not overly clean robe. Several servants stood by with cuspidors [spittoons] which he used occasionally, and another held his bowl of betel-nut juice which gave his lips and teeth the usual dark, reddish-black, unpleasant effect."

The interpreter had instructions to tell the sultan that the group "represented the great American people through the great American newspapers . . . and that everyone was eager to know about the great sultan." JTM was doubtful whether the sultan knew what the word "newspaper" meant. He interrupted the discussion and asked the sultan if he'd like to go out in the sunlight to be photographed. The sultan refused, so JTM asked if he could sketch him: "Inasmuch as this involved no effort on his part, he consented." When the sketch was finished, JTM asked for a signed statement the group could send back to the United States, and they were given the following: "I, Hadji Mohammed Jemalol Kiram, Sultan of Sulu, am like a brother to the Americans and hope they will treat me the same."[23]

The statement was dated 1317 on the Mohammedan calendar and bore the sultan's signature. Elated by their success, the group hurried to return to Jolo where "surprise, excitement and joy greeted our return." The friendly visit "helped make the subsequent negotiations and peace treaty possible." JTM wrote numerous stories for the *Record* about the "queer customs of Sulu, including those of marriage." It aroused so much interest at home that his friend Ade "was moved to piece it all together into his first operetta, 'The Sultan of Sulu,'"[24] for which JTM provided "native names, local color and designed all the costumes."

Meanwhile, after the return from Jolo, one day an inter-island steamboat, the *Churruca*, was headed to Borneo and JTM went along because he seemed always to have been "willing to go anywhere at any time!" While in the city of Sandakan, JTM got the urge to write "an affectionate letter back home to the girl I left behind me." He had been corresponding with her from time to time and would "put a dollar's worth of colorful local stamps on the envelopes to make them look interesting." Since his travel plans were uncertain at best, he asked US consuls in Shanghai and Yokohama to forward all of his mail to Manila. When he returned there in August 1899, he found mail that "had been pursuing me for nearly a year," including correspondence from the girl he left behind:

> The lady indicated her strong suspicion that I would rather stay in the wilds than come back to her. I cabled at once with reply prepaid: "Is it too late if I return immediately?" The answer came: "Too late. Was married July third." [Unfortunately] she continued getting my letters, including the one from Borneo.[25]

A T THE END OF AUGUST 1899, JTM decided to take a steamer to Peking to continue recruiting more correspondents for the *Record* in China and Japan. In China, relations between foreigners and the Chinese "were becoming threatening: it was the first rumblings of the Boxer Rebellion [an uprising in which thousands of foreigners were murdered], which broke out the following summer." Traveling by mule and sleeping on k'angs [a brick platform], JTM toured the Ming Tombs and the Great Wall. In China, JTM hired Robert Coltman as a correspondent for the *Record* and was able to arrange an interview with Li Hung Chang, a politician, general, and diplomat who "was still the greatest figure in China." After a rickshaw ride through Tartar City, Coltman and JTM were "whisked up to the heavy doors off a temple" where Li lived:

> In came old Li, leaning heavily on the arm of a retainer and carrying a stout cane in his left hand. He was bareheaded and was dressed in a common light-blue Chinese coat, white trousers and curious clumsy boots. Low on his nose rested a pair of big steel spectacles; above them looked out the merry, lively eyes that had been made so familiar by his photographs. He shook hands all around and was assisted to his seat. Then we all sat down.[26]

> We had been told that we must not leave until he signaled. The signal was the raising of a glass of champagne. The champagne was already poured out . . . getting warmer and warmer. [When they left the audience, it was] with the consciousness of having been in the presence of real greatness. Unlike our friend in Sulu, Li Hung Chang had an impressive personality.[27]

During the first two years of the American occupation of the Philippines, JTM's days were "satisfyingly full of hiking and fighting, of rumors and alarums [alarms], of infinite romance and adventure. When the Filipino insurrection petered out and the grim necessity of going home loomed ahead, it seemed to me highly desirable to go to Africa." The Boer War (1899–1902) between the British and Dutch settlers in the Transvaal—the land north of the Vaal River in what is modern day South Africa—had been "in progress for some time" and "a siege of Pretoria seemed likely." JTM needed to continue to scratch his travel itch:

> Anyhow, I didn't want to go home at all, and was eager for any excuse to continue this fascinating sort of existence. I knew the *Record* had a man with the British forces, but none with the Boers; I suggested [the *Record*]

send me down. The answer came: "If you think you can join the Boers, go ahead." At the end of April 1900, I left the Philippines, this time for good. Our little bungalow never looked more cozy and charming; my ties in Manila were many and pleasant. There were many farewell dinners before I sailed.[28]

By the time JTM had reached South Africa, the war had entered the guerrilla stage and the "big show was over . . . and South Africa had lost its place on the front page." The *Record* sent a cable to JTM instructing him to "get an interview with Oom Paul and then come home." Oom (i.e., Uncle) Paul was the nickname for Stephanus Johannes Paulus Kruger, also known as Paul Kruger—the state president of the South African Republic (Transvaal). He earned international recognition as the face of the Boer Resistance against the British Empire. Kruger had "moved into a squatty, gabled cottage standing in a soldierly row of gum trees." The interview was in a tiny room that served as both a parlor and office. Kruger was not what JTM expected:

> Oom Paul sat at the farther end of a table in a large easy chair. His silk hat lay on the table. His thin hair was combed straight back from his forehead until it reached his neck. A little gold earring hung from each ear. His eyes were red and inflamed and he kept them closed most of the time. His features were large and coarse. I looked in vain for the fatherly, sympathetic expression of which I had heard so many admirers speak. It was not there. Every line was hard and severe. But as if to make up for a lack of gentleness, there was tremendous power in the leonine head, the huge pear-shaped nose and the stern unsmiling mouth.[29]

Kruger rose, shook hands with JTM, and then settled back into his chair, looking JTM over. It was obvious to JTM that Kruger was not in a good mood. He emphasized his comments "by vigorous smashings on the table with his powerful fist." For twenty years, Kruger had been president of a republic and one of the great figures of South Africa. Now a fugitive, he "was beyond the consolation of good scenery and good cooking." An old man whose wife "was sick in Pretoria and might die before he had an opportunity to see her again, he could not fight [in the Boer War] because he was too old." All that was left was to "sit out the evening of his life . . . and contemplate the procession of bitter memories passing in endless review."

JTM finished the interview, filed his dispatch, and left immediately for the African coastline.

AFTER HE LEFT THE TRANSVAAL, JTM received word from Clara that his brother, Ben, was getting married. He sent his regrets in a letter to her:

> I'm sorry to miss the event, for marriages haven't been very common with us children. As for me, I'll probably get married some time when I get home, although I haven't arranged with any particular young lady. Perhaps I will be too ancient by that time to capture a young lady, but when one of them sees all the loot and souvenirs I've picked up, why, I don't see how she could resist, even if she didn't care for me myself.[30]

At each port along the African coast, he mailed a postcard to Clara: "Am homeward bound. Have the fried chicken ready." His favorite meal was "fried chicken, country style, with cream gravy pleasantly mottled with particles of browned chicken—a source of rapture." After brief stops in Paris and London, JTM sailed for home at last on a transatlantic passenger liner, the *SS St. Louis*. Although his friends had planned a reception, JTM "didn't want that" and without telegraphing ahead, surprised everyone by taking a train that arrived at 7 a.m.:

> Everyone was home except George Barr. We all went down to Lafayette to see my other relatives and friends, and I had fried chicken with cream gravy and blackberry jam and all the other trimmings at every house at every meal![31]

In all, JTM attended twenty-six banquets held in his honor in a month, "some large and impressive, some small and informal, and many receptions." He had to give remarks at most of them and eventually was invited to speak at his alma mater, Purdue University. Then on December 19, 1900, while in Chicago for a dinner at the Chicago Athletic Club, his exotic travels and the numerous exotic bugs to which he had been exposed finally caught up with him:

> I woke up feeling as if a sword had been run through my lung. I didn't know it was double pneumonia. At first it never occurred to me that I was seriously ill. I expected to be out soon and kept making dates ahead. But on Christmas Eve they sent for my brother George, thinking I could not live through the night.[32]

A doctor was summoned to examine him and "declared there was no hope." The dire diagnosis "gave rise to rumors" of his death and "notices went out." A second doctor declared JTM's situation "serious, but there's a ghost of a chance if he can get south where there's better air." Ade, who had come to his side, called Lawson, who arranged for a private ambulance to take JTM to the train at Polk Street Station where "my stretcher was lifted through a car window. The engineer was cautioned to go slowly around curves." It helped lift JTM's spirits, although his battle was not over:

> The minute I began jolting along the tracks my spirits started to revive. George Ade had gone ahead to prepare the way in Asheville [North Carolina]. No ambulance was available, but somehow they carried me to a pleasant house called "Oakholm" on Beaucatcher Mountain. I got better, then I got worse. Various malarial bugs from the Orient put in an appearance. My heart became affected, then my kidneys. My only hope was an operation but my kidneys couldn't stand ether or my heart chloroform. The doctor said he would use ethyl chloride, a freezing mixture. And then he couldn't get the knife between my ribs! Two or three times he tried. My mother held my feet and I clutched the nurse. For half an hour he worked, cutting and prying. Finally the doctor forced the knife

through and a hole was opened in my side big enough for drainage tubes. Improvement set in at once. Later I had vacuum treatments to expand the lung. One day, while the doctor was changing tubes, the pleura [i.e., membranes lining the thorax] was damaged and it was touch and go for a while. But I got over that too. I weighed only 85 pounds.[33]

As spring 1901 approached, JTM began to take rides in a horse-drawn wagon, go for walks, and climb in the hills. By May, JTM found it "all extremely nice . . . with nothing to do, nothing to worry about, lots of people fussing over me." Ade had begun writing his musical comedy *The Sultan of Sulu* and JTM's brother, George, an aspiring author, sent copies to the family of his first book "called by the unprepossessing [title] of *Graustark*," the name of a fictional country in Eastern Europe that George would use as a setting for several novels.

NOTES

1   John T. McCutcheon, *Drawn From Memory* (Indianapolis and New York: Bobbs-Merrill, Inc., 1949), 95.
2   Ibid., 97.
3   Ibid., 99.
4   Ibid., 100.
5   Ibid., 101.
6   Ibid., 103.
7   Ibid., 106.
8   Ibid., 107.
9   Ibid., 108.
10 Ibid., 110.
11 Ibid., 112.
12 Ibid., 113.
13 Ibid., 114.
14 Ibid.
15 Ibid.
16 Ibid., 124.
17 Ibid., 127.
18 Ibid.
19 Ibid., 129.

20 Ibid., 142.
21 Ibid., 144.
22 Ibid., 145.
23 Ibid., 147.
24 Ibid.
25 Ibid., 148.
26 Ibid., 150.
27 Ibid., 151.
28 Ibid., 165.
29 Ibid., 171.
30 Ibid., 173.
31 Ibid., 174.
32 Ibid.
33 Ibid., 175.

4 ~~eeeeeeeeeeee~~

Broke Again and Starting Out Fresh

WHEN THE McCUTCHEONS MOVED TO ELSTON, JTM's brother, George, had formed a relationship with a cousin, Charlie Homrig, who operated a photo gallery in Lafayette. George helped his cousin "every moment that he could escape from other duties." Many days "found him up in the duskiness of the studio" where the business of photography—and Charlie's secret passion—involved "more than met the eye":

> Charlie's soul was not in his art. He lived and dreamed and thought only of a theatrical career. No one, excepting George, suspected Cousin Charlie of these aspirations. He lived a hermit among his tintypes and cabinet-size photographs, amid his plush, his papier-mâché rocks and his tawdry backgrounds of arched and pillared galleries overlooking Italian lakes, with a heavy smell of collodion [a mixture of alcohol and ether] and stale tobacco smoke overhanging it all.[1]

Nor did the family suspect that a sense of adventure was growing in George until they learned that a wagon road show financed by Charlie had begun touring, opening in a small town a few miles to the east in a play called *Linna*. Charlie wrote the play, composed the music, and cast himself in the lead role. George had taken a smaller role and his stage name, "George M. Clifford, Commedienne," appeared in bold letters on the handbills and his "cheap little trunk." The McCutcheons received letters from George occasionally post-marked from towns in southern Indiana and Kentucky. The notes were always cheerful—to the point of form letters—which eventually made Clara worried. "Let him alone," Captain Barr would tell her. "He'll come back." And so he did:

> I shall never forget the day George came back. It was my sister's [Jessie's] birthday. All the good things that went to make up an old-fashioned mid-day dinner were spread before us, and we were in the midst of the meal when a tired, dusty forlorn figure came down the road and hesitatingly turned in at the gate. It was George M. Clifford, the late comedian. Fail-ure was written in every inch of his travel-worn clothes, and there were gaunt lines of hunger in his face.[2]

The family gave George a hearty welcome and no "reproach was uttered, for even we younger children could sense something of the fearful blow his pride was suffering. 'Just in time for dinner, George.'" Clara said, trying to pretend all was well but hardly able to keep back her tears. George replied he had had his dinner and wasn't hungry. George continued to decline a number of his favorite dishes until Clara convinced him to have a cup of coffee in honor of Jessie's birthday.

> The wall of resistance, once breached, crumbled away and from that moment I never saw a human being eat so ravenously. I'm sure he never ate so much again, although passing years and comfortable living gave him a rounded amplitude of form.[3]

It marked the end of George's career as a professional actor and by this time he had "reached the girl stage." Taking advantage of his reputation as a real actor and his "enforced idleness in the field of drama," George launched an active social life in Elston. He organized dance parties at the McCutcheon home and "attended many others at the neighbors." Yet somewhere in George's heart there stirred a need for expression. He began by writing plays:

> One of the first, called *The Old Dominion,* was sent to Minnie Maddern Fiske [one of America's leading actresses at the time] who returned it with a kind comment. It could not be used, she wrote, because the first act would require two weeks to play.[4]

At twenty-two, George joined the *Lafayette Daily Courier* as a reporter. Eventually he was promoted to city editor. Searching for local news day after day was a "monotonous routine," but like Captain Barr, his engaging personality and gregarious outlook helped George turn a boring stroll into an exciting mini-adventure. After a long day of filling the empty columns of the *Courier,* George went home and wrote into the night, producing "reams of stories that rebounded with depressing inevitability." He submitted numerous handwritten manuscripts to literary agents only to see them "returned with a stereotyped note of regret." How he persisted was a mystery:

> We, the family, looked on with wonder that he could weather these discouragements without complete and crushing despair. For fear of touching on a painful nerve, we hesitated to ask embarrassing questions about his literary activities.[5]

About this time, Captain Barr died and JTM was employed up north in the Windy City at a great newspaper, which was looked upon with considerable admiration by people in Lafayette. As time passed and George "continued in his path of disappointment, [local] people began to refer to him as 'John's brother.'" When JTM returned home for occasional visits, he "almost dreaded seeing him and having to tell of the fun I was having in Chicago." JTM suggested a possible story plot to George, who used it and sent the written version back to his brother. JTM used his connections in Chicago and took the manuscript to the Herbert S. Stone and Company, which said it "was too long for a short story and not long enough for a book, so they declined it."

When JTM returned in 1900 from the Far East, George let him know that the Stone Company had accepted one of his books:

> I'm sorry to say I doubted it. I felt that he was trying to save his face, that he couldn't bear to confess that all these years of patient struggle had brought nothing of real accomplishment. "That so?" said I enthusiastically. "What's its name?" "*Graustark*," replied George. My spirits sank. What an awful name! I thought to myself. I was afraid to ask more questions for fear the affair was not really settled.[6]

To JTM's surprise, a copy of the published book was delivered to him while he was recovering in Asheville, North Carolina. "Dutifully, I started out to read it as a measure of brotherly affection," he said. After the first chapter, however, JTM "forgot where I was" and "didn't put down the book until I reached the very end." Some weeks after *Graustark* was initially published, JTM returned to Chicago and met his brother downtown:

> Already the book had demonstrated its success. It was to be found on all newsstands. As [George] went to the Polk Street Station Depot to return to Lafayette, he stopped at a stand to get a book. The bookseller shoved forward a copy of *Graustark*. "It's a great book," he said. "Everybody's reading it."[7]

Over a half million copies of *Graustark* were printed in several languages. Stone and Company also accepted George's next book, *Castle Craneycrow* (a story about the abduction of an American woman), which achieved even greater success. Dodd, Mead and Company inquired whether George would consider writing for them and eventually forwarded to him an advance check for $15,000 for his third book, *The Sherrods,* published in 1903. Stone and Company also wanted a third story, but George "felt it would be unfair to Dodd, Mead to have another of his books on the market to compete with *The Sherrods*." Stone pleaded with George and he finally agreed to write the book for them, but under an assumed name: it was *Brewster's Millions*, by Richard Greaves, and George had his brother, Ben, to thank for the original idea:

The number of people who have read or seen this story on stage or screen must run into astronomical figures. A chance remark by our youngest brother, Ben, "Why not write about a fella who spends a million dollars in a year?" caused George to give Ben one quarter of the royalties for 15 years.[8]

George was "John's brother" no longer. For many years thereafter, JTM became known as "the brother of the novelist, though many people haven't yet got us straight."

Back in Chicago, the players in the newspaper industry had changed. The *Chicago Record* and the *Chicago Morning Herald* merged, and when JTM began working again in September 1901, it was for the *Chicago Record-Herald*. His absence from work and a bank panic that wiped out his savings, left him "10 years older, broke again and starting out afresh, but with a very different setup." As his cartoons began appearing again in the paper, readers inquired immediately about the dog's return. "Had I lost him on my travels?" they wanted to know. It caused him to question whether the time had come for a different direction:

> I wondered if I might not create something new that would have the same appeal. I reflected that next to a little dog, the most appealing thing in the world is a little boy, the barefooted boy with patches on his pants and a battered straw hat—the sort of boy that nearly every man in the Middle West used to be. So the following spring, I drew a picture of such a boy. I called the cartoon "A Boy in Springtime." I reflected that if one dog was funny, perhaps five dogs would be five times as funny, so this boy was accompanied by five dogs, worth in the aggregate about a dollar and a quarter.[9]

At the time, it was a highly unusual type of cartoon to appear on the front page of a newspaper because it was human interest—not political or topical. It drew a pronounced reaction and was followed a week later by another drawing with the same title "showing another common activity of boyhood at that season." From that point on, "a series of these 'Boy' cartoons [ran] through all the seasons."

During 1902, Prince Henry of Prussia toured the United States and wherever he went it regarded as "a big event in the news of the day." JTM drew a "very elaborate cartoon of his reception in one of the first cities he visited." Like the "Boy" cartoon, he had "no intention of following it up." But the *Record-Herald* urged him to continue his coverage and he ended up drawing another dozen or so:

> I have seldom done so much detailed work as I put into that series. Hundreds of figures, great processions of people, buildings, characteristic features of different cities and scenes took a great deal of drawing. Six or eight hours of actual manual labor went into each cartoon. Naturally I was delighted that they created favorable comment, so very favorable that the *Record-Herald* printed them in book form under a caption chosen by someone else, *The Cartoons That Made Prince Henry Famous.*[10]

Prince Henry asked for JTM's original drawings, which were displayed in the billiard room in his castle in the city of Kiel.

In a similar fashion, an "unintentional development from a single cartoon" also served as the genesis for one of JTM's best known cartoon series, the *Bird Center*:

> One very dull day, when ideas were scarcer than hen's teeth, I found myself in desperation for a subject for the following morning. As a final resort I drew a picture of a church social such as I had known in the early Indiana days. Church socials happened to be in season just then, but I am certain I had no definite purpose in mind. I called it "Bird Center," a name George Ade had once used in a fable. People commented and wrote in favorably, so a week later I drew a second cartoon and accompanied it with comments and items as if by the local editor. I introduced types I had known in real life in a country town and gave them definite names which the editor of the Bird Center Argosy used in his list of "among those present."[11]

Regular characters included: the minister, his wife and their numerous children, a local doctor, the judge, the town drunkard, Captain Fry the Civil War veteran, Smiley Green the popular town undertaker, and

J. Milton Brown the tintype artist. Anyone from a small town would recognize the characters as "types to be found in most smaller communities." JTM also added a local rich matron "whose name is always first of 'those present.'" In addition, there was the village Lothario and wag, who was a "great hand" with the girls. No one ever took the Lothario seriously "except the visiting young lady." Two young men played mandolins, and their "dulcet strains evoked 'encomiums' [laudatory speeches] at all social gatherings."

Some criticized the *Bird Center* cartoons as a stereotypical representation of country life, but JTM disagreed: "It may be said that these types are conventional and hackneyed, but if a defense were necessary, it would be supplied by the obvious fact that all small towns are conventional, and the adventures of the social set rather hackneyed."[12]

A "slender plot" began to appear—"never anything very dramatic"—but the *Bird Center* did include "little love affairs" and "little ambitions that were gradually unfolded as the series advanced." One week, the people were celebrating the Fourth of July. The next week, it was a baby show. The *Bird Center* series gave JTM his "widest professional reputation." A new form of literature had been created, declared novelist Henry Blake Fuller, and gift items such as ornaments, plates, sofa cushions, and leather goods were sold bearing the characters. There even was a *Bird Center* card game, "which obtained temporary popularity."

The success of the *Bird Center* series provided JTM "a certain amount of limelight which, combined with the publicity given my war correspondence, resulted in a good many social invitations." JTM was single, "suitable for filling in" at social events, and the combination made him "just about the busiest person you ever saw." It also forced him to find a method for coping with his inherent bashfulness. He chose alcohol:

> During this period I evolved a working relationship with drink. It was customary to serve one cocktail, sherry with the fish, champagne with the roast, then port and liqueurs. After some experimenting, I discovered that I could manage nicely on one cocktail, one glass of sherry, a glass

and a half of champagne, and a small glass of Benedictine [an herbal liqueur]. This quantity gave me a pleasant sense of self-confidence. My bashfulness vanished to the extent that I said the funny things I thought of instead of regretting all next day that I had not, but my syllables were never mixed nor my voice raised. Whether or not I was really a sparkling dinner guest, the fact remains that after those drinks I thought I was—which helped immensely.[13]

Over time, JTM continued to refine his defense of the occasional criticism of the *Bird Center's* representation of country life:

If it seemed to satirize some forms of gaiety in the smaller communities, or to poke a little good-natured fun at some of the ornate pretensions of society in larger communities, so much the better, for then the cartoons might be endowed with a mission. You will find Bird Centerites in large cities as well as in small ones, and it is to be regretted that there are not more of them. For they are all good, generous and genuine people. The poor are as welcome as the rich. There are no social feuds or jealousies, no false pretenses and no striving to be more than one really is. No one feels himself to be better than his neighbor, and the impulse of generosity and kindness is common to all. If there was a "villain" in the piece, it was the old banker whose nearest approach to villainy lay in the fact that he believed a mortgage is no respecter of sentiment. With this single exception, "there is not a cross word in the history of the *Bird Center*," to quote one of its inhabitants.[14]

The *Bird Center* was adapted for theater "and it was the inspiration for many amateur productions throughout the Middle West" despite the fact that "a few country newspapers resented it because they thought [it] made fun of the country style of journalism." Even so, JTM continued drawing the series for another year or so, even after accepting a job at the *Chicago Tribune*.

M cCUTCHEON'S CARTOONS HAD ATTRACTED more than just the
readers' attention; they caught the eye of James Keeley, managing
editor of the *Chicago Tribune*. For some months, the *Tribune* had been
without a cartoonist when theirs, Harold Heaton, took a brief hiatus to
write plays and pursue a stage career. One day, Keeley sent for JTM and
offered to double his salary if he would join the *Tribune*. Keeley's offer
presented JTM with a dilemma for several reasons; he liked the *Record-
Herald*, he liked his editor Victor Lawson, and he was fond of his associates, and said so:

> I told Mr. Keeley I owed Mr. Lawson a good deal and couldn't accept any
> offer without giving the *Record-Herald* a chance to meet the raise. [They]
> jumped my pay from $65 to $110 a week, so I told Mr. Keeley I intended
> to stay where I was. In June 1903 he sent for me again and offered me $250
> a week. "The same condition still exists," I said. "I won't leave without giv-
> ing them a chance." "Name any figure you like," said Keeley. "No, I can't," I
> replied. Back at the *Record-Herald,* there was a great consultation. Every-
> body went into a huddle. Nobody on the *Record,* not even the managing
> editor, was getting that much! It would have thrown the whole paper out
> of kilter. They would have had to raise everyone all along the line.[15]

JTM told Lawson: "I like it here. I'm grateful to you for my start. I'll work
for you for a hundred dollars a week less than the *Tribune* offers me." Even
$150 a week was still more than any other employee received. More man-
agement discussions took place, including among the board of directors
where the subject "raised the devil." Lawson "couldn't bring himself to it"
because "giving any sort of raise was never his strong point."[16]

JTM went back to see Keeley and they finalized his contract. The first cartoon by JTM for the *Chicago Tribune* was published on July 1, 1903. Several
weeks later, on July 20, 1903, news of the death of Pope Leo XIII appeared
in the *Tribune's* noon edition. JTM went to discuss the story with Keeley:

I was still going through an attack of stage fright. The first days in a new job one tries too hard, which is like pressing in golf. We discussed the cartoon and he suggested: "Why not a globe with a band of black?" In as simple a form as possible I drew the world tied with a great band of crepe, the bow draped over the approximate location of Rome. The cartoon was presented to Archbishop [James E.] Quigley, and I have reason to believe it ended in the Vatican among the souvenirs of Leo XIII.[17]

For JTM, the cartoon about the pope was the beginning of a long and satisfying relationship with Keeley—a man "who was called the ablest and most colorful managing editor in the country." Among other attributes, JTM admired Keeley's ability for playing up a news story, and perhaps he saw some of himself in his managing editor:

Behind his abrupt way of giving his staccato orders, he had a venturesome soul; he would have liked to be off doing the things the correspondents were doing. He was always sympathetic with my desire to go adventuring and with any departure I made from the routine cartoon. In after years, I had many occasions to be grateful for the permissions of absence he granted, and the way he played up my stuff.[18]

In an unusual twist of fate, Keeley left the *Tribune* in May 1914 to join the *Record-Herald*, from which he had recruited JTM. Keeley and several partners ended up purchasing the newspaper. When the *Record-Herald* merged with the *Chicago Examiner* to become the *Chicago Herald-Examiner*, Keeley joined the Pullman Company as a vice president.

WHEN JTM WAS NOT PLAYING "HOOKY," as George Ade "so disrespectfully termed my travels," he was a member of the Redpath Lecture Bureau. Redpath was founded by James Redpath, an American journalist, and supplied speakers and performers for lecture halls across the country. Membership required JTM to "keep a notebook, recording the dates and places where I was supposed to lecture":

> My method of keeping these notebooks leaves much to be desired by a historian probing the past, but now and then the entries give a skeleton framework of some of my other early activities. Joining things seems to have been one of them. There is an entry about a meeting at Vogelsan's Restaurant . . . to form the Indiana Society. There was still some sort of odium attached to the word Hoosier—a sort of synonym for yoke—but the Society boldly adopted it and made it a term of honor. Another brief notation . . . reads "Meeting of Club at Wellington Hotel." It is likely that this refers to another historic birthday—the Wayfarers, a small dinner club whose only purpose was to promote good-fellowship. On the preceding page, my notebook says: "Notified of election to Royal Geographic Society of London." I remember clearly the arrival of this document resplendent with red seals. It came on a morning when I was feeling singularly frustrated in a geographic sense. The evening before I had been out on the far South Side, endeavoring to call on a young lady. For two long hours I had wandered around in the cold and dark, then, hopelessly lost, I had walked most of the way home, unable even to rediscover the whereabouts of the cable cars.[19]

JTM's first lecture, titled "A Chalk Talk on the Psychology of the Newspaper Cartoon," was scheduled to be presented at the Art Institute's Fullerton Hall. It was not supposed to be a serious lecture, but "in order that it might be dignified by a claim to serious purpose," the word psychology was included in the title, which "the Redpath people [i.e., his representatives from the Redpath Lyceum Bureau][20] thought . . . was important."

He developed a strategy for keeping the audience's attention:

> Usually upon arrival I tried to find someone who could tell me about eight or 10 recent events in town. Then at the conclusion of my talk I would draw cartoons with local significance. The audience always enjoyed this.[21]

JTM's first paid lecture was at Grinnell College in Iowa, and his career as a lecturer was off and running. He lectured "on cartooning usually about once a week anywhere within 500 miles of Chicago." The experience helped him be comfortable in front of crowds and increased his contacts throughout the Midwest, but he "never became sufficiently acclimated to the lecture platform to escape certain agonies":

> It meant doing a cartoon ahead for the paper, something of a strain. Too, there would be a long, tiresome ride in a superheated day coach and an arrival in the early darkness of a winter night on a wind-swept platform of some small-town station. This would be followed by a ride in a rickety bus up to a hotel where commercial travelers eyed me with gloomy suspicion and wondered what "line" I was selling. Sometimes the blackboard or other equipment failed to arrive. This always meant a very unsuitable substitute. It is difficult to draw on an extemporized board and unfamiliar paper. Supposing the easel was set up and the audience was in the house—except for the late-comers that always blur the point of your opening story with a confusion of shifting feet. Then came the worst ordeal of all, getting introduced. I never knew how it would turn out. Sometimes the man who did it talked almost half an hour himself. At one place the mayor introduced me with a wealth of rhetoric and then forgot my name completely.[22]

After a while, JTM got to know which were the "good parts and the dull parts" in his lecture. "When I told about the little dog or the *Bird Center* episodes, there was a hushed house, not even a cough." When he covered the key points about what guides a cartoonist in his work, attention began to drift immediately among audience members—"Faces drooped, and the younger set began to fidget." Some surprises could not be anticipated:

> Once, when I was in this section of my talk, a part that had never failed as a soporific [an agent for causing drowsiness], I became conscious of a sudden wave of interest that swept the house. People were sitting bolt upright in rapt attention, and I couldn't understand it. I had hoped that at

last my serious message had come into its own, but, a little later, it developed that a cat had walked out on the stage and was marching and countermarching behind me. There is nothing like an earnest cat to enliven a discourse. Another time the evening went off beautifully. The audience was suffused with mirth and good nature, and I felt immensely pleased until I reached the hotel and discovered that I had wiped my forehead with a charcoal-covered hand and left most of the charcoal behind.[23]

JTM preferred not to stay in a town any longer that required, so he always "took the last train in and the first train out when I could." Using rear entrances and backstreet routes, he often tried to escape the lecture halls undetected because he "dreaded seeing people afterward or overhearing unflattering comments." Quick visits had their downsides: "Getting away the same night, especially from the smaller towns, often necessitated sitting up until two or three in the morning to take a short ride to somewhere else to make connections to a Chicago train." Often, it just was not possible to depart that quickly anyway because frequently "somebody had been delegated to entertain me, or some minor league lion hunter wanted to show me off and I was trapped." There were other dangers, like accidentally taking the wrong train:

> I remember one occasion that was especially distressing. I started late to catch a train to Whitewater, Wisconsin. In my hurry, I got on a train to Watertown. It followed more or less the same route, with a change at Milwaukee. Not until I was almost at the hotel did I realize I was in the wrong town. It was then seven o'clock and Whitewater was 50 miles away. I tried to get an automobile, but there was only one man in town, people said, who would dare to try to do it in less than a couple hours, and he was nowhere to be found. I called up Whitewater and got the [lecture hall] manager, who was taking tickets at the door. "I'm in Watertown," I apologized. "I should say you are!" He banged down the receiver, furious. Later, to make amends, I went to Whitewater for nothing. Ordinarily, I received $200 or $250 plus expenses. At one place they paid me with two sheets of five $20 dollar bills each, still uncut, all signed by the local banker.[24]

Another time, JTM was forced to hire a driver to take him the last fourteen miles to an event to reach a town in northern Indiana. He got there nearly an hour late. While he gave the lecture, the driver got drunk and when they set out to return, he got lost. He recalled, "It was a lonely drive, groping in the darkness of a silent country road at midnight, but somehow we finally made a distant railway station." A week later, JTM learned that a farmhouse on the same road had been burned and was the site of a gruesome murder. Good thing they had not stopped to ask directions or he "might not have had opportunity to lecture any more."[25]

JTM continued to remain uneasy about his lecturing. He knew his reputation could draw people to a hall, but he "never had any confidence in his ability to entertain them once they were out in front of me." As one audience member put it: "Well, he ain't much of a talker, but the drawin's were purty pat!"[26]

WHEN JTM BEGAN HIS CAREER in the late nineteenth century, newspapers were the only tool available for reaching the masses. While movies and radio would eventually change that during his lifetime, he always believed that when it comes to the "molding of public opinion for better or for worse the dominating power and responsibility rest with the printed columns and cartoons of the country's newspapers." In a daily newspaper, that meant the relentless challenge of producing editorial content, whether stories or cartoons and illustrations, day after day, with no end. Many people asked JTM one version or another of the following question, "Where do you get your ideas—a fresh one every morning? I should think you would run dry." It was commonly believed that the life of a cartoonist "with its demand for a drawing every day, rain or shine, idea or no idea, must be fairly irksome." For JTM, it was anything but:

Let us assume that it was morning and that I had nothing in mind for the day's work. My first move was to read the papers thoroughly, taking note of the news uppermost in the public mind. Nearly every day presents at least one good front-page story, an election, a notable speech, a prize fight, a war scare and so on through an endless variety. By the time I had finished the papers I might have a half a dozen suggestions, equally good or poor. One might deal with a broad national matter; another with local politics; still another might have domestic interest that would appeal to women and children. This list of suggestions is sometimes submitted to the editor. More often the cartoonist is given discretionary powers.[27]

There were times when reading the newspapers "did not suggest a single idea." On dull news days, if no idea emerged by 4 p.m., "the situation became alarming." Worrying did no good and besides JTM "knew there would be a cartoon in tomorrow's paper, and I would get it out, because I was under contract to do so!" Experience also taught JTM that sometimes the last-minute ideas turned out to be the best, which provided a "cheering consolation." But that did not mean the pressure eased:

When that 11th hour came, however, I really had to dig. I would put down the date of the next day and look at it hard. Was it the anniversary of any historic event? Was it the birthday of anybody of interest? Then I would try to remember whether anybody had said anything startling recently. Once a university professor was credited with saying—whether he did so or not—that [John D.] Rockefeller [founder of the Standard Oil Company] was greater than Shakespeare. Then a doctor came out with the opinion that bathing was unhygienic. Changing fashions offer material; and weather was a last resort—there are enough different kinds in this climate to give us a chance.[28]

Political cartoons generally fall into one of two categories: serious and humorous. Although JTM knew each merited their place on the newspaper opinion pages, he preferred the latter and "enjoyed drawing a type of cartoon which might be considered a sort of pictorial breakfast food":

It had the cardinal asset of making the beginning of a day sunnier. It is safe to say the prairies were not set afire by these cartoons, yet they had the merit of offending no one. Their excuse lay in the belief that a happy man is capable of a more constructive day's work than a glum one.[29]

JTM believed that readers preferred to be amused "rather than reformed." The steady drumbeat of the daily news is "so full of crime, crookedness and divorce" that it can be difficult resisting an urge to "become a muckraker who allows the dark spots to dominate his vision. A cartoon does as much good by reminding people of the blessings of life as by pointing out its shortcomings." That being said, he acknowledged that certain subjects require a serious approach: "Some evils demand more stinging rebukes than can be administered with ridicule or good-natured satire." In those situations, he knew what he had to do, but didn't like it:

> In such cases a cartoon must be drawn that is meant to hurt. All the same, I have not liked to draw that sort of cartoon, and it was invariably with a feeling of regret that I turned one in for publication. It would seem better to reach out a friendly pictorial hand to the delinquent rather than to assail him with criticism and denunciation.[30]

He was particularly disdainful of cartoons pitting one group against another: "A most unwholesome type of cartoon is that which strives to arouse the ignorant passions of one element of society against another." He believed "there are too many good people in every walk of life to justify assailing the group as a whole." JTM preferred telling the truth and avoiding misrepresenting "facts to bolster one's point." That was the philosophy that governed his work:

> If the one who saw [my cartoon] smiled, its mission was fulfilled; and if, on rare occasions, half a million people smiled in unison, then I felt a great work had been accomplished. I tried to be optimistic and constructive rather than iconoclastic and discouraging. It isn't so important if children don't believe in Santy, but gosh, the world would come to an end if Santy didn't believe in children![31]

Humor was not the only criteria for selecting the day's idea. Cartoonists had to be mindful of their newspaper's point of view. A business-savvy newspaper knows not to print cartoons that "needlessly arouse the resentment of large sections of its circulation." A certain respect also was required when cartooning the president of the United States and "most artists seek a manner that does not reflect on the honor of the man or the dignity of the office." Similarly, cartoons about women required the artist to "blunt his barb by somehow flattering her." Cartoonists early on adopted certain stock characters to represent people types:

> An anxious-looking man loaded down with bundles stood for a subur-
> banite; a man in a loud checked suit with a hat down over his eyes was
> a gambler or confidence man; by adding a horseshoe watch charm, the
> same man became a race-track sport. Congressmen invariably wore chin
> whiskers and for years old maids wore spectacles and ringlets. Then there
> was the corpulent gent in the frock coat and silk hat, besprinkled with
> diamonds busily spurting out streams of radiance. Who does not recog-
> nize the trust magnate of the last century or, more recently, the capital-
> ist? He used to have side whiskers. Why I never knew for sure but I may
> hazard a guess. When the first American cartoons were beginning to
> appear, the late Commodore [Cornelius] Vanderbilt [an American rail-
> road and shipping industrialist] was our greatest representative of wealth.
> The older generation will recall that this particular Mr. Vanderbilt wore
> side whiskers and expressed considerable disregard for the rights of the
> public. The capitalists of today look lamentably less and less corpulent.[32]

In addition to such stock characters, cartoonists also regularly employed other figures like Father Time, Cupid, Neptune, and the Grim Reaper. Sometimes certain characteristics were more important in identifying real people than a rendering of their actual portrait. At the height of Theodore Roosevelt's notoriety, for example, "a pair of glasses and a gleaming phalanx of teeth were unmistakable." An overweight man out fishing, "whether shown front, side or rear," instantly suggested to readers the portly ex-President Grover Cleveland, who reacted good-naturedly to a cartoon of him by JTM:

Once when it was incumbent on [President William] McKinley to select an American representative to the coronation of King Edward VII, Cleveland's name was mentioned. I drew him fatter than natural, in a boat fishing, and replying to the President, who beckoned from the shore, "Can't go. Got a bite." A note in Mr. Cleveland's handwriting presently arrived: "The incident and the ideas it suggests are not only amusingly portrayed, but thoughtfully—except that I have not been invited to attend the coronation either officially or unofficially, and the string of fish is wholly inadequate."[33]

JTM found that people in public office "have a kindly feeling for cartoonists even though we sometimes handle them roughly." Publicity—even bad publicity—is a statesman's "most valuable asset, and cartoons are as good as first-page advertising." Associating a public figure in some way with farms suggested honesty, simplicity, and democracy. Conversely, silk hats were to be avoided. Generalities, however, did not always ring true:

At the beginning of Carter Harrison's first race for mayor of Chicago, somebody unearthed a picture of the young man in a bicycle suit and cap, bending low over the handle bars. This picture was not one to reassure the people. Obviously the young man lacked dignity and would not do for mayor of a great city. The bicycle cap became an issue and at another time might have defeated the candidate. As it happened, the campaign was coincident with the bicycle craze, and it is presumed several hundred thousand cyclists rallied around the cap and elected it.[34]

Cartoons predicting the outcome of an election or any other prophesy frequently fall down with "a prodigious flop." The solution to avoid such embarrassment? Two cartoons are drawn the day before, like the time in 1902 when JTM covered a city election:

One of the candidates for alderman was John Coughlin, familiarly known as Bathhouse John; all the reform influences were out to accomplish his defeat. It was a picturesque fight, for the Bathhouse's position in the first ward was well-nigh impregnable and his followers included all the riffraff of the levee district. As the campaign approached its end, the reform elements made a mighty effort and there were some optimistic persons who believed that the legions of the Bathhouse would be routed.[35]

The day of the election, JTM's cartoon showed an egg, "which conformed fairly well to the architecture of the Bathhouse," about to be pushed from the top of a tall building. Bathhouse was about to fall. But when the election results came in, he had won "a mighty victory and [it] necessitated some quick side-stepping on the part of the cartoonist." Next morning, JTM drew Bathhouse landing successfully in a net held by friends and associates down on the sidewalk below.

JTM regarded cartoons as unlike any other picture in a newspaper because "the idea alone is the essential requirement, whether it is meant to inform, reform or solely to amuse." He had the following advice for young cartoonists who came to see him for help:

This idea should be brought out with directness and simplicity, in such a way that people will know it is a cartoon and not a work of art. It has little to do with beauty or grace; it has much to do with strength and uniqueness. It is a peculiar form of art for a peculiar purpose, and presupposes the ability to say a thing trenchantly, humorously or caustically, in terms of line. However, I don't believe drawing has much to do with the success of a cartoon. Eugene Field [an American writer], who had only a bowing acquaintance with drawing, could make sketches overflowing with fun and drollery. Mark Twain, who could not draw at all, made crude pen sketches that are extremely funny. I am always conscious of this dilemma when a beginner comes to me for criticism. Remembering the undoubtedly amateurish samples I brought to Chicago to display to a professional, I hesitate to discourage an enthusiastic aspirant; yet it would not be fair to encourage him to waste time studying when it is evident there is no likelihood of success in the end. New ideas and distinct individuality in methods of both thought and technique . . . are the steppingstones I try to emphasize.[36]

POLITICAL CARTOONISTS at the major daily newspapers in America usually produce their work as close to the paper's publication deadline as possible to ensure accuracy and freshness. Sometimes, however, it becomes necessary "to draw considerably ahead of the hour and even the date of publication," as was the case for JTM in 1904, about a year into his tenure at the *Chicago Tribune*. He began to feel restless for some ocean travel, but what he really wanted was a "look-in on the Russo-Japanese War then in progress." JTM bristled at the idea of a war going on "without seeing at least something of the edges of it." When two *Tribune* correspondents departed for the Far East, "every part of [JTM] capable of itching was busy." He studied timetables for a transpacific crossing and concluded if everything went as scheduled, he could be back in thirty-eight days. It was too much for the adventurous JTM to resist, so he went to see Keeley to ask for thirty days of vacation:

> "Where are you going, up to Wisconsin?" "No," I replied, "I'd like to go to Japan." "Great Scott! You can't do that in a month!" "Yes, I figured it out. I can spend four days over there and be back in a little over a month." "Well," he demurred, "this is a campaign year. I hate to have the cartoons stop for so long." "I'll draw 30 ahead," I said reassuringly. "What! What about?" "Oh, some political ones; some about the St. Louis Fair; three about the weather—we're pretty sure to have at least three kinds of weather. Then some general ones, and—oh yes, the birth of a son to the Czar [Nicholas II of Russia]." "Good Lord! But he has only girls!" "I'm taking a chance it will be a boy this time. I can go and get back without anybody knowing I've been out of town."

Keeley agreed to let him go. During the three weeks prior to his departure, JTM drew his daily cartoon and then worked on the extra drawings that "I hoped would fit any emergency which might arise during my absence." The 1904 World's Fair in St. Louis "was good for three or four," the 1904 presidential campaign between Theodore Roosevelt and Alton

B. Parker would provide another dozen topics. And there was Labor Day, maybe several to fit assorted Chicago weather, child life in the good old summertime, and two or three war cartoons to "fit probable conditions in the Orient." Then there was the blessed event of the czar's baby: "I took a gambler's chance. It represented the Czar smiling broadly as he said, 'It's a boy!' Czar Nicholas did all he could to help me. It was a boy."[37]

There was another reason JTM wanted to get out of town: the opening night was coming for the stage version of *Bird Center*, which would debut in New York. "I dreaded the nervous strain of the opening night," he wrote. "It was being widely advertised." JTM shouldn't have worried. At the time of the opening night, he was crossing the international deadline in mid-ocean, "So I never did live through the opening performance of my first—and only—play."

During the few busy days that JTM spent after arriving in Tokyo, he "sent no dispatches home, but wrote an illustrated account on the way back." When he returned home, it was apparent "the public evidently considered the cartoons as timely as usual—which may or may not be a welcome commentary."

A few years later in 1906, JTM again wanted to travel, this time on a more elaborate five-month trip, but was "not entitled to this vacation either." The prospect of producing five months of cartooning in advance was not feasible, so "I had to find some sort of substitute scheme that would satisfy the *Tribune*." He asked one cartoonist to substitute for him, but was turned down. Then he came up with an interesting solution:

> I would ask 30 eminent cartoonists from all over the country each to do one for a day of the month. This idea, which I called the "Cartoon Symposium," met with immediate approval. I wrote them all, telling them of my projected trip, and of my dilemma, and saying that any subject, in their own style, would be welcome. They responded generously. Many were famous at the time, others have become so since, and still others have gone into different activities. With the substitute cartoon business satisfactorily arranged, I could turn to the red tape of preparations for the trip.[38]

JTM's destination this time was Central Asia with "no more serious motive than to get off the beaten track." No other part of the world had "such an appeal to the imagination." The region was home to Jason's search for the Golden Fleece; Genghis Khan and Alexander "exhausted the fields of possible conquest" here; the land offered a "kaleidoscopic vision of Georgian beauties, Persian gardens, turquoise hills, torrid sands and Mongol hordes." He and an acquaintance, Kirk Brice, began preparations to "the birthplace of the human race," including bracing themselves for unsolicited advice:

> Deafen your ears to the warnings of those who have gone before, else you will never start. But all the drawbacks so persistently offered for our sober contemplation served only to make the outlook more alluring. The difficulties of travel are proportional to the distance you are away from them.[39]

JTM and Brice obtained travel permits from Russian authorities "as the district was under military rule at that time," which went easily. JTM recalled, "If you could prove that you were not an Englishman intent on investigation of Russian activities on the northern borders of Persia and Afghanistan, there was no real difficulty in this." Once they reached Asia, the trip got off to a rocky start:

> We were mobbed once in Persia, arrested once in Turkestan and robbed of some of our luggage in Russia. Odessa was under martial law—"a state of siege"—they called it—and looked like an armed camp. But my main recollection is of a boil on my cheek which was conspicuous and painful, and another on my neck. When we dined with important functionaries I couldn't wear a collar, which was very embarrassing. A Black Sea steamer took us eastward. At Novorossiysk [Russia's main port city on the Black Sea] where we had intended to disembark, we found that rioters had seized the railway and no trains were running, so we remained on board as far a Batum [a Russian city on the Black Sea]. Here we landed during the funeral services of the American vice-consul, who had just been murdered.[40]

At Batum, they boarded a train to Tiflis [in the country of Georgia, which was part of the Russian empire], "a most curious city." The Kura River splits the city in half and pours through a gorge "on the sides of which the city is built." The city was home to numerous ethnic groups who lived in separate sections. Despite the geographical separation, "there was constant strife between the Tartars and the Armenians, with the Russian Cossacks always ready to gallop in with their knouts [whips] and rifles."

In Tiflis, Brice and JTM needed to hire a dragoman [an interpreter, translator, and guide] and "had some trouble finding one." They reluctantly hired a man named Johannes who was seventy years old. They weren't impressed with his knowledge, so they set up a way to confirm he would meet their needs:

> As a starter, to test him out, we made a little side trip down into Armenia, to Erivan [the largest city in Armenia and one of the world's longest-inhabited cities] in the shadow of Mount Ararat [a snow-capped volcano in Turkey], and to Etchmiadzin [site of the Etchmiadzin Cathedral—the oldest state-built church in the world], seat of the Armenian pope. When we left him weeks later, we were convinced he was one of the most adroit, efficient and companionable people in the world.[41]

When they returned to Tiflis following Johannes's test, they learned a bomb had been hurled at the governor and the police chief the day before as they were driving down the city's main street. The explosion killed "a couple of Cossack guards. The chief jumped out of the carriage and shot the two nearest innocent bystanders."

To continue their journey, Brice and JTM had to cross the formidable boundary between Europe and Asia: the Caucasus Mountains, which run from the Caspian Sea to the Black Sea and include a "12,000-foot barrier off ice-capped peaks." They regarded the mountains in awe:

> The pass has been a great gateway since ancient times, and as each century brought its vast armies of conquest surging through from east to west or west to east, there were stragglers left behind in the Caucasus.

There is probably no other place in the world where so many nationalities are jammed together. Ordinarily a mail coach ran through the pass by the Georgian Military Road, but revolts and rioting had . . . upset the service.[42]

So they hired a carriage and four horses and departed the Hotel de Londres on the last day of May. Old castles, deep valleys, ornate watchtowers, and tens of thousands of sheep provided a "wonderfully picturesque drive" along the 135 miles from Tiflis to the Russian city of Vladikavkaz at the northern end of the pass. The carriage was the only vehicle on the road and although they "saw many bands of soldiers in the mountains," none approached them. "In many respects," JTM and Brice marveled that the local residents "were just as they had been 3,000 years before; all the time we were reminded of Biblical characters." They rode past Mount Kazbek "where Prometheus [a Greek mythological figure] was supposed to have been bound" and the "wildly grand scenery of Dariel Gorge, eight miles long and a mile deep." One valley after another crisscrossed the gorge "with little villages, each speaking a separate language." Mishket, "a miserable little settlement," claimed to be founded by the great-great-great-grandson of Noah. The Crusaders had also passed along the same route and left "old French names." The wonders continued:

> On the third evening, we descended into Vladikavkaz and took a train for Baku on the Caspian Sea. We found the town barely recovered from riots of a few months before, in which thousands of people were killed. The burned and wrecked business blocks were eloquent reminders, and the nerves of the community were still on edge. A new outbreak was expected momentarily, and the slamming of a door was enough to send the citizens scurrying to the cyclone cellar. You will, by now, have perceived that the time and place of our trip had been well selected for a couple of romantics seeking relief from the pleasant comforts of conventional summer outings.[43]

They remained in Baku several days to stock up on supplies and food for the rest of the trip. Dinners were enjoyed mightily and included "delectable squab [pigeon] and stuffed chicken" at the hotel where they were staying. A looming crisis involving their supply of cigars was narrowly avoided:

> Just as we had almost run out of cigars, we chanced on a shop which had Corona Coronas and Henry Clays, and Hoyo de Montereys and other good brands. In our excitement we bought up the whole stock, which cost some 300 rubles—$150.[44]

They were glad to depart Baku, a city where "living is hard." Despite his experience as a world traveler and war correspondent, JTM had "never been in a place where the air seemed so full of menace and danger, where there was a threat of tragedy in nearly every face, and where the grim terrors of racial feuds were only half disguised by a barbarous half-drunken gaiety." The evening they departed, JTM wondered if even nature tried to compensate for the hard living conditions:

> When we went on board the steamer in Baku the moon was just rising above the eastern rim of the Caspian Sea. I have never seen a richer, yellower moonrise. Perhaps the fact that the Caspian is nearly a hundred feet below sea level imparts to the atmosphere some peculiar necromancy [black magic]. Or perhaps nature strives harder with its aesthetic effects as a compensation to those who are compelled to live in Baku.[45]

The steamer crossed the Caspian Sea to Krasnovodsk—"the first town in Russian Turkestan." From that point forward, Brice and JTM traveled by military train enjoying "good sleeping and eating," journeying 1,700 miles across the desert to the city of Andizhan in Uzbekistan and on to Ashgabat in Turkmenistan, where they settled down as "diplomatic machinery was set in motion" for the next leg of the trip to Meshed—the capital of the province of Khurasan and the Holy City of Persia—"where a Christian is as unwelcome as triplets."

—{{{{{{{{{{{{←

JOHANNES, THE DEGROMAN they had hired in back in Tiflis, was Armenian but carried a Persian passport "for reasons of safety." His name made him part German, but he adopted various nationalities "to suit the occasion if there was any strategic advantage to be gained thereby." JTM and Brice gave him the job of getting their permits. While they waited for the travel arrangements to be finalized, Johannes asked if they would be interested in seeing some fine carpets. The samples were Tekke carpets—Johannes never referred to them as rugs—and they were excellent indeed and JTM and Brice bought some, which turned out to be "fatal" to their departure plans:

> As long as we could be induced to buy rugs in Ashgabat it could never be arranged for us to start for Persia. The word spread through the bazaars that foreigners were buying. It leaked out through the Akkal Oasis and spread to the desert. Turkomans and Tartars and Persians began arriving at our modest hotel. The air was full of dust from visiting rugs. In one day, Johannes' commission on the sale of rugs to us had doubtless exceeded his wages for the whole trip to Meshed. At last we rebelled, and insisted that unless the expedition to Persia started immediately, Johannes was likely to find himself playing the leading role in a Russian atrocity. So he shrugged his shoulders, mustered up a semblance of energy and fared forth to complete arrangements.[46]

The day of departure arrived, and at 10 a.m. when they were supposed to leave, Johannes brought bad news: the road had been washed away in a flood and would delay leaving "for a day or two." They asked how far down the road it had occurred and Johannes replied "out in the mountains, thirty versts" [a Russian measure of distance; .66 mile]. How did Johannes find out? A Persian brought the news, but had no further details. Brice and JTM decided to depart anyway and Johannes was "crestfallen when we indicated that we would proceed as far as possible, and at once."

A victoria [four-wheel, horse-drawn carriage with collapsible roof] with "four drooping ponies" and Valentine, their Russian driver, awaited them outside the hotel. At noon they drove off, "ponies galloping to the crack of Valentine's whip, and clattered out onto the road across the plains to the foot of the Kopet Dag [mountain range], eight miles away." What awaited was not pleasant:

> Well, it was a terrible trip. The roads were fearful. The dust was fearful. The heat was unbelievable—110 degrees in the shade, and our carriage was open. Mirages hung in the distance all the time—lakes surrounded by trees—yet it was absolutely barren except where a small village surrounded an oasis. At one town the gutters were running with—could it be blood? Our hair stood on end. But no, there had been a decree to do away with all foreign dyestuffs which were replacing the native vegetable dyes that give the Persian rugs such magnificent colors. All was dirty, slovenly and backward beyond words. We stopped at night anywhere— the caravansaries [an inn for travelers] were simply native houses which we had to clean out.[47]

On the first afternoon they arrived at the foothills of the Kopet Dag and worked their way for the next three or four hours "through a series of stony, forlorn hills." They encountered "hundreds of camels feeding by the way, their 500-pound burdens of cotton or oil or rugs heaped by the roadside." Shepherds, who looked like central casting chose them straight from biblical times, attended to the camels. The original plan was to arrive at the frontier before sunset, but the "break in the road delayed us." Just as Johannes had reported, a stone causeway across a gulch had been destroyed: "The rocks that had formed it were strewed for a quarter of a mile down the bed of the gulch." They were able to cross the chasm with "a plunge down a perpendicular bank, a wild clatter across the rock-strewed gorge, and a frenzied pull up the opposite bank." Despite overcoming the washed-out causeway, the group only covered "another 27 versts, or 18 miles that day." At night, their sleep was disturbed by the "most characteristic and memorable sound of the East":

> We were awakened by . . . the sound that marks the progress of a camel caravan. On the trails, bound for Persia or Afghanistan or India, the camels are roped together in groups of 10. The leader carries a bell of a certain note, the eight middle camels wear little tinkling bells, and the end one has a great copper bell that hangs from its side and with every step gives forth a deep, rich boom as soft and melodious as the gong of a Burmese temple. For many minutes before the van comes abreast of the posthouse, the bells may be heard. There are no sounds of footsteps, for the camel tread is noiseless. In the uncertain light, the swaying figures of the animals pass like so many ghosts, silent except for the sweetest music of bells that one can imagine. For hours, it seems, the caravan is passing. You are asleep long before the rear guard rocks by and the jangling of bells is replaced by the "silence of the East."[48]

They arose each morning by 6 a.m. to drink tea from a samovar [a decorated tea urn], eat hard-boiled eggs, and be on their way across the "gaunt and somber landscape." They finally arrived at the walls of the city of Meshed where, Johannes informed them, "no suitable caravansary" existed, so Johannes made arrangements with the head of a British bank who welcomed them into his home, apparently "glad to see a rare outsider."

A holy shrine where the caliph of Baghdad, Harun al-Rashid, is buried sits in the middle of the city with a sanctuary extending for a quarter mile on every side. Christians are not allowed in it. Thousands of Shiite Mohammedans travel each year from all over Central Asia to worship at the shrine. JTM found Meshed to be an active, if not filthy, potpourris of activity:

> In Meshed, the main street is 80 feet wide. Down the center of this Oriental Champs-Élysées runs a canal, or more accurately, a dirty ditch, spanned by frail foot bridges and planks. It serves as drinking fountain, laundry and public bath. It is lined by irregular rows of mulberry, plane and willow, mostly rather decrepit and forlorn, and beyond them is the ramshackle of the bazaars. Within, in a sort of twilight, the teeming life of the Orient goes on amid the rugs and odors. Among the dense

crowds may be seen the white-turbaned mullah and half-caste dervish; the portly merchant and travel-stained pilgrim; the supercilious sayid [a Muslim claiming descent from Mohammed] in a green turban and the cowering Sunni who has ventured into the stronghold of the enemy; black-browed Afghans, handsome Uzbegs, wealthy Arabs, wild Bedouins, Indian traders, Caucasian devotees, Turks, Tartars, Mongols, Tajiks. Everybody was shouting and shrieking at the same time.[49]

The time to depart had arrived, and they packed the carriage and returned to Ashkhabad by the same route that brought them to Meshed. By train, they stopped temporarily at Merv [a major oasis city] where, because they were wearing their English sun helmets, "were mistaken for Englishmen and arrested, but released upon proof that we were Americans." They continued their travels to Osh, and from there set out on horses with five attendants to Xinjiang in Chinese Turkestan—230 miles over the Alay Mountains. JTM wrote, "There would be no houses on the road, only the felt tents of nomads feeding their flocks there in the summer," so they sent a man ahead to "arrange with the headman of a village to have a tent emptied for us and moved to a clean piece of ground." The arrangement worked out well, with one unusual surprise:

> When we arrived, a kibitka [circular tent covered with felt] or yurt [circular tent of skins on a collapsible frame] was beautifully decorated with carpets, friezes [sculpted or painted decorations] and soft sleeping rugs. A sheep had been freshly killed, and curds and milk brought in and sometimes kumiss, which is fermented camel's or mare's milk. Then in exchange, everyone who had anything the matter came to us to be doctored! Being white, we were supposed to know. We prescribed for everything, but drew the line at surgical operations.[50]

At higher altitudes they hunted ibex [wild goat] and yaks. Accompanied by native mountaineers, they traveled by foot to "places I never dreamed I could cross—up to 14,000 feet." There were certain risks involved with this kind of travel:

Sometimes the trails were dangerous. We had to skirt the edge of the gorges, with the river below supposed to be 90 feet deep and the footing for our horses exceedingly precarious. Once the trail was broken and we had to descend and ride through the very edge of water, where we could not see what lay under our feet. Often we were lost entirely. Sometimes there were long rides between drinks, a trying ordeal in the heat, though we carried raisins and chocolate to tide us over.[51]

After two weeks, there was not much left to talk about it, so they would sing a good deal and indulge in fanciful conversations, such as: "How do you like the little sunset I arranged for you this evening?" Or, "I put a good deal of effort into that particular landscape. Have you any suggestions?" Eventually, rations began to run out, including their precious supply of cigars. Brice stretched his by smoking cigarettes and teased JTM about his dwindling stash: "If you're good today, I'll give you a cigar." Eventually, they reached the town of Kashgar, where they proceeded directly to the Russian consul, a Colonel Kolokoloff, who arranged for them to stay at a vacant house—"It was also arranged for Kirk and me to lunch with the *taoti* of Kashgar, the native Chinese ruler. We were warned he would wait on us himself and would follow us out [at the conclusion of lunch] as we backed [away] from his presence." It made for a unique lunch experience:

His was a typical Chinese residence, with several courts and gateways before one reached the main compound. The table was set with a lot of little things, like candied fruit, nothing solid. The taoti poured the tea. We stood up to eat. There was no talking, but a vast amount of smiling and bowing. Finally the taoti and some other Chinese dignitaries escorted us to the door and bowed extra-ceremoniously. Then they followed us to the next gate. We backed all the way as per instructions. Then ensued another formal bowing. From yard to yard we backed, clear to the outer gate, each time repeating the performance. We had difficulty keeping our faces straight.[52]

There were two paths that led out of the city of Kashgar—south over the Karakoram Mountains, which were 17,500 feet high at the pass. The route would take them along the "corner of Tibet" and require an eight-week caravan into Kashmir in northern India, then out through India itself. They decided to head north across the Tian Shan Mountains and up to Russian roads in Siberia. The plan involved a journey of 1,000 miles on the roads until they reached the Irtysh River at Semipalatinsk, followed by several hundred more miles down the river "to the Trans-Siberian railroad at Omsk [a city in south central Russia]."

Along the way, they passed Issyk Kul—a lake in which a city "is said to be buried whose towers can sometimes be seen. A storm broke, with thunder and lightning and at 12,000 feet we traveled along in the storm clouds themselves." They drove to the city of Semipalatinsk where they boarded a steam ship and traveled five hundred miles down the river to Omsk, "then by courier express to Moscow." The trip had lasted fourteen days, and at its conclusion they "naturally wished to sell the carriage, but equally naturally no one wished to buy it." JTM suggested tongue-in-cheek that it be burned, "but we finally weakened and left it to the crafty Johannes, with whom we parted regretfully."

NOTES

1   John T. McCutcheon, *Drawn From Memory* (Indianapolis and New York: Bobbs-Merrill, Inc., 1949), 179.
2   Ibid., 180.
3   Ibid.
4   Ibid., 181.
5   Ibid.
6   Ibid., 182.
7   Ibid.
8   Ibid., 183.
9   Ibid., 184.
10 Ibid.
11 Ibid., 185.
12 Ibid.
13 Ibid., 189.

14 Ibid., 189.

15 Ibid., 190-91.

16 Ibid., 191.

17 Ibid.

18 Ibid.

19 Ibid., 193-94.

20 "James Redpath Breathes His Last," *Chicago Daily Tribune* (1872-1922), February 11, 1891, ProQuest Historical Newspapers.

21 McCutcheon, *Drawn From Memory*, 194.

22 Ibid., 195.

23 Ibid., 196.

24 Ibid., 196-97.

25 Ibid., 197.

26 Ibid., 198.

27 Ibid.

28 Ibid., 199.

29 Ibid.

30 Ibid.

31 Ibid.

32 Ibid., 200-1.

33 Ibid., 201.

34 Ibid., 201-2.

35 Ibid., 202.

36 Ibid., 203.

37 Ibid., 205.

38 Ibid., 206.

39 Ibid., 207.

40 Ibid.

41 Ibid., 208.

42 Ibid.

43 Ibid., 209.

44 Ibid.

45 Ibid.

46 Ibid., 211.

47 Ibid., 212.

48 Ibid., 212-13.

49 Ibid., 213-14.

50 Ibid., 214.

51 Ibid., 215.

52 Ibid., 215-16.

5

IN SEARCH OF
MORE FRESH AIR

W ORLD TRAVEL AND AN ENDLESS QUEST for the next adventure was never far from JTM's mind and in some ways formed his general approach to living: "If I had any conscious plan of action during my life, it may be based on the theory that each passing year will seem longer if it is marked by some distinctive feature, some new experience. Varying the smooth daily routine of life makes for a feeling of accomplishment, revitalizes a person, and gives him a vantage point from which to evaluate the rut he may have fallen into."

So it was that in 1907, JTM embarking on another adventure, this time with his friend, Senator Albert J. Beveridge, who had graduated from Indiana Asbury University (now DePauw University) and was known as a compelling orator. For JTM, he brought all the right qualities as a travel partner:

> Beveridge was a fine companion, always interesting, always amusing. While it must be admitted that in his younger days he was too outspoken, too assertive, overdressy, yet the widespread opinion of his conceit

and pomposity would have changed, could others have seen him as I did. He knew what people said of him and he laughed about it. He had a swarm of devoted friends, whose friendship he could not have held had they not discovered the sterling depth of his character. Never in all his career in the Senate was there a word reflecting on his integrity.[1]

JTM and a good friend, Catherine Eddy, had "long been aware of the Senator's admiration for her." Although Catherine welcomed the senator's affection, "her family were unenthusiastic" about it, but Beveridge was hopeful he could change that. When the Eddy family announced it was going abroad in early 1907, JTM and Beveridge arranged to follow, setting out on their transatlantic crossing on the *Kaiser Wilhelm der Grosse*, where Beveridge told JTM "day after day of his hopes." His hopes came true:

> In Paris, Albert and I stopped together at the Hotel Meurice, and in a few days he was happy to announce that the date of the wedding had been set, to take place in Berlin where [Catherine's] brother Spencer Eddy was Ambassador. He wanted me to act as best man, but my leave was too short. After I knew that the Senator's plans were working out happily, I left for a motor trip through the chateau country [and back to Paris]. I had some romantic affairs of my own on hand.[2]

On his return to Paris, JTM met Booth Tarkington ("Tark") and his wife on the Rue de Tournoy near the Luxembourg Gardens, where they dined together one evening. JTM first met Tarkington at Purdue when he would come to visit from Chicago after graduation:

> The year after I graduated from Purdue, Tark had come there from Phillips Exeter [founded in 1781 in Exeter, New Hampshire, as a private college prep school] to take a special course. He became a Sigma Chi brother and I used to see a lot of him when I went down from Chicago. He drew well, had a remarkable singing voice, was a good actor as well as playwright and had a charm of manner that made him irresistible. Not only the nicest young ladies of Lafayette but a procession of visiting young ladies felt his fascination. The only thing that could possibly

interfere with a brilliant future was the possibility that he might not exert his undoubted powers; that, being able to do so many things well, he might never concentrate on one. Entirely due to the efforts of his sister, he kept at writing until his first stories were accepted, *Monsieur Beaucaire* and *The Gentleman from Indiana*.[3]

Their evening together began normally as they "sang and reminisced until midnight," then went to another restaurant "for a bite before bed," where they remained until the establishment closed at 2 a.m. Then the night got interesting, thanks to the ample imbibing that no doubt was consumed to that point:

> Tark suggested that we walk down the Boulevard St. Michel to the Seine [River]. He had with him his frisky little dog, "Gamin," and, needing something to hold the dog in check, he hailed a fiacre [a small carriage]. Tark bowed low and addressed the cocher [coachman] as "Monseigneur le Prince." The cocher did likewise and asked what he wished. With Chesterfieldian courtesy Tark explained—a strap to tie his dog. The cocher, beaming widely, deprecated the fact that he needed all his straps to keep his harness intact, but not to be outdone in civility he dismounted and produced a bit of string from somewhere. Tark gravely offered him a cigarette.[4]

They walked on together as Tarkington explained in great detail the "historical significance of the places we passed." It was now 4 a.m. and "market carts began coming into the city." An old woman, with a supply of ferns for sale, was sleeping just outside the market place. Tarkington awakened the woman and "he bought an armful" of ferns. They walked on and found an old man asleep on the curb next to his vegetables. Tarkington stopped to look at the figure on the ground:

> Tark removed his hat and, laying the load of ferns on the sleeper, stood in an attitude of great reverence. This awakened the old man who glance with astonishment at the funeral effect on his breast. Then he began to laugh. "Monsieur is most amiable," he said, "but do you not think I will catch cold with these damp leaves on me?"[5]

They concluded the evening, now morning, with breakfast and returned to their hotel. Recalling that night in Paris years later, JTM regretted that their "paths diverged widely. I always intended, if I was ever in the vicinity, to drop in at [Tarkington's] studo—located in the hull of an old ship grounded near his garden in Kennebunkport [Maine]."

NOTES

1   John T. McCutcheon, *Drawn From Memory* (Indianapolis and New York: Bobbs-Merrill, Inc., 1949), 217.
2   Ibid., 218.
3   Ibid.
4   Ibid., 218-19.
5   Ibid., 219.

6

A SMALL EFFORT
OF IMAGINATION
TO MAKE AN
EPIC CARTOON

WHAT BECAME A CLASSIC CARTOON and one of JTM's most famous draw-ings started out by accident on the morning of September 30, 1907.

According to JTM's son, John ("Jack") McCutcheon, Jr. (whose own career spanned forty-nine years at the *Chicago Tribune*), his father "was gazing out across Michigan Avenue trying to come up with an idea. His mind wandered back to his days as a boy in Indiana and the vistas of corn-fields he had left behind."[1]

JTM described his thought process on that morning in a 1943 *Tribune* article marking his fortieth anniversary at the paper:

"I started getting material for that cartoon when I was 3 or 4 years old," Mr. McCutcheon recalls. "I was born in a farmhouse on a gentle hilltop south of Lafayette. It was surrounded by cornfields. Not far away, on the banks of the Wabash was the site of the Indian village of Ouiatenon. Six or eight miles up the river was the battlefield of Tippecanoe. It was in the

111

early 70s. Newspapers were full of Indian warfare. The early fall saw the tasseled rows of corn like the waving spears of Indians, and a little later came the corn shocks, much like tepees in the haze of Indian summer. Undoubtedly in my boyish imagination all these things were registering. Then when I was hard up for an idea they came out."[2]

In 1907, the month of September debuted in Chicago with a heat blast that prolonged thoughts of summertime among Chicagoans. A *Tribune* story noted that on September 1 "early in the morning residents in all parts of the city began to seek the cool spots. The bathing beaches for the first time in a week were the scenes of large crowds, and hundreds of owners of private launches and yachts sought the cool breezes on the blue, placid lake. At least seven out of every ten men seen on the street wore straw hats. 'This is great weather for straw hats,' Professor Henry J. Cox, a weather forecaster told a *Tribune* reporter."[3]

On the day he first drew "Injun Summer", during his walk to work along Michigan Avenue to his office at the Fine Arts Building, JTM no doubt subconsciously connected the smells and feel of an unseasonable return to summer in September with the cornfield images indelibly etched in his soul from his childhood in Indiana.

As he entered the Fine Arts Building and headed up to his studio, perhaps he encountered another building tenant and struck up a light and airy conversation about the day's news and the weather. "Seems like fall has been delayed today," one might have said. "Well, it's a little premature for an Indian summer," JTM might have replied, "but possibly this unusually late heat wave helped create such a notion."

Like countless other mornings, JTM would have settled at his drawing board facing the unforgiving deadline, wondering what in the world he was going to create for the next morning's paper. Browsing through his copy of the *Tribune*, he surely would have noticed a story about the weather and perhaps its effect on Illinois corn crops during the current growing season. The subject of corn also could have been the catalyst for thoughts about the cornfields of his youth and the tricks a cornfield can play on one's mind—especially with help from nature's painting palette of mist, fog, haze, and wind. Then an idea began to form, perhaps like this.

At the top of his drawing paper, JTM wrote the title, "Injun Summer." Immediately below, he began writing a caption, neatly lettering each word in single spacing, indicating it would be placed above the first illustration:

> Yep, sunny. This is sure enough Injun Summer. Don't know what that is I reckon, do you? Well, that's when all the homesick Injuns come back to play. You know, a long time ago, long afore yer grandaddy was born, there used to be heaps of Injuns around here—thousands—millions, I reckon, far as that's concerned. Reg'lar sure enough Injuns—none o' yer cigar store Injuns, not much. They wuz all around here—right here where you're standin'. Don't be skeered—hain't none around here now, least ways no live ones. They been gone this many a year. They all went away and died, so they ain't no more left.

JTM penciled in the first cartoon. On the far right he sketched a white-bearded old man wearing a floppy woolen hat and a long, well-worn overcoat and field boots. He placed the man sitting on a log under a maple tree that had begun to drop its leaves. He rested a metal hay rake on the man's leg as a spiraling river of smoke ascended from the bowl of the corn cob pipe on which he puffed. In front of the man, JTM drew a young boy, about four or five years old. He dressed him in a warm coat, a scarf, and boots. He sketched a low-standing, rough-hewn wood fence in front of them, separating the two from eight corn shocks in the distant field. JTM completed the scene by adding a setting sun on the horizon, partially obscured by a combination of haze and fog.

Below the cartoon, JTM wrote a second caption:

> But every year, long about now, they all come back, least ways their sperrits do. They're here now. You can see 'em off across the fields. Look real hard. See that kind o' haze that's everywhere—it's just the sperrits of the Injuns all come back. They're all around us now. See off yonder; see them

Chicago Tribune Magazine
MIDWEST PORTRAIT
By John T. McCutcheon

INJUN SUMMER

Yep, sonny, this is sure enough Injun summer. Don't know what that is, I reckon, do you?

Well, that's when all the homesick Injuns come back to play. You know, a long time ago, long afore yer granddaddy was born even, there used to be heaps of Injuns around here—thousands—millions, I reckon, far as that's concerned. Reg'lar sure 'nough Injuns—none o' yer cigar store Injuns, not much. They wuz all around here—right here where you're standin'.

Don't be skeered—hain't none around here now, leastways no live ones. They been gone this many a year.

They all went away and died, so they ain't no more left.

But every year, 'long about now, they all come back, leastways their sperrits do. They're here now. You can see 'em off across the fields. Look real hard. See that kind o' hazy, misty look out yonder? Well, them's Injuns—Injun sperrits marchin' along an' dancin' in the sunlight. That's what makes that kind o' haze that's everywhere—it's jest the sperrits of the Injuns all come back. They're all around us now.

See off yonder; see them tepees? They kind o' look like corn shocks from here, but them's Injun tents, sure as you're a foot high. See 'em now? Sure, I knowed you could. Smell that smoky sort o' smell in the air? That's the campfires a-burnin' and their pipes a-goin'.

Lots o' people say it's jest leaves burnin', but it ain't. It's the campfires, an' th' Injuns are hoppin' 'round 'em t'beat the old Harry.

You jest come out here tonight when the moon is hangin' over the hill off yonder an' the harvest fields is all swimmin' in the moonlight, an' you can see the Injuns and the tepees jest as plain as kin be. You can, eh? I knowed you would after a little while.

Jever notice how the leaves turn red 'bout this time o' year? That's jest another sign o' redskins. That's when an old Injun sperrit gits tired dancin' an' goes up an' squats on a leaf t'rest. Why, I kin hear 'em rustlin' an' whisperin' an' creepin' 'round among the leaves all the time; an' ever' once'n a while a leaf gives way under some fat old Injun ghost and comes floatin' down to the ground. See—here's one now. See how red it is? That's the war paint rubbed off'n an Injun ghost, sure's you're born.

Purty soon all the Injuns'll go marchin' away agin, back to the happy huntin' ground, but next year you'll see 'em troopin' back—th' sky jest hazy with 'em and their campfires smolderin' away jest like they are now.

teepees? They kind o' look like corn shocks from here, but them's Injun tents, sure as you're a foot high. See 'em now? Sure, I know'd you could. Smell that smoky sort o' smell in the air? That's the campfires a-burnin' and their pipes a-goin'. Lots o' people say it's just leaves a-burnin', but it ain't. It's the campfires an' th' Injuns are hoppin' 'round 'em.

At this point, JTM might have paused and looked at the clock. Perhaps it was 1:30 p.m., and there was still time before the afternoon deadline. He no doubt would have been pleased with the cartoon so far, but would still need to reproduce the first drawing with the man and the boy, changing the view to nighttime and transforming the cornstalks to teepees, around which danced shadowy figures of Indians with ornamental and feather headdresses.

He then finished the cartoon with a final caption:

You jest come out here tonight when the moon is hangin' over the hill off yonder an' the harvest fields is all swimmin' in th' moonlight an' you can see the Injuns and the teepees jest as plain as kin be. You can, eh? I knowed you would after a little while. J'ever notice how the leaves turn red 'bout this time o' year? That's jest another sign o' redskins. That's when an old Injun sperrit gets tired o' dancin' an' goes up an' squats on a leaf t' rest. Why, I kin hear 'em rustlin' an' whisperin' an' creepin' 'round among the leaves all the time; an' 'ever once 'n a while a leaf gives way under some old Injun ghost and comes floatin' down to the ground— here's one now. See how red it is? That's the war paint rubbed off'n an Injun ghost, sure's you're born. Purty soon, all the Injuns'll go marchin' away again, back to the happy huntin' ground, but next year you'll see 'em troopin' back—the sky jest hazy with 'em and their campfires smol- derin' away—jest like they are now.

JTM took a final look, proofing his handwritten captions and erasing left- over pencil marks no longer needed. He packaged the cartoon for delivery to the *Tribune's* composing room and summoned a messenger to pick up the drawing. With that, he donned his jacket and went home for the day.

Later, when asked where he found the inspiration for the cartoon, JTM pointed to a childhood steeped in cornfields and Indian traditions in the 1870s. He concluded that "30 years later, while groping in the early fall for an idea, it only took a small effort of imagination to see tepees, spears and feathers when the early morning smoky haze and fog of autumn obscured the horizon and made the details in those cornfields murky."[4]

His first clue as to what impact the cartoon came "in the form of a telephone call from a friend, Howard Gillette. 'I liked your cartoon,' he said. 'I'd like to have the original.'" McCutcheon gave the original gladly. Meanwhile, acclaim for "Injun Summer" grew, accompanied by demands for reproduction. Later, Gillette turned the cartoon over to the Chicago Historical Society.[5]

In 1912, five years after the original publication date and countless letters and phone calls from readers later, the *Chicago Tribune* decided to reprint "Injun Summer" in September. Accolades for the cartoon continued to grow through the years. The *Tribune* reported that "Injun Summer" was presented at the 1933 Chicago World's Fair "in life size . . . using cutout figures, a diorama and genuine pumpkins, corn shocks and fall festival equipment";[6] it also was "emblazoned in fireworks at the [World's Fair] and again before 85,000 persons at the 1941 Chicagoland Music Festival."[7]

The *Tribune* continued to reprint the cartoon every year in autumn until October 1992, when "objections about its anachronistic take on Native Americans persuaded the editors that the cartoon's era had passed."[8] Noted a *Tribune* editor: "'Injun Summer' is out of joint with its times. It is literally a museum piece, a relic of another age. The farther we get from 1907, the less meaning it has for the current generation."[9]

Still, such a longstanding autumn tradition—one that extended across a large part of the twentieth century—would not go easily into the forgotten past.

Nostalgia and the sentiments of older generations need their nod, too. Howard Tyner, the *Tribune's* current [in 1997] editor, received probably the most moving request from an "Injun Summer" fan: an Orlando woman whose husband was dying of cancer and wished to see the cartoon one last time.[10]

In 1997, the *Chicago Tribune* celebrated its 150th anniversary by "publishing all kinds of things from the past, from historic editorials to pieces written about the paper," Tyner noted. "For many, this cartoon is very much a part of the *Tribune*. What better year to run it again?"[11]

The annual rite of publishing "Injun Summer" in newspapers across the United States for decades prompted now retired *Tribune* Arts Critic Sid Smith to examine the cartoon's appeal in his 1997 article "Up In Smoke":

> The secret of its appeal? The vision and freshness of the cartoonist's imagination, for starters, and the slyness in selecting an almost obscure festivity, one less celebrated than Christmas, New Year's, Thanksgiving, Easter and the rest. Indian summer is something we all experience and look upon with wonder—a tingling, transitional time of longing, mild regret and hope and a tingling, almost painless sense of loss.[12]

Concluded Tyner, the *Tribune* editor:

> I think the bulk of the people who miss it are older and look upon it in a world of rapid, unnerving, unsettling change as something that evokes a quieter time. That's the essence of this cartoon, this gentle relationship between a grandfather and his grandson. It evokes a time when things could be managed.[13]

NOTES

1   Sid Smith, "Up In Smoke. 'Injun Summer' Is Nostalgic To Some, Offensive To Others. Either Way, It Has Earned A Place in Tribune History," *Chicago Tribune,* October 5, 1997, accessed November 18, 2013, www.chicagotribune.com.

2   Tom Morrow, "J. T. McCutcheon Draws a Steady Job at *Tribune*: Thinks He'll Stay—After Forty Years," *Chicago Daily Tribune* (1923-1963), July 1, 1943, ProQuest Historical Newspapers.

3   Ibid.

4   John T. McCutcheon, *Drawn From Memory* (Indianapolis and New York: Bobbs-Merrill, Inc., 1949), 16.

5   Morrow, "J.T. McCutcheon Draws a Steady Job at Tribune: Thinks He'll Stay—After Forty Years."

6   "Century of Progress," *Chicago Daily Tribune* (1923–1963), November 1, 1933, Pro-Quest Historical Newspapers.

7   Ibid.

8   Smith, "Up In Smoke. 'Injun Summer' Is Nostalgic To Some, Offensive To Others. Either Way, It Has Earned A Place in *Tribune* History."

9   Ibid.

10   Ibid.

11   Ibid.

12   Ibid.

13   Ibid.

7

LOOK WHO'S COMING BACK

ONCE AGAIN, JTM decided to play hooky, as his friend George Ade called it, this time twice in the year 1908. During the winter, he and a friend visited the Grand Canyon where JTM enjoyed his "first view of the immensity through a snowstorm, with blue-black clouds boiling up out of the gorges." They rode mules whose strength was proportionate to their body weight and rode down the trails of the Grand Canyon to the bottom, assured by their guides that "no one had ever been lost in this daring feat on which we were embarked." JTM captured his trip in an article that was published in *Appleton's Magazine*. Years later, in 1931, a reprint of the article was still on sale at a store in the canyon when, "once again in a snowstorm," he took his family to visit the Grand Canyon.

By spring of 1908, he "felt he needed some more fresh air." Looking back, JTM's very first trip outside of Indiana was to Chicago when a group of Purdue University students traveled to see actors Edwin Booth (brother of John Wilkes Booth, Lincoln's assassin) and Lawrence Barrett perform in Shakespeare's

Julius Caesar. While in the city, he bought "one of those vases of wax flowers cunningly mounted under a glass dome" for his mother, Clara, and carried the "contraption around with me" the rest of the trip. When he returned home and presented it to Clara, she "expressed great delight." Uncertain whether she was being totally truthful with him about her gratitude, he concluded "possibly she was as good an actor as Booth or Barrett." Now in 1908, with some adventures under his belt, he "wanted to show [Clara] some of the world which I found so interesting." He booked a thirty-day trip to the West Indies on the Hamburg-American Line's *Oceana*, departing from New York City.

Accompanying Clara and JTM on the trip was Ade, Ort Wells (a friend), and, "as a companion for my mother, a female Purdue classmate, unhappily married and also unhappily grown fat." Clara was suffering from a severe case of neuritis [a form of neuropathy], but that "didn't seem to bother any of us." Even so, at the time of their scheduled departure, it was so serious that JTM "didn't know whether we could even get her to New York." They did, but on the ocean she became seasick, leaving JTM to second-guess the wisdom of his decision to bring her along:

> Why did I do this? I felt that I had inflicted this terrible ordeal on her just because I was so eager to have her share my pleasure in travel. At St. Pierre, Martinique, we had to land at a rickety pier high above water level. Husky sailors leaned down and, one by one, hoisted the passengers up the six-foot gap. Mother's neuritis had settled in her right arm and shoulder, but in the excitement of landing none of us remembered it. One of the sailors reached down, grasped Mother's right hand and, with a mighty yank, landed her on the pier. It must have hurt excruciatingly.[1]

Yet Clara kept her composure because "nothing ever ruffled my mother." Curiously, she reported feeling much better afterward and from that point forward "enjoyed the cruise enormously."

In later years, when JTM would tell his mother about, "one after another, the young ladies who occupied my attention," she always asked: "Would you like to travel with her?" This was her "acid test," and he often wondered if it was a by-product of their trip to West Indies in 1908.

~~~~~~~~~~~~~~~~~

FOR MANY YEARS the center of Chicago's artistic, music, and cultural activities was the Fine Arts Building on Michigan Avenue, and JTM's first studio was located there. The building was a marvelous wonder both architecturally and as a people-watching mecca, and JTM drank it all in:

> In its spacious lobby the patrons of the Studebaker Theater relaxed between the acts of such productions as George Ade's *Sultan of Sulu* and the Tarkington-Wilson play, *The Man from Home*. The shops were famous. On the way up the 10 stories in the elevator, one glimpsed kaleidoscopic strata of antique furniture, etchings, lamps, pottery, foreign glassware, handmade jewelry, artistic photographs, fine needlework and old silver. Down the corridors echoed the mingled jangle of innumerable music lessons, and the penetrating scales of opera stars in the making.[2]

JTM's studio featured a skylight and was "large enough to accommodate my constantly growing collection of things from everywhere I had been." A visitor opening the door to the studio was immediately confronted with "rugs from Bokhara and Ashkhabad, bronze filigree lamps from Japan . . . assorted guns and historic shell fragments, the tattered ensign used by us correspondents in going from ship to shore in Manila Bay, to prevent being fired upon by our own ships." The burlap walls were covered with "flags from Spanish ships, pictures, photographs and other mementoes, such as my pass for the Khyber Pass." He worked there for twenty-three years.

There came many knocks on his door, and sometimes it would be "whole grades of starry-eyed youngsters from the city schools." Occasionally, "Seeing Chicago" tours arrived to see the cartoonist. A list of who's-who types also made the pilgrimage to his studio. If JTM was on deadline or too busy to entertain visitors, he "would not open the door," which on occasion he later regretted: "Once, after a prolonged knocking had ceased, I found William Jennings Bryan's card tucked underneath."[3]

Eventually, JTM invented a work style that, assuming he had his idea for the day's cartoon, allowed him to "draw steadily ... and at the same time entertain visitors who conducted a one-way conversation without in the least interrupting my work." One of his visitors was Charles G. Dawes (a Chicago banker who would become the thirtieth vice president under Calvin Coolidge). "He liked to sit and talk ... and was one of my most frequent callers. He has always been an able raconteur with the keenest kind of wit."[4]

Not surprisingly, aspiring young cartoonists stopped by JTM's studio to show him their work in search of a word of encouragement or advice. The young visitors to his studio who would go on to achieve their own cartooning fame and success included: Frank King (*Gasoline Alley*), Milton Caniff (*Steve Canyon* and *Terry and the Pirates*), Frank Willard (*Moon Mullins*), Harold Gray (*Little Orphan Annie*), and Fontaine Fox, Jr. (*Toonerville Folks*).[5] Taking credit for the success of another cartoonist was not in keeping with JTM's humble personality, but "I should be happy to feel that any suggestions of mine may have helped them up even one rung of the ladder to fame."

The first Commissioner of Baseball Kenesaw Mountain Landis (1921–1944) had served as private secretary to Secretary of State Walter Gresham in Grover Cleveland's cabinet, before he was appointed United States District Judge for the Northern District of Illinois, based in Chicago. He also enjoyed visiting JTM in his studio, as did JTM in the judge's courtroom:

> His sense of humor was superb and an hour with him was certain to be
> rewarding. Sometimes, too, I would sit in his courtroom to watch him
> unerringly put his finger on the essential point in a case. He had an effec-
> tive way of deflating pompous attorneys, and of keeping them down to
> brass tacks. It was he who summoned John D. Rockefeller to come and
> testify in his court; who found the Standard Oil Company guilty of ille-
> gal practices which had been enormously profitable, and who fined the
> company $29 million. Probably no more startling decision or one more
> widely discussed has come from any court. It was promptly overruled by

the higher courts, but there were countless thousands who believed in its justice and were convinced the disclosures fully warranted it. In the more exclusive clubs, to which many of his friends belonged, his name was [cursed]. On the streets, where his striking figure was always recognized, he was cheered.[6]

Landis sought JTM's advice and opinion when baseball officials asked him to serve as a "czar of that industry" to help clean up numerous scandals that "permeated the professional sport—they needed a man of integrity and courage, in whom the whole country would implicitly believe." Landis discussed the opportunity with JTM, who advised him against accepting and to "remain on the bench where a man of his character was needed even more. [He didn't and] I came to believe that he was right and I was wrong. He cleaned up baseball, our largest national sport."

At his studio, JTM received numerous unsolicited ideas from various sources, including the time a knock came on his studio door and he opened it to find a tall woman, "soberly dressed with an unfashionable hat, who stepped inside and without any preamble announced that she had written a poem about the aftermath of the World's Columbian Exhibition, and could I use it in a cartoon?" He offered his thanks and promised to read it. With that, the woman smiled and left. As a rule, he had learned to avoid using suggestions for good reason:

> I didn't like to use contributed poems in my cartoons. Floods of verses would ensue and feelings would be hurt. The chances were infinitesimal that this one would be usable; I glanced at it idly, and to my surprise, liked it. I had no idea who the lady was; the poem was not signed. I used it in a rather elaborate architectural cartoon, about which I heard much favorable comment. But I heard nothing from the poet.[7]

For more than a year, the poet's identity remained unknown. Then one evening while attending an opera, "I recognized her in a box [seat]. The mystery lady turned out to be Mrs. Emmons Blaine—none other than the sister of brothers Cyrus, Harold and Stanley McCormick [of International Harvester fame]."[8]

Despite the outcome of Blaine's submission, "the overwhelming majority of these were for one reason or another not usable. They might be too involved, or too violent, contrary to the policy of the paper, or not sufficiently timely."

On the rare occasion an idea could be used, JTM "made a practice of adding a plus sign after my signature with the initials of the sender."

The studio also hosted meetings of an "unpretentious organization called the McCutcheon Social and Pleasure Club." Among the members were Hazel Martyn Trudeau who later married Sir John Lavery, a renowned Irish portrait painter who designed the one-pound note for the new currency for the launch of the Irish Free State, established in 1922. The design of the note incorporated a woman's head; it was a portrait of Hazel. JTM regarded Hazel as beautiful and talented and several of her sketches hung on his studio walls. Once when Hazel drew sketches of herself and two friends at a meeting of the Social and Pleasure Club in the studio, JTM "had a piano moved in from a neighboring music school."

The Auditorium Theater located next door to the Fine Arts Building provided catering for JTM's studio. For a party he held for "current debutantes," he "spent days in preparation of a little silhouette fantasy called 'A Day in the Life of a Debutante,'" which was influenced by something similar he had seen in Paris. It was a puppet show of sorts and JTM "manipulated the figures by hand." He also composed the lyrics for a song called "A Cocoon Song" and inscribed it: "To a Debutante of 1908" and sent it to "five different buds."

He "let each girl assume what she would!"

THE OPPORTUNITY FOR JTM to achieve a boyhood dream—to hunt big game—presented itself, as did most of his travel adventures, unexpectedly. In the spring of 1909, big game hunter Carl Akeley came to Chicago for a speaking engagement and to show pictures from his travels. Akeley, considered the father of modern taxidermy, was not only a taxidermist, but also a naturalist, sculptor, writer, and inventor. Over his long career he worked for several different museums, including the Field Museum in Chicago where he served as chief taxidermist from 1896 to 1909. JTM attended Akeley's lecture and received an offer he couldn't refuse:

> I must have listened with such popeyed interest that he was flattered, for when I talked with him after he invited me to join his forthcoming expedition. It was to consist of him, his wife Delia, Fred Stephenson, a hunter of many years' experience, and me. Akeley had recently been called to the White House to discuss President [Theodore] Roosevelt's plans for an African hunting trip after his retirement in March, and had arranged to meet him in Africa. Consequently the *Tribune* was only too glad to let me go.[9]

The trip was still five months away and JTM found it hard to concentrate on anything else. He approached his daily work "with a mind half dazed by the delicious consciousness that I was soon to become a lion hunter." One of the objectives of Akeley's trip was to film a rhinoceros charge. The plan called for Stephenson and JTM to "provoke the charge and allow the angered rhinos to approach within a few yards of the camera before springing into action." JTM practiced shooting at a target range on the grounds of Fort Sheridan until "my shoulder got black and blue," and then enrolled in boxing lessons as a way to "improve my wind."

In August 1909, Stephenson and JTM arrived in London and "finished outfitting in those shops that are known to sportsmen from one end of the world to the other." He bought several rifles, including a .296 bolt-action Mannlicher rifle, which was "splendid for long-range shooting," He also purchased a 9 mm Mannlicher pistol—"large enough for nearly all purposes but not reassuring at close quarters" and a .475 cordite Jeffery "which has a tremendous impact." His choices were based on a strategic approach to the hunting:

The presumption was that I would shoot a lion at long range with the .256; then in the middle distance with the 9 mm, and finally, if there was time, with the .475 cordite. Several thousand rounds of ammunition were acquired. This did not mean that several thousand lions were to be killed. Allowing for a fair percentage of misses, we calculated, with luck, to get two or three. I had now assembled such an imposing arsenal that I was nervous whenever I thought about it. With such a batter it was a foregone conclusion that something, or somebody, was likely to get hurt.[10]

JTM and Stephenson finished collecting their supplies for the trip, but an item in the local newspaper caught JTM's eye. It was an announcement for the *Grande Semaine d'Aviation de la Champagne*—the first international public flying event to be held in August near Reims, France.

All the famous fliers in the world were expected—the few there then were! I knew at once I had to see it. So we all went over to Paris, to the Hotel Castiglione. Next morning, in order to reach Reims by 9 a.m., we had to get up at five. It was the third day of the meet. All morning we inspected planes—like a crowd in a paddock before a horse race. The flying began in the afternoon. The course was two miles around, with tall pylons at each end. Louis Bleriot was there with his little monoplane; the Farmans [French brothers Henri and Maurice] and Glen Curtiss. The Wrights were not present in person, but other fliers flew their planes, which were catapulted down a runway. All the planes were supposed to fly around the course, if possible. Some didn't even get off the ground. Most flew at an altitude of 50 or 60 feet. There were two or three smashups during the afternoon, and one or two men hurt.[11]

The crowd gasped at the antics of Hubert Latham [a French aviation pioneer], flying an Antoinette. He "was very daring." Latham climbed in his plane to four hundred feet above the ground that day. After several years of flying, he was killed in Africa "by a Cape buffalo." Frenchman Louis Paulhan flew a biplane and "kept going around and around for two hours and 40 minutes, thereby establishing a world's record" for endurance—

"a tremendous achievement." Paulhan only came down when he ran out of fuel and was "carried to triumph on the shoulders of the crowd and cordially greeted by [French] President [Clément Armand] Fallières."

The next available train to Paris did not depart until the following morning, so JTM and his companions "tried to get rooms in Reims, an utter impossibility. The hotels, the boardinghouses, even the private homes were completely full." So they passed the time in a local restaurant and when that closed, they moved to a music hall "until we were put out." When they returned to Paris, Stephenson and JTM departed for Italy where they sailed from the city of Naples "with the Akeleys on the SS *Adolph Woermann* bound for Mombassa" on the coast of Kenya. The weather was very hot and "on the hottest day of the trip, in one of the ports of call when the mercury was spluttering around the top of the thermometer," the group learned that explorer Robert Peary had discovered the North Pole. The news "cooled us off for a while."

The new governor of British East Africa, Sir Percy Girouard, was a passenger on the *Adolph Woermann*. Girouard invited JTM and the group to make "the long ride from Mombassa to Nairobi in his special train, stopping enroute at Tsavo," where two man-eating lions killed "28 natives" employed as construction workers in 1898 on the Kenya-Uganda Railway. The incident had occurred "nine years earlier" as JTM was "coming up the coast from the Boer War."

Along the way, there were many lion stories told as the group rolled down the railway. One story, which was related by "a gentleman high in government service, a man of unimpeachable veracity," caught JTM's attention:

Once upon a time there was a caravan of slaves moving through the jungles of Africa. The slave drivers were cruel and they chained the poor savages together in bunches of 10. Each slave wore an iron collar around his neck and the chain passed through this ring and on to the next man. For weeks, they marched along, their chains clanking and their shoulders aching sorely. Life was far from pleasant and they watched eagerly for a chance to escape. Finally, one dark night, when the sentinels were asleep, a group of 10 succeeded in creeping away into the darkness. They were unarmed and chained from neck to neck, one to another. For several days they made their way steadily toward the coast. They ate fruit and nuts and herbs. All seemed well. But alas! One night a deep rumbling roar was heard in the jungle through which they were picking their unanimous way! A shudder ran through the slaves. "Simba!" they whispered in terror. Here they were, 10 days from the coast, and quite defenseless. Presently the lion appeared, his cruel hungry eyes gleaming through the night. Slowly, slowly he crept toward them. They were frozen with terror, realizing only too well that the lion's intentions were open to grave suspicion. Being chained together, they could not climb more than one tree, and perhaps no tree was big enough to hold more than nine of them. In any case, the horrid tale goes on to relate how the lion gave a frightful roar and leaped on the 10th man.

The dilemma of the slaves is obvious. They knew better than to disturb a lion while he is eating. They sat still and waited while he greedily devoured their late comrade. Then, surfeited with food, the great beast moved off into the jungle. Immediately the nine remaining slaves took to their heels, dragging the empty iron ring. They ran until they were exhausted and, after a nap, hurried on again, hopeful once more. About suppertime, they heard the distant roar of a lion! Nearer it came, and presently the lion's gleaming eyes appeared among the jungle grass. Once again they were frozen with horror as the hungry beast devoured the last man in the row—number nine. As soon as the full-fed lion disappeared, they scrambled up and hiked busily toward the coast, nine days away.

They began to dread the supper hour. The next night the lion caught up with them and diminished their number by six. Finally, here was only one man left, and the coast was a full-day's march away. Could he make it? It looked like a desperate chance, but he still had hopes. With pleasure he noticed that the lion was becoming fat and probably could not travel fast. But with displeasure he also noticed that he had 40 feet of chain and nine heavy iron rings to lug along, and the extra weight naturally greatly handicapped him. It was a thrilling race—one day to go, life or death the prize. Who can imagine the feelings of that poor slave? But with a stout heart he struggled on. The afternoon sun slowly sank toward the western horizon, and . . . At this point in the story the locomotive screeched loudly, the wheels scraped on the track, and my official friend leaped off the cow-catcher. "Here," I shouted. "What's the finish of that story?" "I'll tell you next time I see you," he sang out.[12]

Others who had sailed on the *Adolph Woermann* included members of the Boyce Balloonograph Expedition. W. D. Boyce was a Chicago newspaper publisher who had been challenged by George R. Lawrence, a noted photographer and balloonist, to finance an expedition to photograph African animals in their natural habitat—from the sky. Lawrence argued that the pictures would help boost circulation for Boyce's newspapers. Unbeknown to JTM, this would lead to his first balloon ride:

> They were going into the big-game country to photograph wild animals from above. When they had their camp set up outside Nairobi and their 12,000-cubic-foot balloon partially inflated—not fully because somebody thought the hot equatorial sun would expand the gas and burst it—they invited Fred Stephenson to make an ascent. Hundreds of natives sat around spellbound. But the balloon would not rise with Fred, who was six feet five and weighed 230 pounds, until he had thrown out his heavy hunting boots. Then it started at once for some trees a hundred yards away, and was hastily reeled in again.[13]

JTM's turn came next. Since he only weighed 140 pounds, the balloon "shot up to 1,000 feet with no sensation of motion, except that the ground dropped dizzily away." He stood up in the three-foot-square basket, "clutching the ropes and dramatizing the situation":

> Supposing the wire snapped? Would I drift 100 miles, perhaps, into some remote wild region, where the natives would hail me as a god? Or the lions accept me as manna? How would I act under this confusion of

identity? I never decided, for I was jerked back to reality with startling abruptness. Everything had been fine so long as we were going up—there was no resistance—but when they started to haul me down, the balloon rushed in wide circles like a kite and the partly filled bag flapped and thundered. That wire looked very frail![14]

But he got down without a scratch and later Delia Akeley made a 200-foot ascent, which would be the last flight for the Balloonograph Expedition. In the end, "this method of photographing animals proved impracticable."

Nairobi sat at the edge of the Athi Plains—"a broad sweep of sun-bleached grass veldt" that extended for many miles. The town was not yet fully gentrified as there were "few of the gentlemen ranchers who later" settled in great numbers in British East Africa [now Kenya]. JTM noted, "Countless numbers of [wild] animals fed contentedly within walking distance from the [train] station." Sometimes at night, as had happened the evening before JTM and his group arrived, a lion attacked a zebra herd, stampeding them through the town's streets where they trampled fences and gardens.

More than one hundred natives were needed to assist the expedition of four white people. One headsman ran the safari, eight served as gun bearers, four *askaris* [soldiers]—armed and wearing uniforms—provided guard duty during the day and night.

> Each white person had also his tent boy or personal servant, who took care of his tent, bedding, bath and clothes. "Jumma" was my tent boy, a Wakamba [an ethnic group from eastern Kenya] with filed teeth. Jumma had the happy faculty of never looking rumpled, a trick which I tried to learn, but all in vain. Instead, however, I learned from him a useful expression. As nearly as I could make out, his word of approval was "umslopagus." Like smacking lips, the sound of it conveyed satisfaction. When qualified by "eighty-eight," the highest number he was able to count, it signified his highest praise.[15]

In later years, whenever JTM would rate a certain woman as umslopagus 37, or umslopagus -3, his family members "unerringly deduced my drift."

The safari also brought one cook and four *saises* [a person employed to take care of a horse]—who were responsible for each horse and mule, "of which we had four." Eighty porters from numerous tribes—including Swahili, Wakamba, Kikuyu, Masai, Lumbwa, Kavirondo, and others—carried luggage and other loads. About twenty *totos* [boys] stowed away and emerged to help "when it was too late to send them home." The *totos* received only food and lodging, but they gained "the experience which would enable them later to become porters." Daily life on the safari was exhilarating:

> For weeks and months on safari you live a nomadic tent life amid surroundings so different from what you are accustomed to that you are both mentally and physically rejuvenated. You are among a strange and savage people in strange and savage lands, threatened by strange and savage animals. The life is new; the scenery is new. There is adventure and novelty in every day of such a life, and it is this phase that has the most insistent appeal. Even if one never used his rifle, one would still enjoy life on safari.[16]

But using the rifle is why JTM came in the first place. He had "two absorbing ambitions" that are shared by "everyone who goes to Africa with a gun and a return ticket: I wanted to kill a lion and live to tell about it." And so he would:

> Finally I encountered my first lion. It was not until I had come within 40 yards that I could get a clear view of him. He was glaring at me with tail waving angrily, and his mouth was opened in a snarl. I could see that he didn't like me. Luckily I got him before he got me. We had many other lion hunts and tried several different methods of hunting them. We sojourned in the rhino country, where we saw at least 100 every day. Then we went on to elephant country. It was of unfailing interest to see how the Akeleys prepared all the animal specimens we obtained for the museum.[17]

In his 1910 book, "*In Africa: Hunting Adventures in the Big Game Country,*" JTM devotes "a good portion to our encounter with the safari of Colonel [Theodore] Roosevelt"—which was "news of the first water." While he was in Africa, JTM carried "an unnecessarily large quantity of Indian rupees in order to send a cable to the *Tribune* in case anything serious happened to" Roosevelt:

> I didn't want to arrive at a telegraph station with a world scoop and then be balked by a demand for cash payment. Years later when I casually mentioned this to Roosevelt's younger sister, Mrs. Douglas [Corinne] Robinson, she was horrified. "Oh, how ghoulish!"[18]

"Yes I suppose so," JTM later wrote, "but that's how newspaper minds work."

The safari returned to Nairobi after more than four months. One day, Stephenson and JTM hired a carriage, "a low-necked affair drawn by two little mules, and took a drive out of town." In a few minutes they had passed 60 impalas, a herd of zebra and "some Coke's hartebeets" [antelope] who watched them "with humorous interest. As long as the carriage kept moving they showed no apprehension. An eland grazed on a hillside and a wart hog trotted away." Then, a final opportunity to kill more lions:

> Suddenly three lions walked slowly out of the mullah and climbed the slope on the other side—not 350 yards away. One was a female, the others were immense males. They stopped to look back, then resumed their stately retreat. Then began a most strange lion hunt. I had heard of the practice of "riding" lions, that is, bringing them to bay on horseback, but to my knowledge no one has ever "galloped" a lion in a carriage drawn by two mules, much less "galloped" three lions at one time. It was a memorable chase. The mules were lashed and the carriage rocked like a [English] Channel steamer. We gained on them, we reduced the distance to 250 yards, we both got out and knelt to fire. But we both missed and the lions disappeared over the brow of the ravine.[19]

Safari hunting evolved dramatically in the years following JTM's Africa trip and "in many respects the technique of hunting has utterly changed since I was there. The hunter now embarks in a well-equipped truck, and in defiance of all obstacles quickly places himself wherever he wants to be in regard to the game." As a result, "danger is mitigated to a very pleasant minimum."

JTM's return from Africa generated "a good deal of publicity," including a cartoon by Clare Briggs, an early American comic strip artist, "which pleased me very much." The cartoon featured a dog—"one of my special brand of flop-eared mongrels, standing on the end of a pier looking seaward toward the smoke of a distant steamer." The caption read, "He's coming back." Over at the *Tribune,* the paper ran a series of advertisements with the headline "He's coming back" and inserted the ads "into the paper almost anywhere." A week later, the *Tribune* ran ads with the headline, "Who's coming back?"

The advertisements were "so timed that it was topped off with the news of my arrival."[20]

NOTES

1   John T. McCutcheon, *Drawn From Memory* (Indianapolis and New York: Bobbs-Merrill, Inc., 1949), 215.

2   Ibid., 221.

3   Ibid., 222.

4   Ibid.

5   Ibid.

6   Ibid., 223.

7   Ibid., 224.

8   Ibid.

9   Ibid., 228.

10   Ibid.

11   Ibid., 229.

12   Ibid., 230–33.

13   Ibid., 233.

14   Ibid.

15   Ibid., 234.

16   Ibid., 235.

17   Ibid.

18   Ibid., 236.

19   Ibid.

20   Ibid., 237.

8

A Man Making His First Flight

Having personally seen an airplane leave the ground at the 1909 air show in Reims, JTM knew he "would never be content until I had flown." Planes fascinated him and he "hung around airmen whenever [he] had the chance." However, flying was still in its infancy and still dangerous so "passengers were not in demand." As a result, his "own efforts to get off the ground were consistently balked."

In 1910, the *Chicago Record-Herald* sponsored a race between a train and an airplane. The starting point was Washington Park on Chicago's south side and the destination was Springfield, Illinois. As "the train had to stop at many stations, [the plane] had no difficulty keeping abreast and at times ahead." Pilot Walter Brookins of Dayton, Ohio, flying a Wright Flyer, won the race and the prize of $10,000. Prior to the start of the race, Brookins gave an exhibition flight on the city's lakefront. "An Associated Press man went with him," so JTM had no chance. Somehow JTM's interest in flying came to the attention of Frank Russell, a plant manager for the Wright Company in Dayton, and he arranged for JTM to fly with Brookins on a demonstration flight in Springfield two days later.

Unfortunately, JTM received a wire saying one of his aunts had died and the "funeral would be, of all times, two days later!" He faced a dilemma:

> I don't know that it is going to redound to my credit, but I was certainly torn by conflicting emotions. Here was everything all fixed for me to make my first flight, a thing I wanted at that time more than anything else in the world. However, I decided to do my duty, and telegraphed that I could not come to Springfield and why. I have always hoped they believed me![1]

Undaunted, JTM corresponded again with Russell asking if he could arrange another flight. Russell replied that JTM was welcome "to come down to Dayton any time." JTM picked a date "on which I had an evening engagement to speak in Indianapolis." He figured the experience of flying "might add valuable matter to my talk." He looked forward to the flight with "eagerness and some apprehension, and hesitated to tell [Clara] of my plans." But he would be late for the appointment:

> What was my chagrin to find myself so delayed enroute to the station that I missed my train! I took another one about 11 p.m. and woke to find that the engine had broken down! We crawled into Dayton toward noon, three hours late.[2]

When JTM met Russell he was very accommodating: "Never mind, we can go out right after lunch." The flying site, Simms Station, was located a number of miles outside of town and JTM was concerned about being able to catch a train back to Indianapolis in time for his evening speaking engagement. Russell "said it would be impossible to reach the field, wait for proper flying conditions and get back by train time."

Disappointed, JTM departed for Indianapolis. Some time later, he tried again and "got as far as the field. But a heavy wind was blowing; in fact the door of the hangar was nearly blown off, and the plane was not even brought out." He wondered whether destiny was conspiring to ground him forever. But he tried again and, accompanied by Harold McCormick, went back to Dayton where "Orville Wright came out to the field with us":

> The plane was brought out and my turn came first. I remember rattling through the weeds at a terrific speed—no concrete runways then!—and circling over the adjoining fields at about 700 feet. I sat on the lower wing of the biplane, with my feet on a small bar below, and clung to the struts. I think the pressure of my grip must show to this day! The pilot sat beside me with two control levers in his hands. The engine was suspended above us and two big propellers, connected by chains, were behind us, between the two wings. It was extremely primitive, crude and awkward, but it did go up, and after 10 or 15 minutes came safely down. On my return [to Chicago], I drew a cartoon expressing the emotions of a man making his first flight.[3]

McCormick—who would become a pioneer in the aviation industry and was immortalized as one of the inspirations for Charles Foster Kane in the movie *Citizen Kane*—went next. He apparently narrowly avoided a disaster: "Harold went up and came down, and as they turned the plane to run it into the hangar, the crankshaft broke squarely in two!"

In the summer of 1911, JTM made his second flight, this time at the first International Aviation Meet in Chicago, where grandstands were constructed in Grant Park on the east side of the Art Institute to accommodate the crowds. Once again, Orville Wright helped him get his wish:

> On the first day I lunched with Charles Dawes, Harold McCormick and Orville Wright, and before I had phrased my hopeful question, Wright interrupted me: "Yes," he said, "you may go in the biplane race." It was scheduled for that very afternoon. The race was to be around four pylons, over a course scarcely a mile long. There were several entries. I learned with some uneasiness that the pilot of the Wright plane was named Coffin—Frank Coffin. After lunch I was asked to go to the Wright hangar to have my heart examined. It was pounding so hard with excitement that I feared it might

not pass the test, but all was well and I walked back to my seat. On my way I passed, still lying on the field, the wreck of the plane in which William Badger [a twenty-five-year-old pilot from Pittsburgh] had just been killed.[4]

JTM tried to be nonchalant about his imminent adventure in the sky and to appear "unconcerned as I saw Coffin's plane trundled out before the crowd." He quickly got into the spirit of it, with the help of a woman attending the meet:

> I had the fun of suddenly arising and handing my hat to one of the ladies in the party. "Will you hold this for me, please? I am going to fly in this race." The resulting sensation was entirely satisfactory, and I strode down the ramp and out onto the field and took my place in the plane. It was the same open type fuselage in which I had flown before. The signal was given; we started. Soon we were up and began rounding the pylons, one after another, at what appeared to me a horrifying angle. On the ground, Dawes was standing with Orville Wright and he has often told me how scandalized Wright was at the way Coffin was banking those turns. At no time were we over 50 feet from the ground.[5]

During one of the laps, JTM looked down an spotted an ambulance "racing across the field below us." He turned "gingerly in my seat" and saw a plane half submerged in Lake Michigan. It had been circling over the water "as a side show" and crashed, killing the pilot, St. Croix Johnstone: "Badger and Johnstone were the only ones killed in the meet, one just before and one during my flight."

Harold McCormick who, like JTM, "had got the flying fever," purchased the first privately owned airplane "in our part of the country" and housed it in a hangar he built on the beachfront adjacent to his home in Lake Forest. JTM learned of it in a phone call one day from McCormick:

> "Hello, John. How would you like to ride home with me in my new plane this afternoon?" "Great Scott! How long have you had a plane?" "I just got it. It's a Curtiss. I flew in it for the first time this morning." "Of course I'll go back with you. When shall I show up?" "Come to Grant Park about five."[6]

Thrilled by the opportunity to fly with McCormick, JTM raced to finish the day's drawing, aware that he "hustled that cartoon through without too much care." He packed a bag and arrived early at the lakefront, where the beaches were jammed because it was a hot day. The takeoff, needless to say, drew a lot of attention:

> There was prodigious neck-craning as we swooped over the water. At 80 or 90 miles an hour, the 30 miles to Lake Forest were covered all too soon. These were my first three flights—one each year for three years. Planes were still a stirring novelty. Flying, for ordinary mortals, was a matter of tremendous interest and news value.[7]

Given his fascination with airplanes, why didn't JTM take flying lessons himself? He noted, "For a fellow who couldn't back a car out of a garage— let alone tune in correctly on a radio football game, even when Purdue was playing—there was never any temptation."

~{{{{{{{{{{{{{<~

DURING JTM'S LIFE only two US presidential campaigns "stirred [him] from top to bottom": the 1884 campaign pitting Grover Cleveland vs. James Blaine, when JTM was fourteen years old, and the 1912 campaign in which Woodrow Wilson defeated Theodore Roosevelt and incumbent president William Howard Taft. Roosevelt had succeeded to the presidency after President William McKinley's assassination in 1901. After Roosevelt assumed the office, "a shudder ran through the financial world. McKinley's boastful promise of 'a full dinner pail for all' was being amply fulfilled for some if not for all":

> If my political observations have proved anything, they seem to indicate that our nation cannot stand prosperity—or too much of it at once. Every great wave of it generates abuses of some kind or other. The "hath-er"

is not satisfied with what he "hath." He must devise schemes for getting more. Most depressions, if not caused by war or market manipulation, seem the result of battles among industrial giants. McKinley's benefi-cent complacency in the face of tremendous growth of business combi-nations aroused a growing indignation. In answer to this rising clamor of protest, my second Presidential champion rose to prominence. Big business was very suspicious of the fire-eating Teddy. [He] shook a warn-ing finger at the captains of industry—men who were not accustomed to having fingers shaken at them. Perhaps it was bad taste, but it came nearer to being heresy [to do this] in those days.[8]

The newspaper cartoonist has a duty to "make a hasty review of the world's doings as chronicled each day in the press," decide which subject is most important, and then "construct a cartoon about that subject." By scanning cartoons from a particular period in US history, one can gain "a fairly complete record of the chief events . . . and grasp the general trend of the big news."

Assuming this to be true, whoever delves through the files of the first decade of the 20th century will come to an inevitable conclusion. The most important news of that time was Mr. Theodore Roosevelt, Pres-ident, politician, statesman, sociologist, reformer, defender of the faithful, exposer of shams, protagonist, antagonist, hunter, diplomat, apostle of peace, wielder of the Big Stick, and founder of the Ananias Club [named for Ananias, who fell dead when he lied to the apostle Peter about a financial transaction]. A historian might be puzzled to decide whether Mr. Roosevelt was an imperialist, a Democrat or a Republican.[9]

Roosevelt had a knack for capturing public fancy and one of his most successful tactics was associating himself with the Rough Riders in the Spanish-American War. The Rough Riders were a hodgepodge collec-tion of cowboys, collegians, gun fighters, cotillion leaders, millionaires, and plainsmen. His adventures with the Rough Riders made Roosevelt a "veritable Golconda [the name of city in India famous for its diamonds] of inspiration to the cartoonist." He displayed a genius in being involved in provocative acts that "stirred interest and aroused the bitterest antagonism and the most devoted loyalty." Roosevelt "kept life in America in a pleasant turmoil," which provided JTM with plenty of cartooning material:

> His variety of mental and physical activities, aided by features that lent themselves gladly to caricature, made him a tempting target for cartoon exploitation. His teeth and eyeglasses became famous almost before he did. When he smiled it suggested a man in ambush behind a stone wall. The friendliness of the nickname Teddy also helped win for him a peculiarly intimate place in the minds and hearts of the nation. It became a habit to think about him, either kindly or otherwise, but certainly to think about him.[10]

Roosevelt's other asset was an ample supply of "good horse sense which he clothed in graphic language." Phrases like nature fakers, muckrakers, the strenuous life, the crop of children is the best crop of a nation—and many other sayings—"owe their vogue to his instinct as a promoter and advertiser." JTM covered Roosevelt his entire career, starting in 1900 when he was nominated as vice president with McKinley. Although Roosevelt was more of an "executor of President McKinley's policies than a proponent of new ones of his own," his "volcanic energy and initiative" eventually asserted itself. Roosevelt's speeches to Congress included "little touches of human interest" that supplied cartoonists with materials for years:

> "Make race war impossible by abolishing lynching," he said. "Abolish lynching by inflicting a summary death penalty on those guilty of assaulting women. Pass a law demanding publicity in corporations; pass another law protecting all corporations from contributing to campaign funds, and a law demanding supervision of trusts." He said also that injunctions should be upheld; that we should save coal lands; that swollen fortunes should be remedied by a graduated inheritance tax; that strikes should be made impossible by a board of arbitration; that we need currency

reform, a reduction of the Philippine tariff, and scientific agricultural methods. He advised us to respect Japan, annex Cuba if it didn't behave, keep up an efficient Navy and perfect our coast defenses.[11]

While some presidents "allowed their mental processes to operate in a limited orbit," JTM admired Roosevelt for extending himself beyond the usual presidential topics of "statecraft and diplomacy." Roosevelt "leaped blithely from a discussion of the Open Door in China" to bobcat behavior habits. A discussion of how to make farm life attractive to boys "came in for the same eager consideration" as the design and construction of the Panama Canal.

As president, Roosevelt spent summers at Oyster Bay, New York, where the nonstop activity made the town's "humble name a misnomer." To be sure, Roosevelt went there to rest and enjoy quiet time, but if he actually got it, "it was not recorded by the humorists of the pencil who were kept busy by the amazing variety of his visitors":

> For instance, on Monday the President entertained the champion tennis player; on Tuesday some old Rough Rider pals; on Wednesday some fellow LL.D.'s [lawyers]; on Thursday a couple of big game hunters; on Friday a few politicians; on Saturday some brother historians or eminent scientists. Between times he would seek relaxation by chopping down a few trees, swimming across Long Island Sound or taking 10-mile marathon walks. No President ever worked so hard turning out material for cartoonists.[12]

If life became too tame at Oyster Bay, Roosevelt would hunt bears in Mississippi. "This activity produced the crowing triumph of Roosevelt's personal popularity—the Teddy Bear," wrote JTM. On one bear hunt, Roosevelt discovered a wounded young bear and ordered a mercy killing. Later, *Washington Post* political cartoonist Clifford K. Berryman drew a cartoon about it and portrayed the bear as a cuddly cub; about a year later, it was produced as a children's toy called the "teddy bear." When Roosevelt bemoaned societies that failed to produce babies and declared it "race suicide," labeling unmarried men as criminals, parents with particularly large families brought their children to the White House in hopes of receiving "presidential congratulations." Cartoonists "hailed him as the 'Advance Agent of Poster-ity.'" When Roosevelt gave a $100 check to a child named after him, hundreds of parents named their babies Teddy and "sent special-delivery letters to the eminent patronymic," looking for their share. Roosevelt took a trip in a submarine, lunched with educator and orator Booker T. Washington, took boxing and jujitsu lessons, and more: "All these sprightly doings kept him in personal touch with more sections of the country and more classes of people than any President before the advent of radio." He gave the public a lot to think about, and a lot of material to cartoonists like JTM:

> I was one of those most benefited by these Theodorian characteristics. It was a dull day when I could not turn to the White House for an idea. He was as dependable as the weather. I drew him so often, mostly with sympathetic friendliness, that I received, in the form of letters and invitations, many evidences of his friendliness in return. I don't think I was thus flattered into my attitude of admiration, because other Very Important Persons have been equally nice to me without converting me into a devoted follower.[13]

When Roosevelt's term expired, "there was a wide clamor for him to run again," but Roosevelt refused to run, explaining he had served two terms and did not intend to seek a third. "Taft was his man," and the nation voted him in confident that "Teddy's policies would be carried out." JTM recounted that "They were. A few weeks after Teddy had gone to Africa to hunt lions, the Roosevelt policies were carried out and dumped over the back fence."[14]

JTM saw a lot of Roosevelt when their safaris joined in Africa where Teddy and his son, Kermit, "killed three elephants for Akeley's group in the American Museum of Natural History." While in Roosevelt's tent one day, JTM asked him whether he would ever run for president again:

> "No," he said. "No, the kaleidoscope never repeats. A lot of people seem to worry about what to do with ex-Presidents. Well, they needn't worry about this one. I can keep myself busy."[15]

Although that was his position in 1909, three years later he ran again but failed to receive the Republican nomination, so he created the Progressive Party (nicknamed the "Bull Moose Party") and ran against Woodrow Wilson. JTM offered his full support, including delivering a very rare (for him) campaign speech:

> It is one of my proudest experiences to have gone through that Bull Moose campaign as a rapt participant. The *Tribune* threw its whole weight behind T. R. My cartoons were 100 percent for him. I even made my first and last political speech in his behalf. "I wish to go on record," I began, "as favoring the Bull Moose cause, in case those of you who see the *Tribune* every morning may still be in doubt as to where I stand! I have no illusions as to my qualifications as a spellbinder. I don't expect you all to rush home after hearing my speech, to vote for T. R., however much I might hope for such a gratifying result. My chief concern just now is that you don't rush home while hearing it!"[16]

NOTES

1 John T. McCutcheon, *Drawn From Memory* (Indianapolis and New York: Bobbs-Merrill, Inc., 1949), 238.
2 Ibid.
3 Ibid., 239.
4 Ibid.
5 Ibid., 240.
6 Ibid., 240-41.
7 Ibid., 241.
8 Ibid., 241-42.
9 Ibid., 242.
10 Ibid., 243.
11 Ibid., 244.
12 Ibid., 244-45.
13 Ibid., 246.
14 Ibid.
15 Ibid.
16 Ibid., 247.

9

AN OMINOUS SHUDDER

Sometimes the best laid plans don't turn out as hoped, and a pirate cruise in 1912 was among them.

When JTM was a boy, he learned from his books that by following the trade winds and careful navigation he should

> in due course arrive in that alluringly vague vicinity known as the Spanish Main. Duties of the farm and the necessity of going to school prevented the carrying out of any plans just then, but as I looked wistfully down the dusty road to where a fringe of maple trees marked the limit of my travels, a spirit of unrest stirred within me which I am afraid I have never outgrown. Every year there comes, like a recurring fever, an irresistible longing to look at timetables and steamer sailings in the hope that somewhere in this busy world I may find a spot where romance and legend have escaped the cruel inroads of the commonplace.[1]

In 1912, the annual travel fever struck again and JTM was "determined to fare forth and lay a tardy wreath on the shrine of Captain Kidd and his long-dishonored crew." He wrote:

> I wanted to sit on the lonely beach where [François] L'Olonnais [a French pirate] sat; I wanted to lie under the palm tree where the swaggering [Bartholemy] Portuguez [a Portuguese pirate] cooled his swarthy brow; I wanted to anchor in the leeward coves where [Captain Henry]Morgan's [a Welsh privateer] vessels swung. Perhaps somewhere I might stumble over the edge of an ironbound chest, in which case the expenses of the trip might be defrayed, not to mention the duty on such buckets of pearls and plate as might be uncovered by my questing pick and shovel. And if, perchance, the islands yielded no such material reward, I felt that the trip would be rich in such other compensations as health and recreation, which are equally beneficial and secured without the irksome exertion of digging for them in the hot sun.[2]

As JTM planned how he would cover such a trip for the *Tribune*, he debated whether news articles that glorified the deeds of pirates "might possibly have an evil effect on the young." Such an "unhappy result seemed unlikely when one reflected that the pirates are all dead—or most of them anyhow." That knowledge could only lead to one conclusion: "a life of piracy is both disastrous to the health and destructive to the hope of living happily ever after."

JTM wrote to his friend Kirk Brice, inviting him on the cruise. Brice agreed and added he mentioned the cruise to Elsie Clews Parson [an American anthropologist] who said "she's coming too." JTM did not know Elsie, but to even out the group, he invited Katharine Dexter McCormick [a biologist and member of the McCormick family, which gained prominence from the invention of the McCormick Reaper and later in publishing the *Chicago Tribune*]. The arrangements required each to pay one-fourth of the expenses. Now all that was needed was "a long, low rakish craft," and JTM located one in Miami—the *Whim*, a "charming suitable schooner with all the comforts. "Fearing to lose her by delay," he chartered the boat immediately. Later that afternoon, a telegram from Elsie arrived: "Have just chartered motorboat *Heather* in your name." JTM felt sunk:

> I couldn't get a release from the *Whim* charter, although they said they would try to re-let her. Besides, I most definitely did not want a motor-boat. But from a rather exaggerated—as I look back on it—sense of chivalry, I didn't say anything. I cheered myself with the reflection that the *Heather* rhymed with "always fair weather."[3]

First JTM, then Kirk and Katherine and finally Elsie arrived at the dock. Elsie brought "an attractive young Englishman she had met one day at tea, she said, and just invited him along." His name was Archibald Clark Kerr; "Perhaps she thought the unmarried couples needed a chaperone." At any rate, they set sail on February 6 and trouble began immediately:

> The *Heather* was built like a destroyer, 105 feet long, her two 300-horsepower engines consumed 42 gallons of gasoline an hour. She was long and low but rather more rockish than rakish, as we were soon to discover. She carried a complement of nine men. There were no sails, nothing but the engines. To satisfy the enormous appetite of these engines in a cruise through parts devoid of filling stations, a great deal of gasoline had to be taken on board. The tanks, containing 1,550 gallons, at 11 cents [a gallon], were filled; nine large 50-gallon drums were lashed to the rails, and 25, 10-gallon tins of oil were stacked on deck. The presence of all this gasoline crowding the living space and clashed a good deal with romantic ideals. Also, it raised our center of gravity to somewhere up in the huge funnel. I thought with misery of the smart little *Whim* and her white sails.[4]

A norther wind had been blowing "fiercely for several days," but at 5 a.m. they got underway and the first thirty minutes went smoothly. Then came a scare:

> We felt an ominous shudder. The *Heather's* propellers raced and she buried her nose in the sea as if she had decided to be a submarine. At last she swung dizzily back and then began to slide down a long hill, at the

bottom of which a mountain of sea dropped on her bow with a crash. This was only the beginning. For the next hour, the *Heather* staggered, reeled, bucked, plunged and trembled, burying her nose and shaking her tail fearsomely. When a heavy norther traveling south meets the Gulf-stream traveling north, the consequences are open to criticism.[5]

Down below deck, the travelers were "confined unhappily beneath tightly fastened hatches." It gave them a sense of security "that is felt by a rat in a trap." Kerr readied his pistol, saying "he preferred that way to drowning." Brice tried to stay in his bunk and was overheard saying to himself he'd "had enough of pirate islands" and that "Manhattan was the only island he was interested in." Finally, after an hour, the rough seas subsided. Unfortunately, when JTM peered out a porthole, he could see they were back where they began the trip. The captain told them "it was the first time in 32 years that he had turned back." A minor mutiny followed:

> Kirk and Katharine announced they were through with pirate cruises and would cross to Nassau on the regular boat. Elsie, her Englishman and I decided to stick with the *Heather*, whatever it rhymed with, and at midnight we made an uneventful crossing and were well on the way to Nassau when Elsie had an idea. About 5 p.m., the sea having calmed, Elsie thought it would be fun to visit Andros Island, then a vast and mysterious expanse populated only by flamingos, myths and a few Negroes who were said to have lapsed back into African barbarism. This was just what our souls craved after the past 24 hours.[6]

They arranged to rent a sixteen-foot launch and loaded it with food, water, blankets, and guns. Accompanied by a sailor, they set out on the short run to Andros. The trip took longer than expected as the launch "chugged bravely on without making any appreciable approach to the fringe of the palms" they could see in the distance." The sun set and after an hour the sea was totally dark. Then, horror:

> We found our craft most clearly where she was not supposed to be— in the midst of the tumbling, sinister white waters of a reef. In the dark the great black uplifts of the waves before they broke loomed like huge

glistening rocks. There was a grinding of the keel and we lurched over into the lagoon. Here more trouble awaited us in the shape of numberless treacherous coral peaks that lurk near the surface, invisible at night. We struck one but slid off without apparent harm because we were going so slowly. We waded the last 100 yards, with only a flashlight to show the way, and lugged our things ashore, floundering over the jagged coral and into pools left by the receding tide. Driftwood furnished a cheering fire, and with all the sensations of shipwrecked mariners, we stretched out on that lonely beach to sleep.[7]

At dawn, they cooked breakfast and walked along the shore. The group decided to set out for Nassau, which was about forty miles from Andros Island. The launch's best speed was five miles per hour, so it would take all day with half the time being spent at sea with land out of sight. They loaded the launch, "offered a prayer that the gasoline would hold out," and departed. Lying between Andros Island and Nassau is the Tongue of the Ocean—a deep trench in the Bahamas. The Tongue of the Ocean is approached—by those who are aware of it—with fearful respect. JTM and his group were not aware of it. Meanwhile, another nautical nightmare awaited them:

A breeze sprang up and the water became choppy. Within 15 minutes the wind had risen ominously and big black clouds were bearing down on us. Incredibly swiftly the seas became so heavy we feared the launch would capsize. She took the big ones on the bow where they stopped her momentarily, broke and sent volumes of water into the little cockpit. It was impossible to keep the boat on a compass course, for the seas beat her off so savagely that we seemed to be making no headway at all. From crest to crest we struggled, the wind and waves growing steadily more formidable. One man worked the hand pump, another bailed. We had no life preservers. The canvas hood was ripping to pieces and everybody was bailing now. Kerr, knee-deep in water, got out his revolver again. Elsie's notion of adventuring to Andros was being fulfilled in a big way.[8]

It became evident that even if the launch held out, their gasoline would not. Andros Island was out of sight and if they turned back, "might we not pass it to the north, the way we were being blown?" They eased the launch in what was hoped to be the general direction of Andros Island and zigzagged for two hours until they spotted land. Elsie and Kerr removed their shoes in preparation for being thrown into the water. JTM did not because he "knew that if the boat capsized, I could not swim the mile to shore with or without shoes." A wild ride lay ahead:

> The reef was roaring like Niagara, and an endless line of foam marked it. Far away on shore we sighted a few houses beneath the palms. Along the beach we could make out figures frantically rushing back and forth and making signals at us. We presumed they were trying to tell us not to cross. But we had to, and we did. A lucky lift of the sea must have cleared us momentarily, for the great purple rocks were so near the surface it seemed inevitable we should strike them and be overturned. Fifteen minutes later, drenched to the skin, chilled and disheveled, we landed on the beach of Mastic Point amid a throng of excited natives. "It was an act of God," they said. "No boat can cross that reef!"[9]

The natives greeted them warmly and provided dry clothes and hospitality. In the evening, the group learned that Morgan's Bluff was not far from their location. Morgan, legend says, used the spot as a refuge and rendezvous point. "Very little imagination was required to see his swift sloop bearing in toward the safety of the quiet lagoon" and the idea of pirates and blockade-runners made it "worth floundering over the reef just to hear the atmospheric words roll out in such a setting."

Before departing for Andros Island, JTM decided to ride on the schooner, *Sundog*, that hauled mail and cargo. He left instructions with the captain of the *Heather* that if they did not return in two days, a search party should look for them along the coast of Andros. With a northwester still raging, it was unlikely anyone would venture outside Nassau to look for them. With no cable or radio available, a weekly mail and miscellaneous cargo run by the *Sundog* was the only communication link. So by mid-afternoon, they loaded the schooner and decided to sail from Mastic Point to Nicholls' Town. JTM wrote, "At daybreak, after a twelve-hour voyage, we tied up at the wharf in Nassau, very bedraggled and very hungry."[10]

Meanwhile, the two storms apparently were enough for the *Heather's* engineer and steward who quit and had to be replaced. More gasoline also had to be purchased and it would be "weeks before we could get more." They also needed meat, ice, and fresh vegetables, and with "fatalistic accuracy . . . had fallen into the hands of a yacht supplier who bore the same name as a famous pirate, and it is presumed that a smoldering ember of inherited iniquity was stirred into action." When they received the bill for their supplies, "they were staggered." The agent and the cook had stowed the supplies—enough to feed the crew of a man-of-war:

> There were items on it that would have jarred a fixed star. Among the things we had not ordered was enough beer to float the boat. None of us drank beer, and even if we had, there was no good reason for getting so much that merely the drinking of it would have left no time for anything else. We refused to accept this item together with others equally preposterous, and the cook was detailed to help the piratical agent carry the stuff ashore. Then in the midst of dinner, the cook announced that he too was going ashore, and he put on his coat and deserted.[11]

Another cook was hired and they set sail for Nassau harbor. They journeyed to Wemyss Bight where natives were terrified by their searchlight; they anchored in a cove at Cat Island where the entire population came out to "inspect us"; at Rum Cay, hoping to make a landing that would impress the natives, JTM slipped on the sea ladder and was "left dangling in the water," which caused a "broad grin to spread over the faces of the Rum Cay reception committee." They sailed south to Tortuga, the "most famous of all buccaneer strongholds." Little remained of the "chieftains who terrorized the Spanish Main" and they saw only a "peaceful valley and a sleepy sprawling little town." From there, they cruised along the shore of Haiti and stopped at the town of Port-de-Paix, where the "evident hostility of the people made us uncomfortable."[12] They journeyed overland by horse to the city of Gonaïves, fascinated by tales of voodoo worship and human sacrifice. After about three days, they reached Gonaïves, "dirty but healthy." The *Heather* was waiting and took them to the coast of Port-au-Prince where they made "a ceremonial call on President [Jean-Jacques] LeConte in his palace." About a month after their visit, LeConte was assassinated.

"Having had all the pirate cruising I wanted just then," JTM departed for home. There remained one last bit of outstanding business awaiting his arrival: "the little detail of paying for the charter of the *Whim*, which had not been re-let."[13]

JTM and his friend Kirk would link up for one more adventure during the autumn of that year. One day, Dr. Carlos Montezuma, an Apache Indian, asked JTM if he would like to join Montezuma's tribe on their annual deer hunt. The plan called for driving from Phoenix to the Indian reservation and then "proceeding on foot with the Apaches for two weeks." JTM recalled:

> [We would be] sleeping as they did on the ground, eating Indian fare, and seeing amazing exhibitions of Indian tracking. It would be an unusual experience because one must be invited by and go with a genuine Apache. There would be 38 Indians and four or five whites. I knew him sufficiently well to ask if I could bring Kirk Brice, and Montezuma agreed. Presently Kirk wrote me in a great state of excitement. He said he had mentioned the trip casually in Elsie's hearing and she said she was coming, too! I told him for God's sake to head her off![14]

When Kirk arrived in Chicago, he telephoned JTM and gave him some bad news; he had recognized Elsie's duffel bag in the Blackstone Hotel lobby. JTM "hit the ceiling." Kirk issued a challenge: "'Come on down and tell her yourself!' he said. I went down and there she was. 'What train are you starting on?' she inquired enthusiastically. 'Now, here, Elsie—' and I started in."[15]

It turned out that Kirk and Elsie had been playing a joke on JTM. Although they boarded the train together, when it stopped at "a lonely little station, Elsie and her duffel bag disembarked on some tour of their own."

Despite the mishaps associated with the ill-fated pirate cruise, unsurprisingly it gave "new life to another of those boyhood ambitions of [JTM's] that seemed to be perennial." Not only had he wanted to visit tropical islands—he sought to *own* a tropical island.

> Often from the airy heights of the haymow [stack of hay] I used to gaze over the cornfields, and after looking intently for a while I could see green seas tossing on my own private coral stand. In the early stages of this ambition the island was not particularly peopled by anybody but me and few trusty retainers. As my reading progressed, I discovered that island life need not be wholly spoiled by the presence of beautiful ladies. But until I was grown up, the only islands I knew were those of my dreams and books. As far as I know, I had never laid eyes on a real one unless at low water a mudbank appeared on the Wabash.[16]

JTM had an opportunity to see lots of islands during his adventures in the Philippines, including "real ones with coconut palms and more or less languorous native girls." Other affairs called to him, but years of "strap hanging and deadlines" failed to fade the long-held dream. In 1914, with his contract about to expire at the *Tribune*, he resolved to "do something about getting an island." He learned that Melville Island in the Arafura Sea near Port Darwin, Australia, was "available at a price within my range—probably because of its inaccessibility." The island had 10 million acres of land and 10,000 head of wild cattle, and JTM decided to go see it:

> Viewed in retrospect, there were quite a lot of things wrong with this idea. For one thing, it would take at least three months just to get there and back. Paying such a large slice of a not very large capital for an island I might never set foot on a second time seemed of dubious wisdom. I think I've always been a practical realist in working for my money, but I suspect I'm something of a starry-eyed idealist when it comes to spending it. I'm afraid I thought it would be worth the money. This point of view may be incomprehensible to those who see life wholly in terms of percentages, invoices and overheads, and I mean this in no way derogatory to businessmen. There are many times when a bank balance is more beautiful than a palm tree waving in the trade winds.[17]

A steamer was scheduled to leave for Melville, Australia, on July 25 from San Francisco. Meanwhile, a dinner marking the sixteenth anniversary of the Manila Bay naval battle was scheduled to be held in Washington, D.C., at the home of Admiral George Dewey. JTM was eager to attend with Ed Harden and so he made plans for "a quick trip east" prior to setting out to see his island at the other end of the globe. As fate would have it, the dinner turned out to be one of those otherwise ordinary events in life from which "arose unexpected consequences." At the dinner, JTM sat between Dewey and Captain Pitt Scott, who had been a member of the admiral's staff when he was commodore.

JTM recalled, "Other old friends were there, a little older, a little stouter, a little less romantic-looking than when they were pacing the quarter-decks in a strange half-known place called the Philippines. In addition to the reminiscences, there was, as I had anticipated, much talk of the recent Vera Cruz incident." In April 1914, several sailors from the crew of the USS Dolphin were arrested and detained by Mexican authorities after landing in a restricted dock area in Tampico. When Mexico refused to apologize, President Woodrow Wilson sent a fleet to the Gulf of Mexico:

> Seventeen of our battleships were flung in a massive crescent before the city, which our soldiers were holding against the Mexicans. Venustiano Carranza and Pancho Villa were heading rival armies in northern Mexico, and [Mexican President Victoriano] Huerta was drinking his brandy when he scoffed at Wilson's attempt to get an apology for not saluting the American flag. The Navy was preparing a formidable demonstration. Pitt Scott had been put in command of the *Marietta* which was outfitting in the Brooklyn Navy Yard. She was a small gunboat which might be sent in closer, possibly up some river to do bombarding.[18]

This caught JTM's attention and he turned to Scott: "Gosh, you're likely to see more action than any of the other ships!" JTM said with a "wistful note in my voice."

"Why don't you come along?" Scott asked. "I'd have to get permission of the Navy Department," JTM said. "Well, here's Admiral [Bradley A.] Fiske right now." The admiral approved the request and the next day JTM went to see US Navy Secretary Josephus Daniels, where he also happened to meet Assistant Secretary of the Navy Franklin D. Roosevelt. Permission in hand, he "proceeded at once to New York. Then a monkey wrench was dropped into my plans." As he stood together with Scott, an orderly approached and handed Scott a long official envelope:

> He opened it and I knew instantly that something was wrong. He read it twice, then handed it to me. It was an order for the *Marietta* to proceed to Guantanamo to relieve another ship on patrol duty at Santo Domingo. She was to go nowhere near Mexico. Well, it was one of those things! I didn't want to go to Santo Domingo! After a few shoulder shruggings, meaning what-the-hell, I took my bags, said good-by to Scott and headed to Harden's office on Wall Street where I immediately called John Callan O'Laughlin in the *Tribune* office in Washington, D.C.[19]

O'Laughlin, who had been the longtime editor of the *Army and Navy Journal*, was "short and dark, vital with enthusiasm" and always "sparkled with good-fellowship," making it easy to understand "why he has always had so many friends." He had served as first assistant secretary of state under Theodore Roosevelt. JTM explained his situation to O'Laughlin, who called Daniels and arranged a transfer from the *Marietta* to the *USS Wyoming*— "our most imposing battleship!" The *Wyoming* was in the Brooklyn Navy Yard, so JTM raced back and found Scott, who led him to the battleship:

> The executive officer, Commander David Todd, turned out to be a Manila friend. He took us to Captain [James] Glennon. "I am to have the honor, sir, of accompanying you to Vera Cruz." "Vera Cruz!" he exclaimed. "We have orders to go to Mexico!" "Why, it's less than an hour since I was told I was to go there on the *Wyoming*." "I'm sorry," said the captain shortly. "There must be some mistake. If anybody knows the ship's orders, I should." It looked like an impasse. I had almost reached the shoulder shrugging stage for the second time when—also, for the second time, like something out of a storybook—an orderly approached and handed the captain a long official envelope.[20]

Glennon read the note slowly and finally said: "Well, you're right, here are my orders to go to Vera Cruz." With that, he directed JTM to bring his luggage aboard the *Wyoming*. The episode was "something to remember— to have been able to give the commander of a battleship his first news of his orders from the Navy Department." Telephoned instructions beat the slower paper-based order that had to "pass through several hands" to get to its destination.

JTM and the *Wyoming* departed the next morning for "one of the most pleasantest seven weeks of my life." The *Wyoming* joined thirty-five other ships at Vera Cruz, including two super dreadnoughts. Admiral [Oscar] Badger, who was in command, transferred his headquarters to the *Wyoming*. JTM was supposed to go ashore, but "to my delight by a general vote of the wardroom I was invited to stay." JTM relished life on board:

> I could continue to enjoy, among other things, those glorious nights of delicious coolness, with the admiral's orchestra and the ship's band, and a thousand sailors perched on the turrets and scattered about the decks to see the moving pictures. The wonderful spirit on the *Wyoming* won for it the name of the Happy Ship.[21]

The world's newspaper war correspondents were on hand, and although there was little to see or do, "the air was full of rumor and possibilities." JTM went ashore every day; one time he accompanied cavalry troops to El Tejar about ten miles in from the coast; another time he joined Admiral [Cameron McRae] Winslow on a destroyer to Puerto Vallarta—Mexican gunboats blocked their entrance. One night he slept with US Marines who were on sentry duty. Later he hosted a dinner for General [Frederick] Funston, commander of the land forces, who JTM first met in the Philippines. As if he wasn't already figuratively flying from everything going on, a real flight was arranged for him a few days later:

> It happened that still another Manila friend, [Captain] Henry Mustin [a pioneering naval aviator who helped establish U.S. Naval Air Station Pensacola], was commandant of the [*USS*] *Mississippi* the aviation

headquarters of the fleet, and he was disposed to help me in my persistent desire to fly. [War correspondent] Dick Davis had been up a few days before and reported that the Mexicans had fired on his plane. This made a fine news story. I was assigned to the care of a naval flier named Geoffrey Chevalier, who took me over the town and the harbor, over the greatest concentration of American naval power up to that time. It was a beautiful flight but without incident.[22]

Effective July 1, 1914, Daniels ordered all ships to go "dry." For the sailors on the *Wyoming*, the loss of alcohol led to a "wake, and a noisy one, and it lasted until midnight, at which moment any leftover liquor was thrown overboard. Admiral Badger and Capt. Glennon immured themselves in their quarters, stopped up their ears and ignored the revelry that resounded through the ship." Most of the newspaper correspondents, known for their fondness for drink, were gone from the battleships once the liquor ban took effect.

Meanwhile, public interest began shifting from Vera Cruz to the Mexican revolutionaries, Carranza and Villa. The *Tribune* cabled JTM and instructed him to get sketches of both men. JTM met Carranza in Saltillo, where he drew his portrait. A meeting was arranged with Villa, who was based in Chihuahua. JTM was uneasy:

> I had some misgivings about drawing this picturesque character whose exploits were filling the columns of all the papers in America. He had been represented as a person of such impetuosity and at times violence that I worried about the form his displeasure might take in case the portrait did not please him. He buckled on his holster and cartridge belt, seated himself at a table and laid his six-shooter in front of him. He wore a light-gray uniform and shiny riding boots; it was evident he had bestowed some pains on his appearance. He had a fine forehead and a well-shaped nose. The one unpleasant feature was the pendulous lower lip which, as he sat listening, with his suspicious eyes darting from one person to another, had a most disturbing effect. In view of the revolver, I wondered whether I should draw this as it was, and yet I realized that it was absolutely essential to a true likeness. So I drew what I saw.[23]

JTM finished the portrait and asked Villa to autograph it. Villa looked at the sketch and "in a sprawling hand, thereby refuting the story that he could not write," signed "Francisco Villa."

Time was passing and as July 25 approached, JTM realized if he did not catch the boat to Australia "in a hurry," he would not return home in time to begin his new contract at the *Tribune*. When the last possible moment for departure arrived, like he did in Bombay where a coin toss led him to the Spanish War rather than a tour of India, he "trusted to luck" what he should do. Thanks to the toss of a coin, he would not be westbound in the middle of the Pacific Ocean when World War I began in Europe.

-ϨϨϨϨϨϨϨϨϨϨϨϨϾ

L IKE THE LIQUOR ON THE NAVY'S FLEET, interest in the Vera Cruz inci- dent had evaporated. In Europe, all the pieces were in place for war and had JTM "dreamed that war was at last so imminent, I would never have been loitering in Mexico covering our little fracas with [Mexican President] Huerta, and fighting mosquitoes." On July 27, 1914, war cor- respondent Fred Palmer received a telegram from his editor, Trumbull White, at *Everybody's Magazine*: "Conditions very grave. Leave at once for New York and Europe." Palmer and JTM boarded a northbound train and separated in St. Louis. Palmer took the *Lusitania* across the Atlantic on August 4; JTM stopped at Chicago long enough to have the *Tribune* arrange "for money and credentials," and then he booked his trip on the *SS St. Paul*, which left August 7. The news from Europe was explosive:

It was a week of terrific climaxes—the flaming bulletins, the staggering succession of crises in Europe as one nation after another declared war. During my few days in Chicago I drew five cartoons: "The Christian Nations," "On Guard," "The Sport of Kings," "The Crime of Ages" and

"The Colors." All five won favor. All were conceived in the profound emotion of the hour and had the advantage of a background of events which were stirring humanity to the depths.[24]

Many news reports said American citizens were stranded abroad with letters of credit but without cash. To prevent this from happening, JTM took a letter of credit from the *Tribune,* plus $5,218 in gold coin, "American, British and French." He carried the gold in "two stout bags"; it weighed over nineteen pounds. On the *St. Paul,* he put the coins in his trunk "where I used to verify its presence several times a day." Other correspondents also were on the *St. Paul*—"all weighed down with coin." The adventures began as soon as the *St. Paul* docked at Liverpool:

> There were no porters on the dock. Passengers had to rustle their own luggage, assisted by cabbies. By Aug. 15, I was in London, and on the 17th in Brussels. [Fred] Palmer had arrived two days before me. We all knew that there would be an iron determination on the part of the military commanders to bar correspondents. We were told no man could go with the French Army unless he spoke French and filed his dispatches in that language. [British Field Marshal Herbert] Kitchener was notoriously hostile to newspapermen as well as supremely indifferent to how they felt about it. Certainly none of us had the slightest hope of seeing anything of the German side because of the widespread belief that in no circumstances would correspondents, German or alien, be tolerated in the German lines. News was not leaking out; no correspondents seemed to be leaking in.[25]

The outlook remained dim and most correspondents felt "the military authorities were more than half right in their wish to exclude writers who might unintentionally betray an important operation with disastrous results." JTM wondered if the day of the war correspondent had finally ended, yet "nearly all the men who had been in on the war game during the last 20 years were dropping down on London like birds coming home to roost." JTM decided to try his luck with the French:

I had all sorts of credentials to impress the French Army. My plan was to stay a few days in Belgium, then return to London, thence to France. Once again, luck intervened. Instead of staying a few days [in Belgium], I stayed eight weeks. Instead of joining the French Army and needing my letters of introduction, I joined the German [Army], against all advices to the contrary—and my letter of credit was good in Germany. It was indeed a piece of journalistic good luck to be one of the first four correspondents to see behind that shroud of mystery.[26]

JTM tried "in every way" to obtain permission to travel to the German front lines. It was beginning to seem doubtful "that I could *see* anything of this war," and in despair he "decided to try subterfuge":

We applied to the American consul, who gave us each a formidable-looking document dripping with large red seals. There was nothing in this to enable us to pass lines. All it said was that we were American citizens. Yet on it four of us started out in a taxicab—Irvin Cobb, Will Irwin, Arno Dosch and I. We all climbed in, intending to go as far as we could and return to Brussels well in advance of the invading legions.[27]

Soldiers stopped his group at every barricade, inspected the documents, "shrugged their shoulders and let us through." Guard post by guard post, JTM and the others made their way past streetcars that had been "thrown across the street" by explosions. Before long, they were out of the city:

JTM wrote, "It amazed and amused us to find how potent our worthless passes seemed to be." They were headed toward Louvain, Belgium, and passed through "large detachments of Belgium soldiers, tired and worn, and machine guns drawn by dogs." They began encountering refugees, first in small groups, "later in solid streams. Some had carts or wagons loaded with household goods. Men, women, children, dogs—a sorry procession, silent, resigned, helpless victims of war." They continued on without trouble for a time:

Nobody stopped us. Nobody tried to stop us. Then it dawned on us that nobody wanted to stop us. When a city is about to fall, all precautions are relaxed. A car dashed by, loaded with newsreel photographers. They waved us to turn back. "The Germans are coming." The taxi driver didn't look happy, but he took us in a reflective sort of way to within a couple miles of Louvain. From a slope, we looked down on the town. The sound of firing came from somewhere beyond. Then the driver got off his perch and made a long survey of the machinery under the hood, coming to the conclusion that the car had arrived in a state in which it would travel only in the direction of Brussels. "I go no further! If I am cut off, they take my cab!"[28]

Concluding that "all persuasion" would be useless, JTM grabbed his raincoat and asked the driver to promise to wait for the group. They started toward Louvain on foot. In town, people stood grouped together in the doorways. They saw some priests waiting "in a walled garden." Gunshots sounded nearer and nearer. JTM recalled, "In the streets there was an absence of hurry and noise, but the silence here was not the silence of unconcern. The king had left two hours earlier. Irwin spoke: 'I understand any correspondent caught in the German Army will be shot.'" Suddenly, a group of Belgian soldiers appeared:

> The soldiers ran out of one side street and into another. A second group darted across. We had gone only a few more steps forward when two figures rounded a corner. It was almost a minute before we realized what we were seeing. One was an uhlan [cavalryman] on a horse, his rifle lying across his saddle. The other was a German soldier on a motorcycle. We flattened ourselves against the wall. The Germans rode slowly by, their steel-blue eyes scanning the street ahead. I shall never forget them.[29]

Concluding war in the streets "seemed imminent," the group hurried back to the taxicab. By the time they got to Brussels, "we found we had been cut off." A column of German soldiers was on the road marching toward Brussels "in clouds of white dust." JTM had been worried about not getting to see the front—"now the front had come to us." He was concerned:

> We were engulfed in the mightiest front in Europe—straw-hatted, without so much as a toothbrush, speaking only English, and I with a letter to the President of France in my pocket. We felt reasonably sure we

could not be mistaken for Belgians. Cobb couldn't look anything but an American if he tried. Indiana stuck out all over me—as it always does. But we decided to report ourselves at the first possible moment, to tell them that we were not there for any malicious purpose, that we were simply there because we had come in a taxi and could not get back.[30]

They watched the "river of gray"—two solid streams of soldiers—pour down the Rue de la Station on the way to Brussels and France and into the history books: "Tens of thousands of infantry, tens of thousands of calvary with poised lances, hundreds of military pieces and thousands of soldiers on bicycles . . . rolled in like a flood that had no end." It was an awe-inspiring view:

> The roar of motors, the clatter of hoofs and the measured fall of thousands of heavy boots on the pavements were both stupefying and hypnotic. The columns flowed in, singing in great choruses. The songs swelled in thunderous strains above the plaza beneath the Hotel de Ville and the Cathedral of St. Pierre. We waited until we saw an especially jovial-looking German officer and then reported to him, explaining in some trepidation how we happened to be there. Instead of ordering us to be shot immediately, he laughed heartily. Then he called other officers and together they laughed over the circumstances of the American correspondents caught between the lines, who had come out in a taxi to see the war.[31]

The Germans denied permission to return to Brussels, which would have been too dangerous anyway because of "snipings and reprisals." They were free to move about the city but forbidden to leave without permission—"partly for their own safety." They looked English, which "in many eyes . . . made us marked men." They checked in to the Hotel Mille Colonnes, which faced the train station, where they watched hour after hour "an unbroken stream of gray-clad soldiers pouring through the town." It went "on without end, forenoon, afternoon, evening and night." The following morning they awoke to find the "same roar in our ears, the same compact volume of German power still surging and singing onward."

There was nothing to eat at the hotel, but the group was able to buy bread, cheese, and a can of pineapple at a nearby delicatessen. A number of German soldiers also were in the shop, and JTM "noticed with some surprise they were paying for their purchases":

> It was a pleasure to find the invaders were not the maddened barbarians we had been led to believe. During the three days in Louvain I never saw a single exhibition of rudeness or discourtesy from a German soldier or officer to a citizen. In the barbershops I saw officers patiently wait their turn while citizens preceded them into the chairs, a small matter perhaps, nevertheless an indication of the desire of the soldiers to avoid giving offense to the people.[32]

Two days later the Germans announced the group was free to leave Louvain. The ride to Brussels was a shock, compared to just three days earlier: "Gaunt walls were all that remained of many houses. Rude mounds with extemporaneous wooden crosses stood by the road here and there." For some reason, the fields with their grains remained undisturbed. JTM continued to be impressed by the apparent civility of the invading army:

> On entering Brussels, we saw where a camp had been made in a park. None of the trees had been damaged, and even the sod that had been removed lay carefully stacked up for replacement. This careful preservation of the park was as thorough as the careful destruction of the Belgian snipers and their homes.[33]

It was not long after that JTM and his group "heard of the tragic outbreak [at Louvain] that shocked the world." For five days, the city of Louvain was pillaged, burned, and destroyed by the German Army. It sobered JTM's view of the Germans:

> In view of the historic importance of events just preceding and following the partial destruction of the city, I described rather fully in my dispatches the events I saw. The fact that I was one of four American newspapermen in a position to chronicle first impressions gave my

observation an interest it might not otherwise have had. Much war news that reached American readers was somewhat one-sided. I endeavored to give both sides.[34]

The seemingly endless flow of German soldiers continued through Brussels and "seemed to have become a fixed feature of the landscape, like the rows of trees or the monuments." So many men and horses passed their way that "the magnitude of the movement benumbed the senses." JTM and the correspondents learned that Britain and France were massing a large number of soldiers near Waterloo. JTM wondered if "a second battle, on a larger scale, might be fought 99 years later on that historic field." Naturally, they were anxious to get there:

> We each obtained a pass from General Von Jarotsky, the German Commandant of Brussels. It stated that Mr. Whosit, American journalist representing the Such and So, was permitted to pass through the German lines. To this brief document was affixed the photograph of the bearer. It was probably intended for use only in the environs of the city, but anything with the stamp of the German Government on it bore a magic potency which we used to such excellent effect that it carried us past thousands of Germans all the way to the French frontier until that ill-fated day when we ran into an officer superior in rank to General Von Jarotsky.[35]

By now, the German Army had commandeered all taxis and automobiles throughout the city. JTM and his companions found "two street hacks"—one of whom "had served in the Belgian artillery and presumably was a man of great courage." They set out at 4 p.m. "with the intention of seeing something of this great battle of Waterloo and getting back in time for dinner." The battle they found was the famous Battle of Mons:

> There were seven of us in the two hacks, plus the two drivers in their rumpled silk hats. Many people in Sunday clothes watched our exodus with amusement. When we reached Waterloo there were no armies, but we could hear the distant rumble of artillery [fire]. A good deal of

diplomacy was necessary to induce the drivers to proceed. At an inn an excited landlord assured us that a great battle was raging only eight miles farther on. The Germans [had] commenced to push back the English and French. Here the English [Field Marshal John] French showed brilliant strategy, saving his army from the enveloping tactics of the Germans. For three days we followed this battle without catching up with it.[36]

That evening the hack drivers refused to go further and "deposited us in front of the L'Aigle Noir in the Grand Place at Nivelles" and left to head back to Brussels, twenty miles away. Will Irwin, suffering from a case of tonsillitis, went with them. The rest of the group went to the hotel bar where the landlord "provided a banquet of cold meat, eggs, coffee, bread and cheese." The correspondents attracted a great deal of attention and drew an "excited, curious crowd." They learned to their disappointment that the town had no form of transportation as the Germans had commandeered the cars, horses, vehicles, and gasoline, so they decided to set out on foot:

> At 6 a.m. we started out. Except for sandwiches and two boxes of cigars, we were unhampered by impediments. A somber hush hung over the country. In spite of the bright sunshine, the orderly fields, the tree-lined roadways, there was that in the atmosphere which betokened sudden calamity. The people who remained stood in little groups, talking in low tones, and regarded us in wonder. Often we caught the word "Anglais." We hoped to reach Mons, 18 miles away, in five hours. We passed through Seneffe and Manage and presently came up with a German column. "Who are you? What are you doing here?" We showed our passes and the officer received us with an address of welcome. Would he honor us by having a drink? we asked. He would, with pleasure.[37]

An hour later, JTM and his companions were sampling army soup. By this time it was noon and they had traveled only nine miles. They worried the "battle would not last long enough for us to catch up with it," but they also were hungry. After lunch, the German column resumed its march

and soldiers called out, "*Auf Wiedersehen*." The correspondents continued their own march and were walking down the road to Bascoup "when
an officer in a passing car hailed us." Feeling confident with their "potent
passes," they told him who they were:

> "I'm sorry," he said politely, "but you cannot go any farther. You must
> go back." "We have passes," we assured him. "It is impossible for you to
> continue. We do not allow newspapermen with the army. You must go
> back immediately." His voice carried conviction. Our hearts sank but we
> extended our passes. He looked at them, whistled low and made a ges-
> ture of despair. "Very well," he said, "you may continue!" Our spirits rose
> like rockets. We forged ahead. But all was not well with us.[38]

Cobb was an excellent walker but "weighed over 200 pounds" and was
wearing a pair of rubber-soled shoes that made every step "agony." Everyone else in the group "were more or less disabled" by the twenty-mile walk.
As they collectively limped toward the town of Binche, it became obvious
that if they wished to go farther that day, "some other means of locomo-
tion" was necessary. The following day they went from stable to stable in
town in search of a horse. By mid-afternoon, "we closed a deal for a roan
mare, aged about 20, an old cart and a set of harness for 775 francs." The
horse's name was Bulotte, or Fat Girl; her alias was Gray Gables, an impo-
lite reference to her prominent hip bones. A young German suggested the
group would be well-served by purchasing two bicycles and JTM "spent the
afternoon learning to ride again . . . as a collection of Bincheans watched
me delightedly." They left Binche the following morning, Lewis and JTM
rode the bikes and the others followed in the cart. In the town of Merbes-
le-Château, they found the first evidence of an atrocity:

> We stopped to investigate. A man had had his throat cut and several
> houses had been burned. From one source we heard that the citizen was
> deliberately murdered; from another that he had been studying the Ger-
> man troops with field glasses; and from still another that English sol-
> diers had been firing from the house at German skirmishers. The last

explanation I believe to have been the most probable one, for the Germans made no secret of the army's policy of killing citizens in houses where sniping had been done.[39]

They crossed the Sambre River and headed to Maubeuge. Their passes were examined by a German outpost "and found sufficient." The young soldier asked if they would like to see where the battle had been waged. The group followed him up a steep path under a bluff below which "town lay compactly." The French had "failed to stem the Teuton advance," despite holding a strong position and the trenches revealed a scene of "great confusion: caps, haversacks, food, tobacco, broken rifles, bloodstained notebooks told eloquently how precipitate had been the flight of the defenders."

The correspondents decided to follow the road to Beaumont and, if nothing was happening there, they would head back to Maubeuge. It was late and a drizzling rain began and there was "great anxiety about approaching the German outposts after dark." French Army scouts were in the area and they were caught between two armies.

> For three days now we had kept on and on, always expecting to be stopped but always, by some freak of luck, being allowed to pass still nearer to the front. Ahead, the road ascended steeply to where it merged into the winding street that led to Beaumont. We knew that if we followed it, we should reach the inevitable square. The town was jammed with troops. We decided to report to the officer in command, as we had done with such excellent results before. The war correspondent, according to popular conception in those days, was generally a dashing sort of person in smart riding clothes. Not so, however, were the correspondents who found themselves on August 26 [1914] down on the French frontier with the sound of great battles to the left and right. We had unshaved faces, soiled linen, dusty rumpled clothes now wet with drizzle. I prefer not to dwell on what we looked like when we drew up before the town hall in the square in Beaumont.[40]

A stern-faced but handsome officer emerged from the hall wearing a coat with white cloth "indicating high nobility." He surveyed the group in "one sweeping glance—an all-embracing glance which missed nothing—not even the fact that two of us wore straw hats." He asked who they were and what they were doing there. Although he spoke fluent English and was polite, his tone had "an absence of that warmth we had hoped for." They were told the German Army allows no correspondents to travel with it. They were asked to wait, "something we soon got accustomed to doing." A general with a more relaxed demeanor arrived to offer some startling news:

> He informed us that if we had gone forward toward Maubeuge as we had intended, and had been found, we would really have been shot; that two men with the same sort of passes as ours had already been found within the lines and arrested. "Those two men will be sent as prisoners to Liege," he said, "but you will be sent back to Brussels tomorrow." Then he asked us, "How did you get your reports in?" We told him we had not sent a word, that there was no means of doing so. Our desire, we said, was to follow the army in order to tell the truth about what we saw. We pointed out that our reports might have the effect of counteracting the stories of alleged German atrocities which were flooding the world, for we had seen no evidence of such things.[41]

The general shook his head and told them they were not being held as prisoners, "but you must not try to escape." He instructed them to return in the morning when they would be sent back to Brussels. It took a while to find sleeping quarters that would accommodate old Fat Lady. They were directed to a schoolhouse. Hunger caught their attention:

> As yet we had not eaten. In our pockets we had some chocolate, sandwiches and 11 hard-boiled eggs, also the remnants of two boxes of cigars and cigarettes. With these we made our way back to a schoolroom where some soldiers were singing, and ate our supper on a bench. Of all the vivid impressions of the days in Belgium, this is one of the most vivid— and how those men could sing! I wish I could have sketched it on the

spot instead of from memory, but sketching is dangerous in an army. The ability to draw focuses suspicion on one's motives. Next to a camera a sketchbook is the surest way to invite trouble.[42]

The following morning the group tried to sell Fat Lady and the cart, but "no one in town would give anything for them." They tried offering all of it to a soldier for one mark, but he refused. Finally, they donated them to a young Belgian "who accepted them without enthusiasm, hitched up and drove away." Following instructions, they reported to the town hall:

> Columns were forming, motor vans pulling out, official cars purring in readiness. In the colorful picture of that quaint plaza of Beaumont, there was only one incongruous note—a group of five very disheveled, hungry-looking Americans waiting by the door. That we were being observed and discussed was painfully obvious. For an hour or more we waited. At 10 a.m. the staff departed. One of the last things that one of the last departing officers did was to turn us over to a tall young lieutenant named Mittendorfer, who informed us there was no way at present of returning us to Brussels.[43]

As long as the general staff remained in Beaumont, the correspondents were free to move about the town. However, when the staff departed for the front, "the responsibility of his charge must have weighed heavily on Lieutenant Mittendorfer, for he placed us under a guard armed with a rifle and bayonet." He gave a short set of instructions:

> "You are not prisoners, but you must not leave this spot." We sat on the spot, which was a stone bench in front of the guardhouse until the middle of the afternoon. At 3 p.m., it began to rain and we were asked to step inside. In another moment, we had been marched into the guardhouse. There we found a French suspect, a Belgian suspect, a Congo Negro chauffeur and a couple of French prisoners of war. The first two were doubtless the ones who had passes like ours, mentioned by the German officer. The room was 12 or 15 feet square and the floor was half a foot deep in straw. A sentry stood at the door, another at the window. Of

course we "were not prisoners of war" but we could not leave the room under penalty of having a bayonet run through us. Our sensations were far from exhilarating.[44]

Eventually they saw the lieutenant and "hailed him earnestly." Mittendorfer apologized profusely and allowed the correspondents to transfer from the guardhouse to a café next door. That's where they stayed—and slept—as "two long days of imprisonment dragged by." Food remained scarce but there was plenty of wine because 20,000 bottles had been found in the cellars of Prince Caraman-Chimay's residence, which was nearby. For dinner, the correspondents enjoyed rye bread and an "old Bordeaux, probably worth many dollars a bottle." Despite the abundance of wine, excessive drinking was verboten for the soldiers:

> We heard the officer in charge giving his night orders to the guards on duty. "My children," he said (he was only 26), "you must behave well, like German soldiers. You must not drink too much, for if you get drunk, no matter how much I like you, I will have you sent to prison for seven years." This was the German penalty for drunkenness while on duty.[45]

The following morning, breakfast again featured rye bread and another rare old bottle of wine. Around noon, one of the correspondents was sent out under armed guard to forage for food. He returned with "a few potatoes, some onions, a can of apricots, a jar of honey and a box of cigars." For the first time in three days, they also enjoyed a hot meal because the "landlady made stew." That evening, they were instructed to be ready to leave on two hours' notice. "Two minutes were all we needed," and at 9 p.m. they walked to the railroad station along with a group of 250 French and English prisoners of war. The correspondents were crowded into a "second-class coach half full of German wounded" and were told to pull down the window curtains because the train "might be fired upon." They pulled out of the station at midnight, but for where, they "had no idea."

By morning their train had covered twenty-five miles to the city of Charleroi; at Gembloux, they had a six-hour layover as seven hundred

additional French and English prisoners were loaded on the train. Breakfast included rye bread, honey, and . . . a Bordeaux wine. For lunch, more
rye bread and honey. During the layover, Red Cross workers handed out
sausages and "we got one or two." The morning of day two, they arrived at
Aix-la-Chapelle where they "were put off" the train. They were instructed
by the Germans to report to the American consul in Aix and obtain permission to leave. After that, they were to "report to the police for instructions." Their arrest would turn out to be good fortune:

> Relieved, but looking scarcely human after the many nights in our
> clothes, we hurried to the consul's residence to find that he was out of
> town. The vice-consul made out papers for us. Then for 24 hours we shut-
> tled between the military authorities and the [German] secret police who
> were reluctant to let us out of their clutches. When the American consul
> came back from Liege, I discovered that he was an old friend, Robert J.
> Thompson of Chicago. He speedily established our identity so that we
> were released from further surveillance; and he verified our newspaper
> connections so that the German officials recognized us as accredited
> correspondents. Thus the circumstance of our arrest at Beaumont, at the
> time a crushing disappointment, turned out to be a real piece of luck.[46]

JTM checked into the Hotel Nuellins, "a quiet, conservative place in
which the great of Germany were wont to stop." Beginning with their first
encounter with the German soldiers at Louvain, "we had been constantly
impressed by the orderliness of the German behavior, not only to us, but
to the native people of Belgium as well":

> "Where are all these atrocities?" we asked one another. We had seen
> none. We had tried over and over to trace an atrocity story to its source.
> It was always elsewhere. Over and over we discussed this phase of Ger-
> man conduct, so very different from what the London papers had led
> us to expect. Here we were, five American newspapermen, who, by a set
> of curious chances, had seen much of the German Army in its passage
> through Belgium, who had followed closely in its wake; here we were

with a news story that Americans should hear. It seemed only fair to the Germans that we should say what conclusions we had reached, wholly independently and without coercion or bribe, about a situation that was stirring the world. Even though none of us was pro-German in his sympathies, it was the unanimous opinion of all of us that the atrocity stories were being tremendously and intentionally exaggerated. I feel I should add that we were not nearly so anti-German as we had been before seeing so much of them at close quarters.[47]

The correspondents prepared a statement containing their views on the matter. Five of them signed it as representatives of their news organizations—the *Chicago Tribune*, the *Saturday Evening Post*, the Associated Press, and the *Chicago Daily News*. It was sent to Berlin to be transmitted by wireless radio to the United States; they chose not to cable it because it would have to be reviewed by London censors. The statement also reached Kaiser Wilhelm, and the correspondents eventually received "a letter of thanks from the Reichskanzler or prime minister." They waited in vain for a reaction from the United States:

We never knew whether it had reached America at all until long afterward. Evidently there was much "interference" in that early wireless message. The AP man in New York had to do a good deal of guessing when he pieced it together.[48]

There was little news to report from Aix, but what was worthy of reporting could be sent from the city of Vaals, "just across the border in Holland." Two of the group departed for London, but JTM and two others remained. They wrote "a respectful letter to the Kaiser" requesting permission to travel to the front in hopes of seeing more of the German Army in action. The letter, along with Thompson's influence, "enabled us to gain facilities which we might never have obtained had we been sent to any other city":

Capt. Alfred Mannesman was sent to take us back through the German lines. Thompson also went along. Except for the car, we newspapermen paid our own expenses for the next 10 days. The contrasts were vivid and striking between our recent sojourn at the front and our present trip, accompanied by an officer with a Kaiser's pass. On the first occasion, as quasi-prisoners, we had slept on straw with suspected spies. Now, Prince [Heinrich] Reuss, ex-German minister to Persia, "bestirred himself to find lodgings for us," as Cobb put it. On the first occasion we ate only rye bread provided by our armed guard. Now we dined in the big hall of the Prefecture as guests of His Excellency Field Marshal von Heeringen, commanding the Seventh Army of the German Kaiser.[49]

A German officer said hello to JTM and "referred to my Prince Henry cartoons," which the officer had seen hanging on the walls of the prince's castle in the city of Kiel. During the ten days with the Germans, JTM "saw the great fortresses of Maubeuge [France] battered and smashed." At Brimont, "with the twin towers of Reims Cathedral only a scant three miles away," JTM stood next to the howitzers that had "shelled it less than a week before." The Germans defended the decision to shell the fortress:

> We were told and retold how the French were using the towers as an observation post; how two German officers under a flag of truce had been sent to warn them to cease; and how those officers had never returned. It became one of those interminable war controversies, in which each side sticks to an opposite story.[50]

JTM had another opportunity to fly in Laon, France, where arrangements were made to take off with Karl Ingold, a pioneer German aviator. What followed was possibly the first flight of a civilian over the lines and certainly a rare aerial view of war-torn Europe:

> A Bavarian staff officer lent me his leather coat. "It has my shoulder straps," he said. "If you fall into the hands of the enemy you will be treated as an officer, not as a spy." I was conscious of a new thrill of interest. "Be careful not to bump against the gasoline tank," I was cautioned. It was just above my head in the biplane, which was not a combat plane and was not even armed. In the open cockpit were two handles to which I

clung. The propeller was in front but high enough so that the blast passed over me. The wind was erratic and full of pockets. I became a fatalist. No amount of anxiety could affect the outcome of the voyage.[51]

Only five years earlier, JTM had attended an aviation meet not far from here in peacetime. Now everywhere was the sign of war:

A smoky blur 70 miles to the southwest was Paris. The entire battle front along the Aisne River [in northeastern France] was dotted with microscopic figures. Huge clouds of belching smoke from the French and English batteries, and answering bursts of unfolding white billows from the German side, told how savagely the great duel was raging, and meant that every moment men were being torn to pieces. But I could not hear the deep growl of the guns above the noise of our motor. From our 3,000-foot height we could watch the battle more or less relieved of the anxiety of being shot. If an Allied balloon gun had fired on us, we could not have known it unless we saw the white puffs of smoke; if a hostile plane were hovering above us, we could not have heard it. Such indeed proved to be the case—a Frenchman was high in the clouds above us but we were happily unconscious of the menace of his movements.[52]

As Ingold and JTM landed, a crowd gathered and cried out: "See the Frenchman!" They watched as "exploding shells, like white flowers," burst in the sky around his plane. It was much ado about very little. They had been in "no very great danger from him, nor he from the shells, but at the time it gave an added zest." JTM filed a story, which received considerable attention:

The *Tribune* gave this flight of mine much prominence. Up to that time I am not aware that any civilian had flown in either a German or an Allied plane over the lines. From that gun emplacement at Brimont, I had gazed out over the broad plains, where only five years before I had attended the first aviation meet ever held. Under the impetus of war necessity already that incredible development was under way which was to scrap all the military strategy that had governed war since the beginning.[53]

McCutcheon and his companions made their way to London where, "as men fresh from the German side of the battle front, we were objects of much curiosity to the London war leaders." Alfred Harmsworth, a British newspaper and publishing magnate also referred to as Lord Northcliffe (in deference to his title of 1st Viscount Northcliffe), received JTM in his "chintz-curtained office" at the *Times* and "was particularly kind." Harmsworth asked who else the correspondents might be interested in seeing while in London. JTM hoped to meet with W. W. Jacobs, author of *Dialstone Lane,* his "favorite book," and William Haselden, cartoonist for the *Daily Mirror,* owned by Harmsworth. Unfortunately, both were unavailable, so instead Northcliffe took JTM and Cobb on October 22, 1914, to visit with Lord Frederick Roberts (i.e., 1st Earl Roberts) at his house in Ascot, Berkshire:

> The great hall was a perfect setting for one who had served his country
> for 60 years, and who now was spending his twilight of his life in peace
> by reminders of his thrilling days. Above the fireplace was a tremen-
> dous picture of a detachment of courageous Gurkhas [a Nepalean serv-
> ing in the British Army] fighting their way up a steep mountainside. To
> the right and left of this [picture] were [mounted] heads of an ovis poli
> and an ovis ammon, those mountain sheep of Central Asia considered
> by sportsmen to be the greatest prize in big game. One had come from
> the Tien Shan Mountains in Chinese Turkestan where I had been eight
> years before. This established a bond of interest and helped me to get
> acquainted.[54]

Lady Aileen Roberts, Frederick's younger daughter, arrived before her father, and he followed a few minutes later. JTM had expected a man with a larger stature and "certainly a much older-looking one." Roberts stood five feet three inches with a ruddy face and hair "so thick that he appeared bald." Deep lines underscored his "alert eyes" with good-natured wrinkles radiating outward from their corners. He appeared to be a man of sixty-five rather than eighty-two, and with a clear voice he immediately made them feel at home:

> "They must have a great army," he said when his daughter told him where we had been. He was eager to know the spirit of the German soldiers, and when we told him that the army, as we had seen it, seemed a unit of enthusiasm and confidence, he nodded as if that were what he had expected. He asked detailed questions about how we had come to be caught in the German advance and how we had been treated. I was struck by the impersonal attitude both he and Northcliffe exhibited when discussing the enemy. They did not show the same bitterness I have found so often among Americans. When we told him that, in our observation, the Germans had been operating with discipline, and that the stories of atrocities were undoubtedly exaggerated, we were surprised to find that this was his own opinion. In the course of his long experience he had learned war psychology thoroughly.[55]

Lady Nora Roberts, his wife, entered on the arm of their elder daughter, Lady Edwina Stuart, and Lord Roberts "went at once to her side." Roberts showed "great devotion and deference" to his wife who obviously was "suffering from the infirmities of age." Lunch was announced and in the conversation that followed, JTM suggested his "family must be finding it difficult to keep him from the front":

> He smiled and said he was sending his grandson instead. Above the mantel in the library was a portrait of his only son, who had been killed at the Battle of Colenso [during the second Boer War in South Africa] in 1899. It is said that at the time the casualty list was posted, officers who had not dared tell him the news watched with concern when he went over to scan the names. He read the list from top to bottom without any sign of emotion, then turned gravely and resumed his place at the desk he had just left.[56]

After lunch, Roberts agreed to sit for a portrait by JTM, and Lady Roberts sat nearby while her husband "patiently, if somewhat sleepily, underwent the ordeal." He then autographed the drawing. It was probably the "last picture made of him before he died three weeks later."

While he was grateful for the hospitality the Roberts family offered, JTM later wondered whether he had been used as a pawn, both by the Roberts and by the Germans, in order to manipulate the war news in their favor:

> It will be evident to readers who have got this far in these memoirs that the courtesies which the officers of the German Army paid us, and the kindnesses now offered by Englishmen in high rank, came at time when, by chances of war, I [was] in a position to be of great service to the cause they represented. We recognized this and realized that these marks of thoughtful hospitality were not without ulterior motives. The Germans wanted us to shade our reports in their favor; the British wished to counteract any influence which the Germans might have used to affect our neutrality. Hospitality, skillfully used, is the most insidious of propaganda. In contrast, the sincere welcome of old friends was a relief.[57]

JTM arrived in Chicago just before Nov. 1 [1914] when his new employment contract with the *Chicago Tribune* was scheduled to take effect. Throughout all of his recent adventures, he "had been nowhere near Melville Island."

Speaking of friends, Joseph Medill Patterson was the coeditor and copublisher of the *Tribune* in 1915, and he and JTM considered each other friends. In August of that year, JTM and Patterson sailed for Paris on the new French ocean liner, the *SS Provence*. Patterson had some hesitation about making the trip with JTM:

> It was the first time I had ever traveled with Joe. He told a friend of ours that he was almost afraid to go with me because he liked me so much, and he felt certain that we would not come back friends. This was his way of

saying that he considered himself very hard to get along with. I had known
Joe ever since I went to the *Tribune* and had always been interested in his
philosophy. He had a keen zest and curiosity about life, a great desire for
firsthand experience. He was intellectually honest, and though one might
not agree with his opinions, one respected his courage in asserting them. I
could not imagine Joe Patterson misrepresenting a fact although the truth
might be awkward and have unpleasant consequences.[58]

Patterson lived a colorful and interesting life. To JTM, Patterson's novels
and plays from "his early days" revealed a "social consciousness which
drove him to give up a promising literary career for more direct public
service." In 1903, he was elected to the Illinois House of Representatives;
"he became a Socialist for a time" and was "appointed Commissioner of
Public Works" under Chicago Mayor Edward F. Dunne, whose candidacy
he supported. JTM recalled, "He was among the first to join the U.S. Army
at the time of the Mexican border trouble and again when the United States
entered the First World War." Despite being related to the influential and
powerful Medill and McCormick families, he enlisted as private both times
because he refused "to use pull to get a commission, although ultimately
he became a captain."

He and JTM shared a "common love of adventure," and on this particular trip to Paris they "had started off together in the hope, this time, of
seeing something of the French side" of the war. During the Atlantic crossing, they shared a suite on the *SS Provence* and "played dominoes a good
deal." Patterson was humble and never "asserted the importance which
his position gave him," so it was easy to forget their relationship was that
of employer and employee. In Paris, they stayed together at the Hôtel de
Crillon, and once they were settled, they applied for permission to visit
the front lines. Once again, airplanes took center stage:

We found the airdromes much the most interesting places. In one, I saw
the first sample of a new triplane, shaped like a ship with a curving bow,
and with places for cannon as well as machine guns. There were three
tiers of gun ports. I observed it carefully, and from memory drew a picture

of this amazing aero-battleship. When all my sketches and reports were submitted later to the French liaison officer, he brought back everything duly O.K.'ed except the picture of the triplane. "I showed it to the Minister of War," explained the officer, "and he was so interested in it he wanted to study it further. I felt sure you would be glad to let him." This was putting the matter with charming and effective indirection. They had, of course, good reason for keeping it, but I was interested to note that they did not black out my written description of the plane. In subsequent years I never heard any further news of this triplane, so I assume it did not work.[59]

Although the first manned airplane flight had occurred a mere eleven years earlier, advances in aviation technology and flying skills moved forward rapidly. Patterson and JTM visited the headquarters of the Morane-Saulnier Company [a French airplane manufacture] at Villacoublay where they were shown "what I think must have been the first of the devices whereby a machine gun could be fired through the propeller" without damaging it. Both Patterson and JTM were "eager to fly and Joe got the first chance." The ride included an aerial maneuver that was still fairly rare at the time:

> One of the Moranes [there were two Morane brothers, Leon and Robert] took him up in a fast little monoplane. When he came down [Joe] was excited and happy. Pretty high up, Morane turned around and said something that sounded like Voulez-vous loop? I wasn't quite sure but I nodded anyhow, and pretty soon we were diving, and then with a terrific whirl I found my head hanging downward. After another dizzy whirl I was straight up again. I congratulated Joe with real sincerity, if also with intense envy, but there was no opportunity for another flight that day.[60]

JTM was able to get a flyover of Paris with "a handsome young Frenchman named Jacques Baudry." They took off in a Parosol monoplane, "a type I had never seen before." With the airplane fuselage suspended "below a broad wing and entirely separated from it, I devoutly hoped the fastenings were secure." JTM and Baudry did not discuss executing a loop, "so there was no unusual thrill about this brief flight."

Patterson and JTM found the city of Paris to be "pleasantly stimulating" during their nonworking hours. Of course, "this was before the air raids, and before Big Bertha, the [howitzer] gun" used by German artillery crews to hurl shells seventy-five miles. During this period, JTM's reading habits may have influenced a business venture Patterson created in 1919:

> Every day I used to bring back to our room a copy of the *London Mirror,*
> a lively tabloid [a paper with pages half the size of standard newspaper
> pages] in which [William] Haselden's cartoons were then appearing. I
> have always felt that I may thus have contributed to the birth of Joe's idea
> for the *New York Daily News,* [a tabloid-size newspaper he founded]
> four years later.[61]

Meanwhile, Patterson departed for home. As for the "conducted tours to the front," they "had amounted in the aggregate to disappointingly little that was worthwhile from a news point of view." JTM had little doubt that Patterson could have wielded influence, but as far as anyone would be able to tell from the way he carried himself, Patterson the paper's copublisher "was merely another correspondent" of the *Chicago Tribune.*

The Paris trip, instead of straining their relationship, made them "better friends than ever." It was the first of many trips they ended up taking together. In 1924, they went to the Texas border where airplanes were patrolling "day and night, partly to prevent smuggling, partly as a gesture to Mexico." It was an opportunity for another flight, this time over the "Mexican side, in spite of the fact that Mexicans considered planes over their territory in the light of invasion," which would make circumstances very uncomfortable for the plane's occupants if they were forced to land. Unfazed by the possible danger thanks to his war experiences, JTM felt the "novelty of this particular flight for me consisted in flying over the mountains . . . I had never done that before." Still another time, they went hunting in New Brunswick in eastern Canada where "Joe got his moose; I didn't." Along the way, JTM developed a closer understanding of the heirs of Joseph Medill, the founder of the *Chicago Tribune*:

It is an interesting fact that the four grandchildren of Joseph Medill turned out so well. With all their wealth, power and influence, they had every facility in the world to spend their lives in self-indulgence or the excesses of extravagance. Yet each of the four led a life of usefulness and achievement. They were all hard workers. They were born to their jobs, of course, but they could hardly have held jobs like theirs without native ability and personal effort. All three boys gave their services to public affairs. J. Medill McCormick served in the legislature, then as congressman, and ended his life from the lofty eminence of the United States Senate. His brother, Robert R. McCormick—or Bert as he is known to his closer friends—served in the Chicago city council and as president of the sanitary district. Joe Patterson served in the state and the city government. Joe's sister, Elinor, better known as Cissy, the fourth grandchild, had a literary career of merit and was herself a newspaper editor.[62]

As a testament to Joe and Bert's leadership, the departure of Jim Keeley from the *Tribune*—while impactful—did not result in a "serious loss" to the business. Within a year, the newspaper's circulation grew by forty thousand. As joint editors and publishers of the *Tribune*, Joe and Bert "alternated each month in the direction of the editorial policy." Although the policy worked surprisingly well, "it was not ideal." When Patterson founded the *Daily News*, its rise to the newspaper with the "greatest circulation in the United States" required Joe to relocate to New York. As a result, Bert assumed sole control of the *Tribune*.

Upon reflection, JTM regarded Patterson as a "very considerate employer" who was "behind me, believed in me . . . and was sympathetic with my point of view"—a view that often departed from conservative:

He liked cartoons that differed radically from the conventional, no matter how unusual or bizarre they might be; I think he approved of anything that aroused curiosity, speculation or interest of any sort among the readers. He had confidence that my cartoons sensed what people were thinking about, and represented and analyzed public opinion correctly. He was often kind enough to tell me that he had great respect for my judgement in consequence. It is true that he said, "John feels; he doesn't think!" But he also said—and this pleased me very much—that I was the only person with whom he really liked to travel. I have always regretted that his fortunes took him away from Chicago. I saw little of him after that.[63]

McCormick, on the other hand, was "a different type," and JTM never had an opportunity to know him "as intimately as I knew Joe." He appeared to "enjoy and exercise the reins of power" and didn't "thaw out and sit about with the crowd"—because that wasn't his nature. At six feet five inches, McCormick was "powerfully built" and regularly hunted and played polo "to keep in good physical condition." While Patterson's purpose in life was to get as much out of it as he could "largely for the adventure," his cousins Bert and Medill embarked on a political life to "make something of themselves." Like Joe, Bert was one of America's great newspaper publishers, which JTM observed firsthand after Patterson's departure:

> His devotion to work and attention to detail has been amazing. Weekly conferences with the heads of all departments, held at luncheon in the directors' room, keep him in the closest touch with everything about the paper. Daily conferences with the editorial writers, cartoonists and managing editor and other key men in the organization fill his days. When not actively occupied at the office, he is generally attending meetings in other cities and making addresses; or he is tramping for miles through the *Tribune's* timberlands around Shelter Bay [in Washington state]; or he is reading until late at night. He has a keen, historically trained mind. Bert has a great sense of pictorial journalism and the *Tribune* has made a larger demand on the cartoon than most papers. My relations with Bert, while not so close as those with Joe, have always been marked by a consideration and kindness on his part for which I shall never cease to be grateful.[64]

The women of the family also bore strong personalities. The Medill daughters, Katherine McCormick and Elinor Patterson, had "rapier wit which they were too often apt to use against each other." It was JTM's understanding that the *Tribune's* cashier had standing orders to buy a ticket for the one to leave town at once, should the other arrive. One time JTM received a letter from Elinor complaining he had been too critical regarding the Republicans. "Why is youth so harsh?" she wrote. "As you mature, you will grow kinder." The ladies were fearless when it came to speaking their minds and sprinkling in salty language for effect:

> A day or two after the United States had declared war against Germany in 1917, I was looking into a bookstore window on Michigan Avenue. Suddenly I heard a voice at my elbow: "What do you think of this goddam war?" It was the elderly Mrs. McCormick.[65]

AFTER PATTERSON LEFT JTM IN PARIS, he moved to "a small room up on the mansard [a sloping roof, under which an apartment is located] floor of the Hotel de Crillon where from a little balcony I could look across a sea of treetops to the Arc de Triomphe." The "agreeable days" in Paris ended, however, when a cable arrived from the *Tribune*: "Go to Saloniki stopping in Athens for interview with [Greek Prime Minister Eleftherios] Venizelos." JTM, accompanied by Bill Shepherd of the United Press and [photographer] Jimmy Hare of *Collier's*, left for Athens by "way of Messina and the Corinth Canal." They anchored in Piraeus, Greece, and JTM had "three hours to get my interview." He needed arrangements and got an audience set up, thanks to a local American minister:

> But a correspondent cannot drop into an ancient capital and find its eminent statesman sitting about waiting to be interviewed. Neither diplomacy nor personal dignity works that way. By the time I walked up the steps of Venizelos' house, two of my three hours had elapsed. The prime minister was dignified and polite. He talked frankly and without reservations. Venizelos, Greek's greatest statesman, was pro-Ally, but Constantine, the

Danish King of Greece, had a pro-German slant. Conditions in Greece at the end of October 1915 were of concern to all of Europe. But my mind was on the clock. The interview seemed to last a long time. Finally, I rose, thanked him respectfully and departed, making a mighty effort not to show the haste I felt consuming me. I dashed to the cable office. There was not censorship to delay me, but the painstaking care of the operator, counting words and then recounting them, was a terrific ordeal. Then he had to figure out the amount due, and he did that twice.[66]

Finally, JTM hailed a taxi and sped to Piraeus to the pier where he boarded a rowboat. Another small craft blocked his departure route. It looked like he was going to miss the boat:

I looked at my watch. The time was up. I looked at the ship. The anchor was up. I . . . waved frantically. Shepherd and Hare were [already on Piraeus] watching for me and rushed to the Captain. We reached the ship's side. Rather than risk an argument, I pressed on my boatman an amount liberal enough to leave him almost as breathless as I. I caught the sea ladder and climbed to the deck of the moving ship, gasping and panting. I felt 10 years older.[67]

At Saloniki JTM found "a bewildering confusion of ships and soldiers and monumental uncertainties." On the way to the Olympos Palace Hotel, JTM stopped to photograph some Greek soldiers. He narrowly avoided getting arrested:

I escaped arrest and detention only because [a] Greek policeman spoke English and had lived in Chicago. "Where do you live?" he asked. "Corner of Astor and Schiller," said I. "Ha!" he said. "I lived on Division." Only a few streets apart. We became friends at once.[68]

The hotel had only one room available, so the three newspapermen settled into it. A couple days later, Richard Davis also arrived in the city. Since no other rooms were available, he was invited to move in with them, but later a room became available and he moved out. When JTM first arrived in

Saloniki, "there were few correspondents," but two months later "there were at least 20, representing the leading news agencies of the pro-Ally or neutral world." The British debacle at Gallipoli and the ensuing evacuation to Saloniki jammed the bay with "warships, battleships, transports and hospital ships." Suddenly, the "ancient Thessalonian city had become an important news center"—albeit reluctantly, if the military authorities could help it:

> Every morning we could be seen at the daily news conference held in the office of the commander-in-chief of the Allied forces, [French] General [Maurice] Sarrail, where the general or a member of his staff revealed as much as was prudent of the news of army movements. Questions were permitted; some were answered, some were not. The custom of seeing and talking to correspondents is a good one, although it was most unusual in that war of official aloofness. No one was permitted to talk to General Sarrail. He did not give out interviews or talk for publication, but in a situation as complicated as that in Saloniki where rumors and alarums spread like wildfire, it was well to have some place where authoritative statements might be obtained.[69]

In fact, the general summoned the newspapermen on December 10 when rumors continued to persist about Allied "reverses" in the fighting. Leaning against a window sill, Sarrail "confronted the correspondents who were standing, paper and pencil in hand":

> He announced that the British and French were retiring [retreating]. There was no further value in retaining an advanced and dangerous position in Serbia. Prudence required withdrawal to a strategically safer line of defense. Bridges were being burned, tunnels destroyed, all materials and equipment were being saved. In its first few days, the retreat had been remarkably free from casualties. Only about 30 men had been lost. There was complete silence in the little room in the Mission Sique Francaise. No one was taking a chance of misquoting a general who was explaining why his troops, after two weeks' fighting, were giving up their positions and retreating.[70]

At the conclusion of the briefing, Shepherd, Hare, Bass, Davis, and JTM "caught an empty freight train headed for the front." They got as far as Gradek and Strumitsa, where they "saw the first detachments of the retreating French Army," but they were "not allowed to proceed farther." They took a detour, traveling to the nearby border of Bulgaria. There they found themselves "under fire from a Bulgar battery." They caught another freight train back to Saloniki, a "long, halting night trip . . . in a freezing-cold freight car, without blankets" that was "utter wretchedness."

As the retreat continued, the "Bulgarian forces pressed forward relentlessly and the casualty lists increased." Finally, the Allied forces reached the Greek territory. One question was on everyone's mind:

> Would the Bulgars follow? Greece had indicated she would resent the Bulgars advancing alone and stipulated that German troops must lead the invasion and guarantee that the integrity of Macedonia would not be violated. The Greek Army marched out of Saloniki and massed west of the border. To the north were the Allied lines, with the Central Powers beyond; to the south was the harbor crowded with battleships. It was a four-sided front, the whole situation loaded with TNT. In the midst of this electric tension came the German air raid of Dec. 30, the first move in German hostilities against Saloniki. On a day of brilliant sunshine three planes flew over and dropped about 40 bombs. One struck near the Greek barracks while [a general] was reviewing a calvary regiment; another killed a shepherd near the aviation camp; three British soldiers on a transport were wounded; and a few bombs landed in the French camp. Enormous crowds watched the raid, which had instant repercussions.[71]

Because the Allies had an overwhelming presence in Saloniki, they "at once arrested the consular staffs of Germany, Austria, Bulgaria and Turkey, and imprisoned or interned them on a French warship." The previously normal but "scrambled" evening affairs at the Olympos Palace Hotel—where "German officials sit cozily alongside British officers—were over." Prime Minister Venizelos "quickly capitalized on the raid" and Greek neutrality was "put aside," with King Constantine's support.

Despite the "supercharged days," JTM had an "amusing experience." He had sent a note to a Captain Metaxas, the aide to Crown Prince George of Greece, requesting an appointment for the "honor of making a sketch of His Royal Highness." Prince George, it so happened, had come up from Athens to Saloniki for a few days; JTM "had never seen the Crown Prince." After some delay, he received a note from Metaxas to come for tea at 4 p.m. the following afternoon at the headquarters of Prince Andrew, brother of King Constantine:

> I appeared with my sketching pad and materials, which were deposited with my hat in the reception hall. I was led into a salon where I was presently joined by two gentlemen in Greek uniform. The older one introduced himself as Prince Andrew; the younger, from his manner, I guessed to be an officer on Prince Andrew's staff. Tea was served and the conversation was easy and pleasant. I assumed an attitude of deference toward Prince Andrew, a brother of the king, but with the younger officer I quickly reached a state of friendly comradeship in which I invited him to come to America sometime. "Yes," he replied, "I'd like to. My uncle had a great time everywhere he went over there." His uncle? For the first time a glimmering of the true state of affairs penetrated. His uncle could be none other than Prince Henry of Prussia—then this must be the Crown Prince! I am afraid my sudden realization must have been evident.[72]

Prince Andrew turned to JTM and asked: "Well, do you want to sketch this young man today, or would you rather wait until tomorrow?" JTM had already been "enjoying himself immensely for an hour or more and it was getting late," so he decided to postpone the sketch until the following day— "at any time convenient to His Highness." At 11 a.m. the next day, JTM enjoyed another couple hours with the Prince—"and the sketch turned out pretty well." The prince was a "friendly, well-bred, English-appearing young man, with an Oxford education and an extremely magnetic personality."

Back at the hotel, JTM's "huge bedroom" had become a "gathering place for all kinds of people." The events of the war continued to make their mark while JTM and his companions played dominoes:

We played and we played. Once on a short trip back from Monastic, we forgot the set and made a new one out of the paper. Hours of earnest endeavor were spent at this ancient and beguiling game. I usually kept score, one vertical mark for each point, one horizontal mark across four vertical marks representing every five points. By the time we had played an hour or so, these scores looked like long files of marching men. Being, like everybody else with a pencil in his hand, a doodler, I made rough sketches of Shepherd and Hare and what not. Shepherd kept one particular score sheet as a souvenir. But when it came to light [in a search by authorities] on the Italian frontier, there was a terrible to-do. It looked like nothing so much as cryptic notes made by Enemy Spy Number One. His bags were turned inside out; he was put through a long and rigid cross-examination; and only when a young woman in some way recognized the scoring system and explained it to the authorities was he allowed to proceed.[73]

Bass gave a dinner for Davis on the evening before "he left for home and comfort":

Everyone was gay; there were many stories told over the wine. After dinner, we all rowed out to his ship with him, and he waved from the sea ladder until we reached shore again. It was the last time I ever saw him. Back in New York, while talking . . . on the telephone, he dropped dead.[74]

JTM first encountered Davis in Vera Cruz the previous year. He had heard Davis was "conceited, a little brother of the gods . . . and many stories in support of this impression floated around." Davis was a "striking figure wherever he went." Dressing the part, his "background was impressive, his acquaintanceship wide, and his ability outstanding." JTM spent a lot of time with him in Vera Cruz and Saloniki, and found he had "none of the qualities that I had heard criticized." JTM knew him to be "congenial, friendly and unspoiled." JTM had "known his first wife, Cecil Clark, for years." The fact that JTM could reminisce about Cecil, even though she and Dick were divorced, "was a bond that he greatly enjoyed."

The Germans had captured Monastir [Tunisia on the north coast of Africa] by this time and driven the French back along Strumitsa, and the battle lines were now drawn in around Saloniki. It was a deadlock leaving little likelihood of "further military activity." Davis was now gone, Shepherd was out of action in the hospital for a minor operation, and Hare was attempting to obtain a new passport to replace the one he lost. As a result, JTM "was rather glad to get a cable from the *Tribune* to come home." [75]

They made a last attempt to obtain permission from French officials to fly over Saloniki and received approval to take off from an airport a few miles outside of the city. They took off in a Farman biplane designed by French aviator Henri Farman:

> We sat in a balcony effect sticking out in front of the wings. Five thousand feet up I took photographs of the city and harbor, crowded with all its varied shipping. When I landed, my exuding enthusiasm was so evident that the officer offered to take me up again in a Nieuport two-seater combat plane, the fastest small plane in use at the time. All my impressions of flying heretofore were changed at once.[76]

On the way to the "little Greek ship" the next day JTM stopped to get his films developed. The film included "several other things as well as the flight" and as usual "there was a delay." The boat was scheduled to depart in thirty minutes, so JTM had to carry off a "great mass of film still dripping wet." Disappointment met them when they reached the ship and saw their mode of transportation:

> Our hearts sank. It was tiny, not over 600 tons, crowded to suffocation, with cattle and pigs on deck. Very kindly the Greek captain let me drape my films around the pilothouse, where there was a cooling breeze and a minimum of disturbance. The little room was festooned in shiny black. Surprisingly enough, the films were not hurt. In fact they were so good— especially those of the new French lines surrounding Saloniki—that they landed me in Scotland Yard. Of this however I was happily unaware on the trip through the Greek Islands.[77]

While transferring ships, a customs man at Dieppe, France, immediately spotted JTM's film and saw French uniforms, guns, and trenches. "'Aha!'" JTM recalled the man saying. "He raised his eyebrows, shrugged his shoulders and shunted me aside until all the other passengers had been passed." JTM was allowed to board the next ship with the understanding that he would "get the photographs later." He did at Folkestone in England, where he was met by a Scotland Yard official who had his pictures. JTM was escorted to his London hotel and instructed to report to Scotland Yard the following morning at 10 a.m.

He arrived on time but dreaded "any sort of delay, for I was sailing for home the next day on the *Nieue Amsterdam*":

> Time passed. I waited longer and longer. My anxiety increased. Finally a man came and said peremptorily, "Follow me!" I followed him into a huge office where I waited some more. Then Sir Basil Thompson appeared, head of that grim organization. "These films," said Sir Basil, "have been examined by the War Department. All pictures showing buildings, together with troops, have been held. The buildings could be identified and reveal troop locations. The rest of your films are here." And he handed them to me. Then he questioned me in such a way as to reveal a complete knowledge of my previous trip to the German front the year before. It was evident to me that a dossier relating to me was in his files. "Wasn't the Countess Gizycka connected with the *Tribune*?" "Yes." "Wasn't she a friend of Count von Bernstorff?" "I believe so." "What are your sympathies?" "Pro-Ally, naturally." "Whom do you know here in London?" "Mr. Selfridge, Lady Lavery, Lord Northcliffe."[78]

Mercifully, JTM was granted permission to sail for America the following day. He departed "from those sinister portals feeling considerably relieved."

NOTES

1   John T. McCutcheon, *Drawn from Memory* (Indianapolis and New York: Bobbs-Merrill, Inc., 1949), 248.

2   Ibid.
3   Ibid., 249.
4   Ibid., 249–50.
5   Ibid., 250.
6   Ibid., 251.
7   Ibid., 251–52.
8   Ibid., 252
9   Ibid., 253.
10 Ibid., 254.
11 Ibid., 255.
12 Ibid., 257.
13 Ibid., 259.
14 Ibid.
15 Ibid.
16 Ibid., 260.
17 Ibid., 260–61.
18 Ibid., 261.
19 Ibid., 262.
20 Ibid.
21 Ibid., 263.
22 Ibid.
23 Ibid., 264–65.
24 Ibid., 266.
25 Ibid., 266–67.
26 Ibid., 267.
27 Ibid., 268.
28 Ibid.
29 Ibid., 269.
30 Ibid.
31 Ibid., 269–70.
32 Ibid., 270.
33 Ibid.
34 Ibid., 270–71.
35 Ibid., 271.
36 Ibid., 271–72.
37 Ibid., 272.
38 Ibid., 273.
39 Ibid., 274.
40 Ibid., 275.
41 Ibid., 276.

42 Ibid., 276-77.
43 Ibid., 277.
44 Ibid., 278.
45 Ibid.
46 Ibid., 279.
47 Ibid., 280.
48 Ibid.
49 Ibid., 281.
50 Ibid.
51 Ibid., 281-82.
52 Ibid., 282.
53 Ibid., 283.
54 Ibid., 284.
55 Ibid.
56 Ibid., 285.
57 Ibid.
58 Ibid., 286.
59 Ibid., 287.
60 Ibid., 287-88.
61 Ibid., 288.
62 Ibid., 289.
63 Ibid., 289-90.
64 Ibid., 290-91.
65 Ibid., 292.
66 Ibid., 292-93.
67 Ibid., 293
68 Ibid.
69 Ibid., 294.
70 Ibid., 295.
71 Ibid.
72 Ibid., 296.
73 Ibid., 297.
74 Ibid.
75 Ibid., 298.
76 Ibid.
77 Ibid.
78 Ibid., 299.

10

A Good Day to Start Things

Throughout his career, JTM was acutely aware that "small circumstances affected" the direction of his life—including one "which even more profoundly affected my personal life." A small circumstance so pivotal that "all of the things I have most to be grateful for may be credited to this rather trivial happening":

> One Saturday [in 1892] when George Ade and I were loafing around our little hall bedroom on Peck Court, our meager resources depleted until payday, there came a knock at the door. A handsome stranger stood there. It seemed he had bet on the wrong end of the Sullivan-Corbett [heavyweight championship boxing match] and wanted me to draw 10 place cards for the dinner he was to give in payment of his debt. He had seen my name on the *Record* drawings, had secured my address from the office and subsequently made his devious way up the two darkened stairways to our door. He was a tall gentleman, pleasant

and courteous. I was glad to do the drawings for him—they were to be pictures of some of the striking moments in the fight—and I said they would be ready at five.[1]

JTM completed the illustrations in a couple hours and then faced an important question: what should he charge for the drawings? "You'll never see him again," said Ade. "Why not soak him?" At 5 p.m., the stranger returned to Peck Court and was very satisfied with JTM's work:

> That served to stiffen my "soak the rich" platform. So when he tactfully asked what he owed me, I braced myself and blurted out the exorbitant ultimatum, "Five dollars." He never flinched. He met the shock like the thoroughbred he was and paid the price in a spirit of utmost cheerfulness. In fact, we afterward thought we could have asked six or even seven dollars.[2]

Ade was mistaken about never seeing the guy again. The stranger turned out to be Charles T. Atkinson and the acquaintance JTM had "thus begun led to a close friendship which lasted until [Atkinson's] death." It also led JTM to marry Atkinson's niece.

As they got to know each other better, JTM dined with Atkinson and his wife, Martha, in their small apartment on the second floor of a narrow-fronted house on Groveland Avenue near 29th Street. In time, he was introduced to Martha's sister and brother-in-law, Frances and Howard Shaw, who lived on the floor above the Atkinsons. In March 1894, it was Atkinson who hurried out "on a blizzardy night" to summon a doctor for the birth of the Shaws' infant daughter, Evelyn, whom JTM met "soon after her arrival." The Atkinsons and Shaws eventually moved to "a pair of gray-stone houses on Lake Avenue" where Evelyn, then about three years old, "welcomed me on the stairs with a wide grin."

A variety of events would take place and a number of years passed before JTM's thoughts "were to linger romantically on this young lady."

> I was busy drawing cartoons, and my love life made but slight encroachment on my daily cartoon life. Matrimony was not on my agenda. When something of that sort conflicted with other adventure, the entangling alliance was always routed.[3]

When JTM departed on the *McCulloch,* he was "more or less engaged to a young lady." When he returned from that "eventful Odyssey," the young lady had long since married a "handsomer man." In the meantime, the Atkinsons and Shaws had moved to houses in the northern suburb of Lake Forest. When JTM visited "Ragdale," the name of the Shaw family compound, a "lanky seven-year-old listened spellbound" as he told of his world travels. JTM was pleased by her attention:

> I was quite conscious of this flattering attention and definitely pleased to be the object of her childish favor. She still has a framed drawing I made for her on a sheet of Ragdale notepaper, of herself mounted loftily on camel, and an illuminated acrostic [a line of verse]: "For Evelyn Shaw on her Eighth Birthday." By now, she was a slim girl with bobbed hair, not yet emerged from the gangling stage, yet showing evidence of the distinction of appearance which has always been hers. However, I kept this particular romance entirely detached from others of a more mature nature that came and went.[4]

JTM continued to regularly dazzle Evelyn with his stories as "it seemed that I was always going away on long trips, then coming back to tell her about them in front of the fire." JTM's tales from "remote, almost mythical lands"—including Africa, with its exciting lexicon that included words like jungles, elephant guns, safaris, lions, and charging rhinos—did not fall on deaf ears:

> [It was] all calculated, perhaps not unintentionally, to transform a rather mild man in his late thirties into a somewhat heroic figure, especially in the eyes of a young girl who was predisposed to regard him in an admiring light.[5]

On JTM's return from Africa in 1910, he discovered that Evelyn, now a statuesque girl of sixteen, "was charming in her riding clothes as we cantered [went horseback riding] through the fields west of Lake Forest." In those fields, JTM came to realize this "little girl, grown-up man" relationship was changing—which "came as a surprise" to him. When Evelyn expressed admiration for one of JTM's cartoons, "it was at once sent to her, appropriately autographed." Later, when Evelyn attended Bryn Mawr College, he liked to think that his cartoons "stood guard as sentinels which kept me from being obliterated by the new interest that four years [of college life] presented."

During the summer of 1916, after he returned home from the battle zones in Europe, he rented a cottage in Lake Forest near the "Aldis Compound, charming and informal gathering place of literary, social and artistic circles." He called the cottage the Chateau Chic, and in it he drew several cartoons that became his personal favorites, including "The Rhyme of the Restless Rover," "The Munition Maker's Daughter," and others. It was also here that Evelyn and JTM entered the next level of their relationship:

> On a nearby tennis court Evelyn and I began a new phase of our relationship. My tennis helped my cartoons, and Evelyn Shaw helped my tennis. Soon I became aware that this pleasant companionship seemed to take no heed of dates and years. Whether or not by comparison I was elderly, I was certainly given no reason to think so. In her mother's open electric [car] we took our first moonlight drive down the curving road to the beach, and I began to wonder very intensely just what she was thinking—whether I was for her only the 'old family friend' whom she had always known. It was natural that I should fall in love with her. I remember how pleasantly and easily we advanced through the twilight zone of uncertainty to the point where I became very sure of how I felt.[6]

Years later Evelyn would reveal to JTM that in college she told a group of friends that "she would probably never marry, because the only man she could imagine wanting to marry—the cartoonist John McCutcheon—was not likely to be a candidate." In August, Evelyn traveled west to "a ranch in Wyoming." In his letters to her while she was away, JTM wrote that their time being with each other and playing tennis had "been more court than tennis."

Shortly after her return from Wyoming, Evelyn and JTM were engaged.

It was turning out to be the year of dreams come true for JTM, again thanks to Charles Atkinson. After JTM's return from Saloniki the previous March, Atkinson asked if he was still intent on purchasing an island. Atkinson knew about one that was for sale near Nassau in the Bahamas—"in the heart of the pirate belt." Although JTM had been to Nassau, he had never seen this island. It was enough, however, that Atkinson had:

> The late owner, Abraham Van Winkle [wealthy president of a manufacturing company], had looked the world over for such an island, had settled on this as the best to be found for his purpose, and had put in 14 years developing it. It seemed to have all the necessary requirements as to location, climate and piratical antecedents, including some splenderiferous beaches with all the Atlantic Ocean to bathe in and all the sunlight in the world to dry in. The war still raged in Europe; the demand for tropical islands was in the doldrums. Nobody wanted any—except me. It was likely that this one could be acquired for a fraction of what had been spent on it, which might bring the price within the means of a newspaper cartoonist.[7]

JTM spared no time in contacting the agent in Nassau to make an offer. It was rejected. He made a second offer—"somewhat larger, and waited anxiously." Events happened quickly after that:

> Presently the agent appeared in person—to gauge my sanity, I have always suspected. Doubtless he mistrusted a fellow who wanted an island he'd never seen. However, he must have been convinced of my financial, if not of my mental, responsibility, for we got together on an amount halfway between the asking price and my last offer; the trustees were honorable enough to suggest the wisdom of my looking at the island before paying the money. In September 1916, Salt Cay with all its improvements, buildings, goods and chattels, including a small yacht, none of which I had ever seen, passed into my possession.[8]

At long last, JTM finally had his island. Over the years, whenever George Ade was asked what in the world possessed his close friend to buy a tropical island, he would quip: "To refer to." He was on to something; JTM

frequently found himself "referring to it with much pleasure." Friends and
associates referred to it as well:

> The news of my island purchase followed by the announcement of my
> engagement made a combination that my newspaper friends were not
> slow to make the most of. The linked headlines struck the romantic sense
> of the public. Syndicated Sunday features glamorized our prospective
> wedding trip. The island theme and the pirate background were played
> up, with plenty of palm trees, rakish schooners and buried treasure.[9]

Naturally, JTM's fellow cartoonists noted his "belated entrance into the
bonds of matrimony" with both humor and sympathy. As the excitement about his news began to settle down, JTM wondered what surprises
awaited him at Salt Cay because the "only photographs we had were old
and poor." Questions loomed:

> How handsome or how simple the dwelling might be remained a mystery.
> The inventory of contents was scarcely more illuminating. We speculated
> in bewilderment over its odd sequence of items: "11 bedsprings, three bird
> cages, nine sadirons [a flat iron pointed at both ends with a removable han-
> dle]; eight bridge tables; two galvanized tubs; plates for 125; one telescope"[10]

Meanwhile, Evelyn and JTM set their wedding date for Saturday, January
20, 1917. He called it "a good day to start things (in 1933, Congress chose
it as the day to end things, specifically the terms of the vice president and
president). Wedding invitations, as they do for most couples, presented a
challenge. JTM, with his extensive network of friends and acquaintances,
"found it so difficult to reduce my [invitation] list that we sent out an
absurd number!" His friends, according to press reports, had been "brush-
ing up on their [author Robert Louis] Stevenson and [English writer Dan-
iel] Defoe to aid them in the selection of appropriate gifts." These ran the
spectrum from chronometers and picnic baskets, to "fancy cages for the
housing of tropical birds." The bachelor dinner for JTM, contrary to cus-
tom, was hosted by the Indiana Society at Chicago's Blackstone Hotel, and
a who's who of celebrities spared no details in roasting JTM:

Across one end of the Blackstone ballroom extended a backdrop of azure sea. A coral strand in the foreground was strewed with casks of rum and chests of gold. The waiters were swarthy buccaneers. Judge [Kenesaw Mountain] Landis, General [Charles G.] Dawes, [sports columnist] Ring Lardner and others made remarks bearing on the earlier activities of the groom, and there were many variations on the theme, "Good-by, girls, I'm through."[11]

JTM and Evelyn were married (he was forty-eight, she was twenty-three) in the Fourth Presbyterian Church in Chicago, "the interior of which [Evelyn's father, a noted architect] Howard Shaw had designed and which he took pleasure in decorating for the event with Flemish tapestries borrowed from the Art Institute." Wrought-iron candlesticks and bay trees studded with roses—also from the Art Institute—decorated the church interior. JTM's brother George handled the honeymoon suite:

> My brother George had reserved a suite for us at the Ritz in New York and filled it with flowers. A fire glowed in the grate. It was hard to leave such a friendly spot even for the theater and a drive through Central Park in a hansom cab.[12]

Meanwhile, plans for the next stage of the honeymoon needed to be finalized. JTM wrote to E. N. Todd, Van Winkle's son-in-law, to inquire "how to have the island prepared for us. He answered that all I had to do was to notify an agent in Nassau that we would arrive on a certain date." So JTM and Evelyn "set out happily and hopefully," but JTM wanted the trip to Salt Cay to be the "climax of our honeymoon." Should it not, "and prove in any way to be disappointing," JTM arranged "to go elsewhere first." As usual, adventure would follow:

> We were in Jamaica when the United States broke off diplomatic relations with Germany; in Colon [Panama] we found the officers of several interned German ships quartered at our hotel. One of the usual Costa Rican revolutions was brewing, and armed sentinels patrolled the governor's palace in San Jose. In Cuba we expected to connect with a ship

for Nassau, but as we sailed in under the walls of Morro Castle [a fortress at the entrance to Havana Bay, Cuba], we passed [the ship] outbound. There was no other for a week. However, a fierce uprising was in progress in Cuba also. We met Junius Wood of the *Chicago Daily News* on his way to the front, and while war corresponding is not normally part of a honeymoon, we presently found ourselves provided with passes from the Minister of War and boarding a train for the interior. The big battle was vaguely scheduled for some time in the future and, the week being soon up, we started back [by train] to Havana. Even that way lay excitement. A vast forest fire was sweeping through the cane fields. For some minutes our train was an inferno of flame. We had to lay face-down on the floor, thus obtaining a measure of relief.[13]

It was a hell of a honeymoon. At last, Evelyn was "getting her [own adventures] first-hand—instead of being relayed to her by someone else in front of the fire at Ragdale." Finally, their convoluted journey brought them to Nassau but left them "eager and apprehensive." Charles and Martha Atkinson—"inveterate Nassau lovers"—had arrived at Salt Cay before them to "see that all was in readiness." Readiness, as it would turn out, was a relative idea:

Our ship anchored in the roadstead beyond the bar. Nassau lay smiling on her hillside above the gay harbor. So far, so good. A tender came out. Charles greeted us affectionately, but to every question concerning the island he countered with another about our trip. It seemed to us he was evading direct answers. Our imaginations were full of misgivings which increased when we joined Martha for breakfast. She showed equal skill in parrying questions. Subdued and disheartened, we asked no more. Perhaps it would have been better never to have come—always to think of it in the bright colors of imagination.[14]

Then they spotted the *Alice*—"a 50-foot yawl [sailboat] with towering spars." She was manned by the captain, "a coffee-colored Carib, one of the few remaining in the West Indies, and a couple of dusky sailor boys in spotless white." It lifted JTM's spirits:

This was something at least. We embarked, and the Atkinsons waved us off with sphinx-like faces. We steered down the harbor among the shipping, past flat little Fort Montagu on its flat little point. With expectations keyed to the utmost intensity as we turned through the Narrows where, out to sea a couple miles, lay a long, low reef-like affair—our island! From charts we knew it to be about three miles long. There was a brisk sea running, making a landing on the south side difficult, so the captain chose the other side.[15]

They rounded the eastern point where the "true island met our eyes." The beaches were long and white, thousands of coconut palm trees dotted the landscape, and "red roofs topped a 30-foot bluff."

From then on it was a succession of "Oh's" and "Ah's" [and] we have since learned to anticipate the sudden shock the visitor receives when he rounds that point or, more often, climbs the steps from the south and gets his first glimpse of the color and luxuriance beyond.[16]

The *Alice* lowered its anchor and the newlyweds went ashore in a dinghy "to a landing place on the rocks where our staff and their families awaited us, shy but smiling." About a dozen people greeted them—"the entire population of the island." What they saw next took their breath away:

After climbing from the beach up the steep hillside, we followed an aisle of clipped casuarinas to the house, a low, rambling bungalow, with broad porches and cool airy rooms, the most suitable dwelling imaginable. There were coconut mats, wicker chairs, a faded rosewood sofa and a wide desk, a roll of charts, a telescope and a case of seafaring books. The windows were salty from spray. Gloucester hammocks hung in the sheltered corners. Two bedrooms adjoined the living room with cedar closets, and beyond—an honest-to-gosh bathroom. The long veranda connecting the main house with the service quarters was bordered with potted palms. A stone kitchen was immaculately whitewashed; a glowing wood stove was set back in the chimney breast.[17]

The newlyweds wandered about the island "in a haze of wonderment." For JTM, it was "far beyond my most optimistic flights of fancy!" Now they understood what Charles and Martha had been up to:

> At once we realized the reason the Atkinsons had been so mysteriously evasive. They did not want to take the slightest edge off our first impressions. Their reserve had only heightened our thrill of discovery. We couldn't explore the whole island the first day. Marveling and ecstatic, we sank into the hammocks and lay there until the tinkle of the supper bell broke our raptures.[18]

Over JTM's chair at the table on the porch was a painted wooden sign with a familiar old verse, from the "Solitude of Alexander Selkirk": "I am monarch of all I survey, / My right there is none to dispute; / From the center all round to the sea, / I am lord of the fowl and the brute."[19]

JTM knew he was not really a swashbuckler, but "the legend has swung over my head for over 30 years." On his first day at Salt Cay—a long cherished dream—the legend "suited my frame of mind to perfection." As they ate dinner by candlelight, singing suddenly filled the air. It was the staff:

> Josephine the cook, Beatrice the maid, Loretta the laundress, Barabas and Sammy with his guitar—they had come out into the shadows of the long veranda. The wind rustled the palms, the surf murmured gently on the beaches, accompanying the plaintive local melodies. No South Sea idyll, no Louis Becke [George Louis Becke, a prominent novelist] story, could improve on this.[20]

The rest of the newlyweds' days passed quickly, and they were filled with swimming, sunning, sailing, and sleeping. As their honeymoon came to a close, war loomed and "the international cloud was growing more ominous, more insistent on our attention." On their return voyage, security precautions required them to "draw dark curtains across all our seaward windows at night."

Two days after Mr. and Mrs. John T. McCutcheon returned to Chicago from their honeymoon in Salt Cay, the United States of America declared war on Germany in April 1917. Later that year on November 8, Evelyn gave birth to a son, John T. McCutcheon, Jr. The proud parents nicknamed him "Jackie."

McCutcheon returned to Salt Cay, now nicknamed Treasure Island, for a second visit in February 1918. He, Evelyn, Jackie (now three months old), and the Atkinsons sailed from New York on the *SS Esperanza*, which was forced to observe various security measures dictated by the reality of World War I. German submarines continued to sink ships—"even outside the war zones"—and rumors about the enemy raiders were "incessant, insistent." New York Harbor was mined to protect against sneak attacks, and US destroyers were "actively patrolling the sea lanes" along America's East Coast. As the *Esperanza* left the harbor, a US destroyer "camouflaged in large blue and yellow diamonds raced past us and disappeared seaward."

Around midnight, as the *Esperanza* passed Barnegat Bay on the New Jersey coast, it steamed slowly through a thick fog "with all ports darkened." JTM was laying in his berth listening to the occasional foghorn:

> Suddenly there came a blast of an alien whistle, short and sharp with a note of danger, followed by a frantic and prolonged shriek from our own. On the instant our ship shook with a frightful impact, there was a ripping crash, the screech of rending steel, then utter and sinister silence. I leaped down from the upper berth. "Get up. Get dressed. We've been hit." "What is it? What has happened?" Evelyn was hardly awake. "We've been hit," I repeated. "From the sound I think we must go down very soon." "How soon?" "Oh, few minutes, maybe five."[21]

The ship's gangways quickly filled with scurrying passengers but "there was no panic or rushing water." JTM got dressed and put on a life preserver. Evelyn prepared herself and Jackie to board a lifeboat. It was midwinter and the thought of having to enter the frigid water was "not a pleasing prospect." Suddenly, Howard Shaw, who had gone below ship, returned and reported the sinking was not expected to happen immediately. It was a collision and not a torpedo they felt, but it was unclear who or what struck the *Esperanza* and the ship's officers were not forthcoming with any information.

JTM and Shaw went below a second time and learned the *Esperanza* had been "struck amidships on her starboard side—our side" (their four cabins were all in a row on the ship's lower deck). The collision gouged a fifty-five-foot-long gash three feet above the *Esperanza*'s water line. Bolts were ripped out and heavy steel plates curled back "like tin foil." They learned a surprising clue about what hit them:

> The cabins just under ours had been opened to the sky, and a camouflaged anchor had been deposited at the feet of the chief engineer who was shaving. Near it lay broken lengths of anchor chain freshly painted in bright blue and yellow diamonds! Providentially the sea was smooth. Even the slightest roll would have foundered us. The ship turned and limped to New York. Two Navy tugs were sent out to bring in the destroyer. Thirty feet of her bow had been telescoped, but her bulwarks kept her afloat until help arrived. No publicity was given the incident.[22]

The baby, Jackie, slept through it all. In all of his adventures, JTM regarded the collision as "far and away my most terrifying experience." It would take many years before he could "not hear a foghorn without a shiver of dread." But despite the scare, the powerful lure of their beloved Treasure Island caused them to ship out again immediately, and in three days they fell into an "idyllic routine of existence, apparently established through the years by Mr. Van Winkle, and carried on by our staff, several of whom had been with him on the Cay." Life on Treasure Island was delightful:

> As far as we were concerned, there was little to do except enjoy ourselves. The housekeeping seemed to do itself. The cook made out a daily list of articles desired for the kitchen and handed it to the captain, who, being unable to read, handed it over in turn to Cyril Solomon in Nassau. Mr. Solomon was perhaps as vital a part of the [Treasure] Island regime as were the sea and the sun. I was frequently disposed to wonder whether the island could function at all without him! Officially, he occupied the position "agent" for the Cay. He was our liaison officer ashore. He saw to it that the cook's order was filled and aboard next morning for delivery

on the Cay; also the mail, the Nassau Guardian and any errand we had written over about. There seemed to be nothing that we could send for that he or his able assistant Oswald Sweeting was unable to produce. He handled our finances, hiring and paying the staff, and occasionally acting as peacemaker in an emergency. He supervised the opening and closing of the house and all we had to do was to walk in and walk out.[23]

Solomon's responsibilities as Cay's agent was merely a sideline for him. He and his brother Eric operated a tobacco shop on Bay Street called the Pipe of Peace. They sold smoking accessories along with tortoise shells, pink pearls, and other gift items for tourists visiting from the winter cruise ships. Located in the center of everything, "nobody passed up or down Bay Street without stopping in."

Decades later, Solomon would end up turning over the care of the Cay to his nephew Gurth Duncombe in 1946 with "many expressions of regret on both sides at the severance of such a long and pleasant association." He died a couple years after that. Over the years, other members of the Treasure Island staff came and went. Positions in the "kitchen descended from mothers to daughters. Sammy, our first caretaker, was followed by Levi, still later by Josephas." Sammy served JTM and his family for twelve years:

> He was a man very much out of the ordinary. He was smart and likeable and could tell native stories and sing an endless number of beguiling local songs to his guitar. He and his assistant and their families lived on the island the year round. Their job was to guard it and its belongings, to keep it neat, to plant new coconuts, sweep the paths, rake the groves, keep the bathing beaches free of seaweed, tend the rain-water tanks (our only fresh water supply), keep the kitchen in fuel for the wood-burning stove, collect driftwood for picnics, raise and lower the drawbridge and to understudy in anything else that might be required.[24]

Each morning they greeted the supply boat and "soon we heard the wheel-barrows clattering house-ward on squeaky wheels" with the dripping ice, flopping fish, and often a large bunch of bananas on top of it all. Sammy usually dressed with a "conspicuous lack of fastidiousness," but for special occasions, like serving as a butler at a chowder party, "he appeared in crisp white and passed the cocktails with a distinguished air." One eye was droopy, but there was "always a twinkle" in the other eye. Sammy's wife, Josephine, was JTM's first cook, and when she died, Sammy married Priscilla, her younger sister. After the marriage, when JTM and Evelyn came down the next time, "we discovered Priscilla established in Sammy's cottage with a ready-made family, aged two and four." Such an arrangement might cause blushes in polite society, but was common on the Cay:

> In the Bahamas it was not uncommon to be "bo'n outside," meaning out of wedlock. There was apparently no odium attached to this little oversight of the legal preliminaries, and the children become respected members of the community. Sammy told me with no feeling of embarrassment that he himself was "bo'n outside." His father used to visit us occasionally, a very dignified and self-respecting old gentleman.[25]

Native island superstitions spawned numerous curiosities. Sammy always kept a *jibdog*, which in the local language is the female version of a bulldog. Sammy believed that ghosts come out on moonlit nights, and if they meet a bulldog, "every hair on the dog's back rises in horror and can be counted, whereupon the bulldog" is rendered powerless. The jibdog's hair does not rise and she can keep the ghost cornered "until you can take measures." These measures, JTM suspected, referred to some sort of *obeah* [a system of belief among blacks chiefly of the British West Indies and the Guianas that is characterized by the use of magic ritual to ward off misfortune or to cause harm]:[26]

> Whether the more intelligent of our staff believed in obeah and voodoo charms or not, they were clever enough to use the signs to terrorize a big, lazy second-man into leaving. He found the well-known marks on the paths about his cottage and dared not step over.[27]

The McCutcheons had been given a chow as an engagement present. The chow, Shenzi, was just a year older than their first-born, Jackie, so Shenzi became "in the course of his 13 years just as much one of the family." They wondered how Shenzi would spend his time on the island, including how he would get along with Sammy's jibdog. They got their answer following a change of season:

> [Shenzi] favored her with haughty indifference. She was always in the offing, but Shenzi gazed over her head with Oriental aloofness and appeared to us to spend his entire visit in resigned boredom. The following winter, however, Sammy proudly [delivered] a group of most strange animals. Their hair was short, their architecture lean and hound-like, but their slim rattails curled up over their backs absurdly, they had Shenzi's perky ears and coloring, and unmistakable chow black tongues![28]

The fun of owning an island includes being able to lose one's self in fantasy and role playing. Pretending to be king and queen, JTM and Evelyn held audiences on the beach, conferred honors and decorations, and issued mandates and "pronunciamentos when not otherwise and more pleasantly occupied." They also formed a cabinet of officials whose appointments followed the tradition of Kentucky governors naming their colonels, of which JTM was one:

> Charles Atkinson, whom we justifiably consider the patron saint of the island, was at once made Admiral of the High Seas Fleet, consisting at that time of the yawl Alice, a smaller fishing sloop, two rowboats, a canoe and Winnie-the Pooh, a strange craft, four-square, which drifted onto the beach. His duties in the ministry involved anything that concerned water. Thus, he collected blossoms to fill the finger bowls for chowder parties. Also, when a female figurehead we bought in Barbados arrived, sadly in need of attention, it devolved on the Admiral to give her a bath. He doubled in the job of poet laureate and spent much of his time playing the banjo.[29]

Like Jackie, the two other McCutcheon sons (Shaw and Barr) all made their first visit to Treasure Island "when they were brand-new, then not again until they were four years old, owing to commissary complications" and disapproving in-laws. *Their* children would face no such complications:

Today our grandchildren come at any age, accompanied by a suitcase full of all the necessary goods. In 1918, our friends were scandalized at the idea of taking a baby to an island "way out in the middle of the ocean." But Jackie thrived, acquired a fine tan and appeared to enjoy the scenery as much as we. When Evelyn and I dined ashore, we took him with us so as not to upset his schedule. On such occasions we usually parked him on a pillow in the bureau drawer. Left half open, this makes an excellent crib. There is always one handy; a baby can't roll out and he is free from drafts. An empty suitcase will do as well. Of course this particular baby was brought up to be as obliging as possible in such matters. He quite understood that life on an island would have been impossible on any other terms. He could be trusted to sleep anywhere at any time. The ears tuned for his cry were never pressed into service.[30]

On one night, returning to the island with friends after "some festivity ashore," a choppy sea picked up, the "night became darker and darker," and the captain changed his course for a rendezvous point with the dinghy where the "water would be quieter." The dinghy came alongside "where it rose and fell perilously":

"You're not going to get down into that," someone exclaimed. "There's no other way of getting ashore," JTM said. It was indeed a piratical setting—the black heaving water, the mysterious uplift of the island, the glow of the lantern casting shadows on the rocky steps. As the captain steadied my wife, while she "picked chance" to step down into the dinghy, I descended into the cabin, and emerged, grasping the knotted corners of a large triangular bundle which I held gingerly over the side until it was seized from below by Evelyn. "What's that?" asked a curious guest, struck by my evident caution. "Oh, that's the baby," I said casually. "The baby! Has there been a baby on board all this time? Don't tell me you take the baby back and forth like this!"[31]

Everyone spoke at once and when the talk quieted, JTM said: "He always travels with his meal ticket."

When World War I began in 1914, JTM never considered the possibility of America getting involved. During the early part of President Woodrow Wilson's term, JTM looked on him favorably and "took pleasure in drawing several complimentary cartoons about the conscientious effectiveness of his work in redeeming his platform pledges." But his regard for President Wilson "cooled" when it became clear he was moving America closer to war—"a course to which my cartoons had been consistently opposed." In JTM's view, America's eastern states supported the allies, the Midwest was more "restrained," and the far western states very carefully controlled information about their position on the war. His cartoons reflected how he sized up the nation:

> I drew a cartoon expressing this idea, and from the letters I received, it was evidently considered by many a fair statement of the sentiment of the country. The people of America did not want to be drawn in. Nearly two years of insistent pressure, of skillful propaganda and Eastern editorial clamor, at last got under the skins of our citizens who, it has been my observation, are very allergic to sob stories of atrocity propaganda. However, the first month after Wilson declared a state of war to exist brought fewer than 4,100 recruits. Where, one asked, was this widely heralded eagerness to leap to arms?[32]

For JTM, that summed up the viewpoint of an average person in the Midwest and he tried to avoid producing cartoons to help "inflame the public sentiment." He had reached a point in his life where his earlier adventures in the European war zone and the birth of Jackie "combined to hold me at home during 1917 and 1918." Thus it was that he found himself in Chicago as the war neared its end. A great anticipation seemed to energize the entire city:

> I was still in Chicago on that memorable day when the whole city went stark-staring mad; when the papers were literally afraid to print bulletins denying the report for fear of having their windows smashed, or worse damage by the hysterical crowds. [Then] early on the morning of Nov.

11, my wife and I were on a train to Washington. As we passed through Pittsburgh, the long, sustained chorus of engine and mill whistles advised of the Armistice. That night we were part of the milling mass on Pennsylvania Avenue when searchlights and planes crisscrossed the skies and President and Mrs. Wilson waved from an open automobile to the delirious crowds. It was a highly satisfactory and deafening celebration, but not nearly so explosive as the fake one.[33]

JTM was hoping to cross the Atlantic for a firsthand view of the end of the war. Getting the arrangements finalized proved difficult, even though he enlisted the influence of *Tribune* correspondent Arthur Sears Henning, the *Tribune's* veteran Washington correspondent and political analyst who would become famous twenty years later for the erroneous "Dewey Defeats Truman" story, and Secretary of the Navy Josephus Daniels—all for naught. They tried to speed things up, but "it seemed unlikely I could be wedged into a steamer until the following week." Then he got a lucky break—and a scare:

We went on to New York. On the train, Edward N. Hurley happened to pass through our car. He was head of the [U.S.] Shipping Board [which operated merchant ships owned by the U.S. government], and czar when it came to sailings. "Going over?" he said. "Well, you must come on the Olympic tomorrow with Herbert Hoover [then head of the U.S. Food Administration under President Wilson] and me." I was elated at this chance of getting away so soon. Next day I found myself in a palatial cabin called "Louis XVI," with three beds and a bath, but my first night in my sumptuous quarters was something of a nightmare. I had been given a three-in-one typhoid shot. Soon after I turned in, everything began to happen to my vitals. I wondered if I was on my way out, and in a panic of alarm I telephoned the doctor who explained the probable cause of my misery.[34]

In London, JTM secured an invitation to the weekly lunch given by ex-Prime Minister Herbert Henry Asquith and Mrs. Asquith. JTM sat to Asquith's right, as he was the only American attending the luncheon. The time was past for using war propaganda, so JTM assumed that the preferential seating was afforded to him because Asquith "was feeling grateful to America." He traveled on to France, where he found a country reeling from four years of war:

> I found France rubbing its eyes to make certain that the long agony was over. There were scenes of great confusion in the railway stations. Swirling throngs of troops and civilians battled for places on the trains. Even if you reserved a seat, the chances were that at least two others would be firmly established in it before you reached it. Taxicab drivers were independent to the point of insolence; they wanted a short haul and a big tip. Once when I returned to Paris after a trip of several days, I had to try 12 hotels before getting a room. Even the second-rate places were asking 60 francs a day and the franc was still 20 cents [in U.S. dollars].[35]

One reason for a scarcity of hotel rooms was the arrival of thousands of diplomats and others from around the world attending the 1919 Paris Peace Conference, which would determine the surrender terms for the defeated Central Powers. It was quite a collection of people. The city was a "seething swarm of delegates, journalists, soldiers of nearly all nationalities, women war workers, visiting committees and investigating junketeers, joy riders camouflaged as Red Cross and YMCA workers and a hundred other classes, all jostling about the city." JTM found that "a little of Paris this time went a long way" and he was happy when he was finally able to depart the city.

At the Ritz in Paris, JTM came upon General Charles Dawes, who had a private table in the hotel dining room where at lunch every day he "collected around it whomever he might have come across during the morning." He held court with the famous and the not-so famous:

> It was always a variegated group, male and female, high and low. Those were the days before the underslung pipe, when he smoked long Invincible Perfectos [cigars] and gave them out lavishly to his friends. French generals, royalty and other assorted noblemen, American politicians

and friends from home all would go miles for the luxury of one of those
cigars. At night to mitigate the harassments of the busy day, he would
seek nepenthe [forgetfulness] over at the Folies Bergère where a rollick-
ing slapstick revue was playing, ZigZag. It was a great palliative, guaranteed to take your mind off whatever it was on.[36]

Dawes' kindness and authority would end up providing JTM with oppor-
tunities that otherwise would have been out of his reach. He traveled on
General James G. Harbord's (chief of staff to General John Pershing) private train touring the Service of Supplies [SOS] districts, "where I saw
miles and miles of warehouses, bewildering mazes of tracks crowded
with American cars, acres of shells, which had come too late, mountains
of food; and on every hand the brisk, unornamental but exceedingly
capable Yankee doughboy doing his muddy job in a way that filled my
soul with pride."

JTM sketched portraits of the American members of the Paris Peace
Conference, but he was most concerned about getting a good sketch of
US Commander-in-Chief of the Allied Expeditionary Force General John
Pershing. JTM tried, but the subject matter got the best of him:

> His busiest days were over and he was able and willing to pose. In the
> early days of my war correspondence, I discovered the ability to make a
> portrait sketch offered an easy and valuable way to make contacts. I devel-
> oped what in retrospect seems to me a remarkable facility for catching
> likenesses in simple line drawings. Pershing had a face rich in individu-
> ality and strength lines. It should have been easy, but in my eagerness I
> must have tried too hard. Three separate times I tried, and I began to feel
> helpless as if I'd never drawn a line in my life. The last time I was licked
> before I started. Since then I have drawn from photographs of him for
> cartoon purposes—likenesses as good as I had hoped to get in Paris.[37]

JTM moved from the Ritz to the Continental, where he shared a room with
Tribune theater critic Percy Hammond. Although they had known each
other for a long time, their "trails at home seldom converged" because "he

was active mostly by night, I by day." Hammond's "scintillating mind and *bonne camaraderie*" continually drew people to him and as a result their "room was a mecca of congenial spirits at all hours." In Paris at the time, it was possible to run into luminaries anywhere. When they dined at the Continental's restaurant, "we would see a group of four always together— Feisal, King of Iraq, and Lawrence of Arabia with two others, doubtless retainers of the handsome king."

Hammond and JTM went on a twelve-day drive around US outposts in Germany and up to the cities of Bonn and Cologne. In the German city of Coblenz, General William "Billy" Mitchell was in charge of seizing German airplanes as part of terms of surrender. The airport at Coblenz was crowded with many types of airplanes "radically different from any I had ever seen." Mitchell took JTM up in his Lorraine-Dietrich Spad, which he piloted himself, and "up and down the Rhine [River] we went at 200 kilometers an hour, not much in view of present-day speeds, but a star experience then." New Year's Day 1919 was celebrated with Mitchell and the sons of a well-known president:

> Percy and I had dinner with General Mitchell's mess in a little town outside of Coblenz. The centerpiece was a cheerful Christmas tree which played "Stille Nacht" ["Silent Night"] as it revolved on its base, and across it I talked with the [Theodore] Roosevelt boys, Ted and Kermit, about their father. I had not seen him when I came through New York, but I had the impression that he was in good condition after his recent illness. Nothing was said to indicate that either of the boys felt any concern about him. We spoke of his chances in the 1920 election. "Your father's opposition to Wilson," I said, "has made him the logical opponent of any Democratic nominee on a Wilson platform." We could not suspect that on this very day he was being stricken with the relapse that carried him off six days later. Percy and I had no more than reached Paris on the sixth of January when we were thunderstruck by news of Colonel Roosevelt's sudden death.[38]

At times, JTM "tried to list the 10 greatest events I ever witnessed." His short list always included the World's Columbian Exposition, William Jennings Bryan's "Cross of Gold" speech, the Battle of Manila, and the march of the German Army through Louvain. The spectacle of President Wilson's arrival with his wife in Paris on December 14, 1918, was another:

> At that time, in the eyes of Europe, he was little less than a Messiah. From before dawn the people had been converging on the Champs-Élysées to see him pass. Traffic was excluded. Many people carried stepladders. Every window, every roof, every tree was packed with eager eyes. From where I looked down from General Dawes' offices in the Élysée Palace, it seemed that not another human being could be wedged into the picture. Into this breathless expectancy came two open carriages. President Wilson and [French] President [Raymond] Poincaré were in the first, the ladies in the second. There may have been other things in the procession, Guards of Honor, French calvary; there probably were. But I did not see them. As the carriages passed, there was not a cheer, not a rustle; it was as if the millions that lined the way were observing some solemn ceremonial in a vast cathedral. That was Wilson's greatest moment—before the Peace Conference, before they began to remove his statues, before they changed the street names back to something else.[39]

The creation of the League of Nations, the first international organization whose principal mission was to maintain world peace, found most people supportive of "a body which could act collectively against further war tendencies." JTM was among those favoring the league, and during the months following the Armistice, the *Tribune* asked its correspondents to "write occasional personal letters not for publication, giving their private opinion of things." JTM wrote a letter expressing his "hope that the League might be saved from defeat." He came to change his mind about the League of Nations in the wake of the Versailles Treaty:

It seemed to me that the League, far from being an impartial body of cold justice, was to be a manipulated device designed to secure Britain and France the immense advantages they had gained by the treaty. As this became more evident, my sentiments recoiled and I became intensely skeptical of its honest purposes and possible benefits. Only a few years of its operation bore out these misgivings. My cartoon indicated that "according to the autopsy, she was constitutionally and economically unsound, but meant well."[40]

After President Wilson departed the Paris Peace Conference, the *Chicago Tribune* began reassigning its foreign correspondents to other locations. JTM received an urgent cable he'd been "half expecting" from the *Tribune's* Joe Patterson that read, "Urge McCutcheon return at once. He's been off the front page long enough." Such an order would clearly put an end to his "cherished plans for a reunion on the island," which would leave him keenly disappointed:

I had already arranged to have the house opened and the boat put in commission. Nevertheless, I realized that my enjoyment of the lazy days down there might be seriously diminished if I were buying them at the expense of my relations with the paper. There was a gleam of humor in the situation. That was Joe's use of the word urge. As if I needed urging! Never before had I felt this tugging at me to return home! A far greater calamity would have been a cable saying, "Have McCutcheon remain abroad until peace is concluded." There's no use talking, things were different. I was finding that a family crowded out a great many other interests.[41]

JTM's return to America included an assignment to sail across the Atlantic on the armored cruiser *USS Pueblo,* which was transporting fifteen hundred discharged US soldiers. He was the only civilian on the ship whose captain, Brooks Upham, "was an old friend from the *USS Olympia.*" JTM stayed in Upham's quarters, since the captain "slept on the bridge during the entire voyage which was delayed four days by tempestuous buffetings of weather." Evelyn and his brother George greeted him in New York, and after some time relaxing in Atlantic City—"a poor substitute for the island"—he settled back into drawing cartoons.

Never one to settle for too long, and "in order that the year might not be without its distinguishing variation," JTM planned to attend the thirtieth reunion of the Purdue University Class of 1889. He wrote:

> Now a reunion dates you. Any undergraduate with a pencil and a cuff can figure how much of a fossil you are. Therefore, since travel by air for civilians was still sufficiently unusual to be of real news value, I determined to return in very up-to-date style. My plan was to circle high over the Class Day celebrations on Stuart Field, tailspin down for a few thousand feet, then spiral out for a neat three-point landing before the grandstand, to the admiring amazement of my bride and the assembled multitudes, where I would step jauntily out of the cockpit, yawn slightly and adjust my straw hat with a maximum of nonchalance. That was the plan.[42]

All went according to the plan until the pilot recovered from the spin, surveyed the landing field—and didn't like what he saw. So they flew off and landed in a "nice comfortable alfalfa field—without a soul in sight." As a grand entrance, "it was something less than zero—proper penalty for a fellow trying to show off!"

FOR SOMEONE WHO HAD MOVED willingly around the world in search of adventure, two local moves in 1925 also added adventure and excitement to his life.

For ten years prior to his marriage, JTM lived at 39 East Schiller Street in the "friendly old-fashioned apartment on the top floor overlooking Lake Michigan and the lawns and brownstone turrets of the Potter Palmer castle." He and Evelyn continued to live there for another seven years until they moved to an apartment at the corner of Lakeview and Arlington Place. It looked across Lincoln Park to the lagoon and "it was near the Francis Parker School where [their] children went." The apartment included a den and a "jolly playroom papered with giraffes and elephants and porcupines and other things equally suitable for small boys or the president of a zoo." Evelyn's father had designed the building, which replaced "a handsome gray stone house that had to be torn down." The occupants of the house had included Lizzie Allen, "the notorious queen of the red-light district." From his breakfast table, JTM could look out the window and see what used to be Allen's horse stable—"a drab reminder of those gay nineties."

The change in address required JTM to learn "not to get off the bus too soon" on his commute home from work. Another move would require him to "get off the morning bus much sooner."

In 1925, instructions came to JTM from the top of the *Tribune* to move his studio from the Fine Arts Building to the Tribune Tower by the Chicago River—about 1.5 miles further north. It was a difficult decision for him:

> This time I was torn by sentimental emotions of a different caliber. Many considerations entered into my decision to accept, among which was the usual one of expediency. There would be no rent to pay—mine had doubled from $45 to $90 a month—and it was much more convenient to my new home. Even more compelling was the fact that Colonel McCormick wanted me to attend the editorial conference held daily in his office. This could not very well be done from the old studio. As further inducement I was offered my choice of a number of locations, to be partitioned off as I wished. I selected the 31st floor, up among the flying buttresses, with fine north light, and on clear days a wide view over the lake and the city roofs. Four hundred feet below, the boulevard traffic came up to me as only a faint hum. My segment of the "lantern" which rises 10 stories above the main body of the tower, had nice possibilities as a studio. It was 40 feet long and paneled in warm brown oak. The arched windows were on the floor level, leaving the upper half of the room in the romantic dimness I enjoy.[43]

JTM quickly put his mark on the space. He hung red-tasseled horn lanterns he bought in Peking from the fourteen-foot ceiling. A narrow woven runner from Turkestan, "designed to fit round and round the interior of a Turkoman's kibitka [tent], fitted nicely [along] the length of the long wall." Other trophies were displayed carefully around the studio.

The studio was not only a place for work. From time to time, JTM used it to host parties. He entertained various organizations and Evelyn "served box lunches to that group of Chicago ladies who call themselves the Scribblers and whose programs are not always intended for mixed audiences." The studio also welcomed a number of famous visitors, including Winston Churchill who "came up to see me when he was in Chicago." JTM also shared the thirty-first floor with some colleagues, including *Tribune* cartoonist Carey Orr, who had a "scrumptious studio with a fine view of the river and the Loop skyscrapers." Orr, a Pulitzer Prize winner himself who worked at the *Tribune* from 1917 to 1963, was admired by JTM:

> Carey's style is vigorous and forthright, and its apparent simplicity shows a profound understanding of the art of cartooning. He was the cheeriest kind of neighbor, genial, kindly and obliging. However, the two of us were not always there at the same time. There was a detached atmosphere up among the wind-wrapped buttresses quite unlike the camaraderie of the noisy Fine Arts Building.[44]

Despite the occasional parties and encounter with his floor mates, the quiet of the studio more often was disturbed "only by the telephone, a device whereby much valuable time is swallowed up." Many of his cartoons were finished ahead of deadline "with the receiver in my hand, and many people might be piqued to know how little attention their words were receiving." US mail also was a "problem I never satisfactorily solved":

> The tables and chairs were heaped high with things I meant to answer or had saved for reference. Every once in a while Evelyn conducted an archaeological expedition, excavated me from the accumulation and brought my correspondence up to date. She was amused when she found

expired financial rights and warrants in the pile, and mystified by papers blackened with pencil marks. I spent a lot of time and pencil lead making these, my own mediums for tracing cartoon outlines. Sometimes by mistake I made them on my scalp. "Why don't you put the ones already made in this drawer where you can find them when you need them?" she would ask. "That would be contrary to my whole scheme of life, Evelino," I would tell her.[45]

JTM freelanced frequently in his early days when he "seemed to have endless energy to spare" and would "take on almost any outside work that came along." In fact, his philosophy was to never refuse a paying job "if it was along lines that I liked." His freelance work was wide-ranging in subject and included varying compensation:

> When the first cafeteria started in the YWCA building on LaSalle Street, I did the chalk drawings that often hung in the doorway to lure the sidewalk trade to the feast within. For those large sketches, dashed off quickly, I received 50 cents apiece, and thought it was easy money. When Morgan and Wright [Chicago-based Morgan & Wright Tire Co.] started *Wheel Talk* [a magazine] to stimulate the newly developing automobile industry, Schmedtgen and I did scores of drawings which amplified our modest salaries. We also did work for the *Inland Printer* [a monthly publication covering the printing industry], then one of the most artistic exponents of the printer's art. I did World's Fair sketches for the New York Herald at five or 10 dollars apiece.[46]

Although such fees for freelancing seem small by today's standards, JTM "never felt that I was underpaid." By way of comparison, his salary at the time was $25 a week. Big money eventually came, however, in the form of a half-page drawing for Harry Selfridge, a partner of businessman Marshall Field, to be used in a newspaper advertisement. The drawing, "a view of the central court of the [Marshall Field] store with many little figures busily shopping," earned JTM $500—"a princely price." JTM continued to "sandwich in a little extra work" for many years. He contributed political cartoons to *Collier's* when Norman Hapgood (writer and American ambassador to Denmark) was editor, most focused on the Progressive period. His drawings illustrated articles and stood on their own in such publications as *Appleton's, Metropolitan, Cosmopolitan, Saturday Evening Post, Hearst's International,* and others.

Over time, JTM put a limit on the outside work because the "pressure had reached a point where I had to choose between the magazine and the advertising fields." He did not have time for both, so he chose "the one I preferred, although it paid less." This career decision would undergo a significant test, thanks to the reimbursement associated with it:

> In the late 1920's the representative of an Eastern advertising company called at my studio, a very agreeable gentleman with the dynamic go-getter approach then pervading business. This was shortly before the chilling blast of the '29 crash withered the world of industry. The young man asked me to do a weekly cartoon advertising a certain brand of cigarette. "I'm sorry," I said, "but I have not been doing any advertising work for a long time, and besides, I don't smoke cigarettes." The young man said that made no difference, that no one cared whether the artist smoked or didn't, and offered me $40,000 for one cartoon a week for one year. Again I demurred, but he was not impressed. He had risen to the top by getting things done. "How about two cartoons a week for $80,000?"[47]

Not surprisingly, JTM found it to be a "most flattering offer" and decided he "owed him consideration and courtesy." So he told the man he would speak to Colonel McCormick, which he did:

> I told Bert of the offer. I also told him I had no intention of accepting the job even if he were willing. He said he did not like the idea of my doing any sort of cartoons which would appear in other newspapers. At my next meeting with the determined New Yorker, I reported the colonel's sentiments. I added that the increased pressure of another regular job might prove a physical strain too great for me to assume.[48]

Unimpressed, the New Yorker thought the situation came down to simply "reaching a price." What followed was an "amazing crescendo of offers":

> He asked if I would do two cartoons a week for $100,000. When I refused, very politely of course, he asked if I would do the cartoons if they provided the ideas. When I once more refused, he asked if I would accept if they provided not only the ideas but a ghost artist to do the drawing. My only contribution would be to allow the use of my name. Once more, and finally I refused. I was refusing partly because I didn't smoke cigarettes, and partly because in those days I felt there was something slightly—just slightly—infra dig [beneath one's dignity] about advertising. Probably the main reason was that I stood in no great need of money.[49]

JTM's fame as a cartoonist also had its downside. Another "unusual caller" emerged, but this time it was JTM's friends who received the visit. A man saying he represented JTM claimed that the cartoonist was creating a book of portraits. Would they honor JTM by posing for the book and, more importantly, subscribing at a cost of $250 each? A number of his friends did pay. JTM found out by accident:

> Judge [William J.] Calhoun telephoned me to know where to send the check. I was horrified. I told him to make an appointment with the man and then had an officer there to arrest him. When the case came up in the old Harrison Street station, I testified, and it was proved that he had forged my name. But there was some loophole by which he squirmed out.[50]

Then there was the McCutcheon impersonator who passed himself off as JTM in Texas. He lived the high life using JTM's name. The man was "hospitably entertained, put up at clubs, signed chits, borrowed money, and lived for some time on this misrepresentation." The charade came to an end when JTM happened to read a newspaper story "about myself attending all these functions in Austin with persons I had never heard of." JTM immediately sent a letter to "disillusion the chief of police."

-{{{{{{{{{{{-

A LIFETIME OF ADVENTURES AND WORLD TRAVELS can result in a world of personal souvenirs. Naturally, a man "likes to have a place where he can leave things around, things that are full for him of all sorts of associations." Unfortunately, a world-class collection of souvenirs is "not apt to fit well with the home scheme of decoration." What to do with these souvenirs required some marital compromise:

> My wife adjusted herself to a dining room that contained African animal heads, an enormous Japanese gong over 300 years old in which the children rejoiced, and a gigantic ironbound chest once used by the governor of Puerto Rico to hold customs collections after undoubtedly more dramatic piratical services. Finally it had found its way to the Chicago Art Institute. Probably they said, "My, my! We haven't any room for this! Let's send it up to John McCutcheon." Anyhow, one day we found it in the front hall.[51]

To accommodate his collection, JTM had a "couple of overflow studios, also decorated in the Afro-Indiana period." When they built their house in Lake Forest overlooking the meadow at the Ragdale compound, the McCutcheons converted an "ex-cow shed into another repository for such things as my Philippine saddle with the bullet hole in it, and my screened African hunting bed—which in point of decorative value is surpassed by almost everything I have ever seen." He spent most of the summer there.

Although his studio at the Tribune Tower was a dramatic setting with "architectural distinction," somehow it "lacked the spirit" of his studio in the Fine Arts Building. Over time, his heart and the main focus of his life gradually shifted to "my home and my family," and he spent less and less time at the studio. That he was not to be found "more often in the studio" was not always his fault:

Early in 1936, at a reception, my hand was shaken by a large earnest man who represented the League of Nations; he used all the pressure of his 200 pounds. I could hardly keep from crying out. Next day I made the horrendous discovery that I could not use my hand. I was unable to put on my clothes, much less write or draw. It was eight long months before I could once more close my fingers comfortably around a pen.[52]

McCUTCHEON REGARDED CARTOONING as a "peculiar form of art." The mechanics involved in the drawing of cartoons changed little during JTM's long career. Few mysteries remain about the craft and the required tools, which is "usually only a bottle of ink and a pen, a piece of cardboard, an eraser—and sometimes an idea." After JTM had "settled on this last item"—the idea—he followed a set process:

> I blocked it out roughly on scratch paper so that I would know where I was going to place the major figures. Then I transferred it, either freehand or by tracing, onto a cardboard about 16 inches wide, and went over it with black drawing ink, altering, cutting out, adding. If the subject happened to be a good one, there was no little pleasure in elaborating it. If I found I needed refreshment of memory as to faces or detail not supplied by illustrations in the current magazines or my own library, I telephoned down to the *Tribune* morgue, presided over by August Bartz, and told him what I wanted and which view of it would be most useful; in a few minutes these accessories would be on my desk.[53]

JTM smoked cigars when he worked, following a set ritual that started with "two cigars on the desk beside me." Once he settled on the idea for the day's cartoon, he lit cigar "Number One and began the process of transferring the idea to paper." His ritual went as follows:

While my right hand labored assiduously, my left hand carried the cigar to and from my lips. It was constantly going out so that much time was spent in relighting it. Number Two followed. There was more motion up and down than there was smoking. But the cigar and the motion had a psychological effect with a precedent of many years to back it up. I began smoking when I was 12. Every Saturday night in Elston, I scrubbed out Johnston Brothers saloon and was paid in five-cent cigars—75 cents worth of Pride of Weas. My mother suspected there was dirty work at the crossroads, but she reasoned that I would get sick and cure the situation that way. I did—but not for 50 years.[54]

When he was sixty-two he received "a warning tap from old *Anno Domini*" in the form of a "bronchial condition with a duodenal ulcer." His doctor recommended he spend the winter in Arizona, along with a stronger prescription:

He added in the slow reflective way that made his ultimatums sound so casual, "I believe I'd cut out alcohol, if I were you . . . and I don't think I'd do any more smoking." While I had always enjoyed a cocktail, particularly our Treasure Island brand of Bacardi sour, I felt I could kiss the Demon Rum good-bye without wearing crepe. But smoking! That was a major calamity! It worked out differently. When the doctor's ukase [command] struck with its reverberating clunk, I wasn't feeling very well. I wasn't feeling at all like smoking. The first few months passed without a wrench. Finally I emerged into circulation again and the moment arrived when the Corona Coronas were being passed. Can I resist those long brown sleek beauties? I asked myself in panic. I could and did. Thousands of cigars have passed since then but I never wavered.[55]

JTM had another habit when drawing "that may be unusual." He used his own face to model the emotions he needed to draw. It was an unconscious act, done perhaps to make him "more *en rapport* with my subject." There were times when he was drawing with people in the room that he became aware "of the cessation of all other activity, of a suspicious stillness, and upon looking up . . . found everybody regarding me with merriment."

For most of five decades, JTM created a cartoon seven days a week. The work was never routine or dull as each cartoon "presented a new problem." He tried to add variety, choose new subject matter, and keep "changing the form and nature of my cartoons to provide as great diversity as possible." His first try at changing things up was the *Bird Center* series. Others followed:

> I was careful to end each one at a moment of suspended interest; consequently they proved effective circulation builders. *The Heir at Large* was especially lucky in striking the public fancy, and each time I began to draw the threads together for a suitable ending, the *Tribune* would stop me. This necessitated continual mental agility in reshaping the plot, introducing new characters, holding up the love interest, giving it a start in a new direction. It ran for nearly two years. Even then Joe Patterson remained adamant: he wanted me to continue, and to continue with the hero unmarried! For a week or two I conceded in spite of the universal opinion of my friends that enough was plenty. Finally, not wishing to go on yet scarcely daring to finish it off, I wrote an ambiguous sort of installment announcing the hero's engagement.[56]

That was it for *Heir*, or so JTM thought.

As an indication of the power of newspapers in general, and front-page cartoons in particular in that era, on the following Monday, the *Tribune* received 1,500 telephone calls from readers wanting to know "why there was no *Heir at Large*." As a result, "pressure from the paper was such that I was obliged to start a new one which ran almost as long."

In late 1927, the *Tribune* decided to increase the price of the *Sunday Tribune* by 42% from 7 to 10 cents. JTM was recruited to help win over the readers:

> In an effort to prevent the discontinuance of subscriptions which they feared might follow, they asked me to start a Sunday serial six weeks before the change. It was called *The Master of the World* and was the one I most enjoyed writing. It concerned a young scientist who solved the

mystery of the cosmic ray. In view of the fact that this story antedated the magical results of splitting the atom by more than 10 years, I have always considered it one of my more successful prophetic attempts.[57]

His work provided moments of intense satisfaction. When he completed a cartoon that he personally liked, JTM felt a "delightful glow that made the whole world seem warm and friendly." The most satisfying feeling of happiness "comes from something one has done, and done well, with one's own hands and brain." Even so, he went through some periods when "not a single cartoon seemed to have merit," and he paid an emotional price for it:

> A deep blanket of despondency enveloped me. Each time I struck such a sterile streak, it seemed to last longer than usual, and I became very blue. I thought my cartooning days must be over. I dreaded the mornings. If I noticed a streetcar reader looking at the cartoon, I averted my eyes so that I would not see the tired resignation settle over his face. The merit of my work seemed to go in waves. There was no use trying to analyze them. It helped a lot when kindly folk wrote in expressing approbation. The day was brightened. But the old self-critical censor still stood guard to keep me from being too satisfied.[58]

In hindsight, he found his own reaction peculiar because when he "looked back with fresh eyes at the work I had been so gloomy about," he found the cartoon wasn't as bad as he originally thought. In fact, many of the drawings that generated the most feedback "were drawn in those periods." JTM felt he was unable to consistently judge what the newspaper readers would regard as good. When Theodore Roosevelt was elected president in 1904 by a large majority, JTM had an "opportunity to draw an amusing cartoon of the landslide." He was ready to submit the finished work when Jim Keeley called to say late election results indicated that Missouri, typically a Democratic state, "had gone Republican. Thought you might want to do something on that," Keeley said:

> I thanked him and hung up. How futile, I thought, to draw another cartoon after completing such a masterpiece! However, we find it wise to humor the managing editor, so I sat down again and drew a cartoon

on the Missouri situation. I represented Missouri, frock-coated, with a broad-brimmed hat, having left the ranks of the Solid South and gone over to join the Republican states, while the Solid South looked on dismayed and thunderstruck. I couldn't spend much time on it, just hurried it off in less than a half an hour and forgot to give it a caption. Then I sent the two cartoons over to the *Tribune*, confidently expecting to see the masterpiece on the front page. This rosy expectation was 100 percent unfulfilled. It was tucked away in the back behind pages of election returns, and to this day no one has ever referred to it. The Missouri cartoon was on the front page, and because I had drawn the figure of Missouri like that of the mysterious stranger in the *Bird Center*, Keeley had given it as caption the simple phrase "The Mysterious Stranger," a stroke of genius. It drew an instant flood of letters and has retained its place among my better-known cartoons.[59]

Sometimes the smallest of details in a cartoon generated the most comments, something JTM "continued to be surprised by" even after all his years of experience:

> One Christmastime in showing a crowded street with much movement and activity, I drew a streetcar turning a corner. To heighten the sense of motion and make it more amusing, I drew the car itself bending in crescent form as it made the curve. A deluge of letters descended on me. In the utmost seriousness I was assured that a car did not bend when turning a corner; it remained stiff and straight.[60]

From time to time thereafter, JTM curled his streetcars around corners, "and in no case did there fail to come the reminders of my indifference to physical laws." If the readers were always "as vigilant in defending their vested rights as they are the habits of streetcars," JTM thought, America "need have no fear for the future."

Cartoons sometimes created a hornets' nest like one JTM drew in the summer of 1931. It suggested America's steel industry "was languishing" and offered the novel idea of reviving it by "constructing steel and glass houses, durable and easily moved!" Although the first letters of complaint came spontaneously, later "many communications from widely separated sources were phrased in so nearly the same language that it became evident an organized pressure was being brought to bear" against the *Tribune*. Another time, JTM's telephone rang on a December night at some point after midnight. It raised an alarm:

> It was near vacation time; the boys might be driving or even flying home. My wife was out of bed in an instant. An angry lady representing the League of Irish Women Voters demanded an immediate explanation of the next morning's cartoon. Evelyn soothed her as best she could. "What in the world did you do to the Irish?" she asked as she came back to bed and reported the irate lady. The Irish? There was nothing about the Irish in the cartoon I had sent in that afternoon. Hold on a minute, though! I fetched the telephone and called the office. "Is there still time to make a little change in the cartoon?" "Sure. Time for the last edition. What do you want?"[61]

JTM had drawn Central and South America with every nation represented by a face. At the tip he drew two little faces, Pat and Terry, which represented "Patagonia and Tierra del Fuego—who could have resisted giving Pat and Terry an Irish cast of countenance?" The names Pat and Terry had no significance to the point of the cartoon, so "if they're going to be taken as a slur, they might as well come out." Thanks to JTM's call to the *Tribune*, in the morning, the "names were mysteriously absent." Reader wrath was an occupational hazard:

> If they touch on controversial subjects, cartoons will usually have an immediate response. It has been significant of the wide diversity of taste in the reading public that again and again I received bitter denunciation and ardent approbation about one and the same cartoon. In the great majority of cases, letters reviling me were scrawled in pencil and showed ignorance. But there were occasions when persons of obvious intelligence appeared to be sincerely distressed. These were harder to take.[62]

When a cartoon was a "hit," JTM knew immediately, thanks to certain clues. "The elevator man greeted me with gratifying approval; the doorman spoke of it, and the barber." Sometimes the day's news was "uninspiring," and at other times JTM ran into "one of those unhappy streaks and found myself pressed for an idea." When he faced such doldrums, he solved the problem "with one of my reserves." Like Mr. Gladd and Mr. Blue:

> These were not drawn ahead of time; they were simply types of cartoons not dependent on news. One was captioned "Mr. Lugubrious Blue and Mr. Smiley Gladd Discuss the Situation." To emphasize his ultra-pessimistic attitude, I showed Mr. Blue, crushed by despair, about to jump off a high bridge or throw himself under a train, while Mr. Gladd points out on all sides evidences of cheer. These two began airing their views back in 1902. After that they debated most of the controversial issues which tore the nation, expressing extremes of opinion with a freedom which in many cases might not have been acceptable in the columns of the paper unless attributed to imaginary persons like Mr. Blue and Mr. Gladd.[63]

Another reserve cartoon character that saw lots of service was J. Raglan Patchmore. He was a man who "never recovered from the depression of 1893 when he lost his whole fortune of $3.70—a cheerful city bum who depended for sustenance on his wits—and never on work." Patchmore's eyes peered over "a sunburst of whiskers" and his clothes were "ancient and air-conditioned." The Patchmore cartoons were set in a newspaper office and typically the nation faced a crisis. The city editor would assign his "star financial reporter" to find Patchmore. The "resulting interview was run as a news article, illustrated by several [cartoons]. Mr. Patchmore made many friends. At critical times, when 'all the world's ajngle and ajar,' readers asked to know what the Apostle of Inertia thought about things."

JTM used a third form of reserve cartoon starting in 1913 that he called, *The Changing World*. He used it to compare "things of the past" with "things of the present. It permitted a wide range of subjects—artistic, international, athletic, educational, military—in fact nearly everything that had a past and present."

In his constant search to add novelty to his work, JTM sought ways to cover the news without being tied to his studio. In the summer of 1919, he decided to make a drawing of the Jack Dempsey-Jess Willard heavy-weight champion boxing match in person—in Toledo, Ohio. To meet his deadline, this would require him to "fly back from Toledo that same after-noon with the sketches." On July 4, 45,000 people were in attendance at Bay View Park in Toledo to see a fight that lasted less than ten minutes:

> It was 112 degrees on the wooden benches of the enclosing saucer. The gigantic [6-foot 7-inch] Willard was knocked to the floor seven sepa-rate times during the first round. The bell started ringing the count; the referee held up Dempsey's hand. He was carried away on the shoulders of the crowd, buffeted among his friends. But something had happened; I think the bell got jammed and had not rung the count of eight! So Dempsey was called back and re-entered the ring far more tired than when he left it, with the added disappointment of losing $110,000 by not finishing in the first round.[64]

Dempsey defeated Willard, and when the fight ended after the third round, JTM "hurried off through the confusion." As he struggled to find his way out among "the upright timbers of the understructure, I came upon Wil-lard, his face battered and bleeding, apparently lost and alone." Although he gave it his best shot, JTM missed the deadline for the following day:

> It was already after six when I reached the golf course where the plane waited. The menacing trees at the end of the fairway grew higher and higher; we cleared them by inches. The pilot had no strip map; he flew west by compass as long as the light held. Then, without radio beams or beacons or lighted airports, he dared go no further and landed in a pasture near Goshen, Indiana. I had made my sketches at the ringside. I had tried to finish them more carefully as we flew. However, since my mind was distracted by the uncertainty of our position and the oncom-ing darkness, I fear they were inadequate; naturally, they were too late for the morning paper.[65]

In another bid to escape the studio and cover news firsthand, he "tried to take advantage of the newly publicized mechanism for sending photographs by wire." JTM thought it "might [also] be possible to send drawings" using the device. In Washington, D.C., the trial of Secretary of the Interior Albert Fall and Edward Doheny of the Pan American Petroleum and Transport Company was underway. Fall was accused of taking a bribe from Doheny in exchange for leasing US Navy petroleum reserves at Teapot Dome, Wyoming, for low rates without requiring competitive bidding:

> No photography or sketching was permitted in court, but the *Tribune* arranged for me to take one of its seats for an hour. Doheny was being examined by his attorney; Secretary Fall sat within a few feet of me, slouched in his chair. As I listened, I studied every line of their features, their expressions, their attitudes and costumes. As soon as I left the building, while these impressions were still fresh, I made the sketches. They were rushed to Philadelphia where the nearest machine for sending was located. Thus, the following morning, the *Tribune* contained the only pictures of the Teapot Dome trial.[66]

Whatever attention these "early efforts at speedy delivery" attracted was largely lost as the technology for distributing news and images rapidly evolved quickly in the 1920s.

The use of color in newspaper illustrations was a development that began in 1903 in a JTM caricature of Mark Twain printed on the *Tribune's* front page. It was also used shortly thereafter in a JTM retrospective cartoon about the 1871 Chicago fire. In the beginning, the addition of color required a process that "required several days." Later, it was "sufficiently simplified to use every day." Even so, JTM never fully embraced it:

> While I appreciated the appeal of color, I never felt that it helped my own cartoons. Perhaps I had come to rely too much on detail which was apt to be submerged. Or perhaps the change came when I was not longer flexible to adapt myself to it.[67]

From time to time, some cartoons rise above a limited use and display a timeless or evergreen quality that "lend themselves to repeated reproduction in later years in their original form. JTM's seasonal cartoons like "Injun Summer," "Jack Frost," and the "Hunter's Moon" fell in this category. To give his drawings a fresh feel and lasting relevance, JTM tried adding poetry, tabloid fiction, dialogue, monologue, woodcut drawings, Egyptian style, *McGuffey Reader* style, modernism, and silhouette. In the end, there was no formula to accurately predict reader reaction: "On some I never heard a syllable of comment, kindly or otherwise; for some there were friendly words; and for some I took the javelins in my breast."[68]

IN EARLY 1921, the possibility of expanding Lincoln Park Zoo was "so limited that even as far back as 1909 the need for a new modern park adequate to the importance of the city was recognized by Daniel H. Burnham in his plan for the future of Chicago." On the encouragement of Charles L. Hutchinson, longtime president of the Art Institute and one of "Chicago's most valuable citizens," in 1921, JTM was elected president of the new Chicago Zoological Society. He was selected, in part, because of a book he wrote about his trip through Africa with the Akeley expedition. He held the position for twenty-eight years. After the Cook County Forest Preserve donated 105 acres to "be used for a zoological park," construction of the zoo began in 1927. On June 30, 1934, the Chicago Zoological Park (now known as the Brookfield Zoo) opened officially at a preview attended by over 2,000 guests:

> There were speeches, music and a lot of sight-seeing. It was my privilege and honor to preside at this memorable event. "If he should see more elephants than donkeys," I said in introducing Governor [Henry] Horner of Illinois, "I hasten to assure him there is no political significance."[69]

NOTES

1   John T. McCutcheon, *Drawn From Memory* (Indianapolis and New York: Bobbs-Merrill, Inc., 1949), 303.
2   Ibid.
3   Ibid., 304.
4   Ibid., 305.
5   Ibid., 305–6.
6   Ibid., 306.
7   Ibid., 307.
8   Ibid.
9   Ibid., 308.
10 Ibid.
11 Ibid., 309.
12 Ibid.
13 Ibid., 309–10.
14 Ibid., 310.
15 Ibid., 310–11.
16 Ibid., 311.
17 Ibid.
18 Ibid., 312.
19 Ibid. JTM does not name the author of "the old familiar stanza," but see "The Solitude of Alexander Selkirk, William Cowper (1731–1800)," accessed November 14, 2013, www.bartleby.com.
20 Ibid., 313.
21 Ibid., 314.
22 Ibid., 315.
23 Ibid., 315–16.
24 Ibid., 317.
25 Ibid.
26 "Obeah," *Merriam-Webster Dictionary*, accessed November 15, 2013, www.merriam-webster.com.
27 Ibid., 318.
28 Ibid.
29 Ibid., 318–19.
30 Ibid., 319.
31 Ibid., 320–21.
32 Ibid., 327.
33 Ibid., 328.
34 Ibid.

35 Ibid., 329.
36 Ibid., 329–30.
37 Ibid., 330–31.
38 Ibid., 331–32.
39 Ibid., 333.
40 Ibid., 334.
41 Ibid.
42 bid., 335.
43 Ibid., 371–72.
44 Ibid., 372–73.
45 Ibid., 375.
46 Ibid., 373.
47 Ibid., 373–74.
48 Ibid., 374.
49 Ibid.
50 Ibid., 375.
51 Ibid., 375–76.
52 Ibid., 376.
53 Ibid., 377.
54 Ibid.
55 Ibid.377–78.
56 Ibid., 378–79.
57 Ibid., 379.
58 Ibid.
59 Ibid., 380.
60 Ibid.
61 Ibid., 381–82.
62 Ibid., 382.
63 Ibid., 382–83.
64 Ibid., 383.
65 Ibid., 384.
66 Ibid.
67 Ibid., 385.
68 Ibid., 386.
69 Ibid., 424.

11

Anatomy of a Pulitzer Prize Cartoon

A S THE GREAT DEPRESSION took hold of the country in the 1930s, it presented Americans with a miserable state of affairs. Thousands of banks failed and wiped out their depositors' savings. More than 13 million people—25 percent of the US labor force—lost their jobs, and wages plunged to as little as a nickel an hour.[1]

Not surprisingly, bank failures caused panic among depositors. As consumer confidence in the US banking system plummeted, "bank runs" became increasingly common. During 1930 alone, 1,350 US banks suspended operations;[2] some were forced to closed their doors due to financial hardship, while the assets of others were placed into receivership by court order. To the average person, the reason made little difference—the reality was terrifying. One day, the savings they had worked years to accumulate existed; the next day, they vanished.

Naturally, fear and panic gripped the nation, spreading even to those still lucky enough to have their money deposited in banks that were regarded as sound. Reassuring answers remained elusive and a paralyzing doubt took hold of the American psyche.

Against this backdrop, JTM arrived at work at the Tribune Tower on the morning of August 18, 1931. He would have settled into his desk and lit his cigars. As he shuffled through his hastily scribbled meeting notes from that day's editorial conference, his mind could have been mulling lost savings, about how animals store food in the wild, like the squirrels who are wise enough to save nuts for a dark future while they still can. Minutes or maybe hours passed, but at some point that morning an idea surfaced. "That's it!" he might have said to himself.

He began to rough out the shape of a man wearing a white fedora with a black band, dressed in a rumpled shirt under a tie and suspenders. He gave him a down-and-out look—as if he were penniless. He draped the man's suit jacket over the park bench and positioned a label on it that read, "Victim of Bank Failure." He drew the man leaning slightly forward with his elbows on his knees, smoking a pipe. A squirrel, standing upright a few inches in front of the man with his front paws gathered to his chest asks him: "But why didn't you save some money for the future, when times were good?"

To which the man replies, "I did."

JTM might have sat for a few minutes smoking the rest of his cigar. All that was left now was to give the cartoon a headline. He would have put down the cigar and reached for his pen to letter a headline at the top of the drawing: "A Wise Economist Asks a Question." A copy boy would have been summoned and the cartoon delivered to the composing room.

Each year since 1917, the Pulitzer Prize has honored the best work in US journalism, literature, and drama. In 1922, a new category was added for editorial cartoons. The award was originally created by

"A Wise Economist Asks a Question" by John T. McCutcheon, originally published August 18, 1931, and winner of the 1932 Pulitzer Prize for cartoons. From the Chicago Tribune, *July 22 ©1951* Chicago Tribune. *All rights reserved. Used by permission and protected by the Copyright Laws of the United States. The printing, copying, redistribution, or retransmission of this content without express written permission is prohibited.*

Hungarian-born and pioneering newspaper publisher Joseph Pulitzer, who willed his money to Columbia University to launch a journalism school and establish a prize named after him.[3]

As of 1931, no *Tribune* staff member had yet received the honor, but that did not bother Colonel Robert McCormick one bit. He held a very cynical and contrarian view of the awards, regarding them as a bribe and another manifestation of the snobbish New York scene:

> (McCormick) regarded the Pulitzers, he told his New York cousin, as the work of "a mutual admiration society" of cultural gatekeepers in the east. As for himself, he maintained, there were only two standards of excellence, "individual taste and public acceptance."[4]

Nevertheless, someone, it is not known who, completed the nominating papers for "Wise Economist" and submitted it to the Pulitzer Prize committee. In 1932, the administration of the Pulitzer Prize awards was divided into individual juries that focused on the specific categories. The Editorial Cartoon jury included Carl W. Ackerman, an American journalist, author and the first dean of the Columbia School of Journalism; Walter B. Pitkin, Jr., an American author, publisher, and literary agent; and Charles M. Morrison, a foreign correspondent for the *Boston Herald*.

After reviewing the cartoon submissions from around the country, the jury could not agree on a unanimous vote. It sent a preliminary report to the Pulitzer Advisory Board, which oversaw all juries. Ackerman wrote:

> Complete agreement as to any single cartoon has not developed after some correspondence and an extra long search for a compromise. We have, however, compromised somewhat by moving toward the idea of putting H.M. Talburt of the *New York World Telegram* in first place, while John T. McCutcheon of The *Chicago Tribune* would be presented as a *close* second. Please be advised that a cartoonist for the *Boston Herald* also was briefly considered, as was a cartoonist for the *Detroit News*. It is impossible to list all of the powerful pictures of the past year. Thereby, all of the nominations on hand are being considered as high quality. We will advise.[5]

And so they did in short order. The next day, the Pulitzer Prize Editorial Cartoon jury, after an additional six hours of deliberation decided in favor of the man they originally intended to present as a "close second"—John T. McCutcheon.

On May 3, 1932, Columbia University announced the winners of the prestigious prize—including the award for the Pulitzer Prize for editorial cartoon. Of JTM's award, the announcement said:

> During the last year the world has been so filled with events and person-alities arousing the highest type of social criticism that our newspaper artists have had rare opportunity. The noblest traditions of the cartoon have been singularly easy to maintain. This cartoon touches upon one of the greatest national issues.[6]

JTM received a cash award of $500.[7] An article in the *Atlanta Constitution* about a week after the announcement noted that McCutcheon earned the prize "for excellence in the field of journalistic illustrative art for his inter-pretation of a grave national condition."[8]

As time passes, it can be difficult to understand a cartoon's meaning when it is removed from the context of the era in which it was created. Yet some cartoons overcome this. "A Wise Economist Asks a Question" con-tains themes that reverberate from generation to generation. JTM's "Victim of Bank Failure" sign could easily be replaced with "Victim of Technology Bubble," "Victim of Enron," or victim of the string of too-big-to-fail bail-outs and collapses on Wall Street in the twenty-first century. The squirrel metaphor touched a chord in people facing "a grave national condition" in 1931, and it still touches us more than eighty years later.

NOTES

1 *Our American Century: Events That Shaped the Century* (Alexandria, VA: Time-Life Books, 1998), 82.

2 "Managing the Crisis. The FDIC and RTC Experience: Chapter One—Pre-FDIC," *Federal Deposit Insurance Corporation,* accessed November 21, 2013, www.fdic.gov/bank/historical.

3 Seymour Topping, with additional editing by Sig Gissler, "History of the Pulitzer Prizes," *The Pulitzer Prizes,* accessed November 26, 2013, www.pulitzer.org.

4 Richard Norton Smith, *The Colonel: The Life and Legend of Robert R. McCormick* (Boston: Houghton Mifflin Company, 1997), 343.

5   Heinz-Dietrich Fischer, *The Pulitzer Prize Archive: A History and Anthology of Award-Winning Materials in Journalism, Letters and Arts, Vol. 13: Editorial Cartoon Awards 1922–1997* (Munich: K. G. Saur Verlag, 1999), 27.

6   "Pulitzer Award is Given Cartoon by McCutcheon," *Chicago Daily Tribune* (1923–1963), May 3, 1932, ProQuest Historical Newspapers.

7   "Pulitzer Prize to 'Of Thee I Sing.' Indianapolis News Wins Public Service Award," *Daily Boston Globe* (1928–1960), May 3, 1932, ProQuest Historical Newspapers.

8   "The Pulitzer Awards," *The Atlanta Constitution* (1881–1945), May 8, 1932, ProQuest Historical Newspapers.

12

AN EQUATORIAL BAPTISM

EVELYN ALWAYS SAID ONE of the reasons she married JTM was "because I took such interesting trips." When the *Graf Zeppelin* airship began regular crossings of the South Atlantic in 1928, JTM "wanted to make the trip at once" and mentioned it to Evelyn. The idea, to his surprise, "did not strike the happy, responsive chord in my wife that I had hoped." But he kept at it:

> For a couple of years I presented the idea in various circumstances, always without noticeable success. In the spring of 1935, I approached from a different angle. Jackie was about to graduate from Milton Academy. Already he was writing home to know what was going to happen in the summer. I suggested that we should give him a trip as a reward for good scholarship. I added that it should be something interesting and unusual and thoroughly modern—like flying around South America to Rio, crossing to Germany on the *Graf Zeppelin* and sailing home on the

Normandie. Evelyn still felt there were some arguments in favor of her staying home with the two younger boys, but came to the conclusion that she would rather take active part in any disaster than read about it in the papers. In the end, I made our reservations and the initial payments, and so we were committed.[1]

As departure day grew near, they gathered their passports, letters, credentials, health and police certificates, a full set of fingerprints required by Chile, and "oh, a lot of things." McCormick, also a flying enthusiast, "suggested that I send a short daily dispatch to the *Tribune,* chronicling the course of the trip." While on layover in Chile, the flight over the "sheer wall to the eastward, almost four miles high, occupied much of our thoughts":

> When we finally made it, that hop over the Andes, through the pass below Aconcagua at 14,000 feet, was for me one of the most outstanding of my flying experiences. Dizzily we dropped and tipped and bucked, just skimming the sawtooth ridges. Our wingtips seemed almost to scrape the scarps. The gigantic peaks glistened with the pink and gold of the sunrise, then disappeared as we started the slow descent to Mendoza through a couple of miles of thick white cloud.[2]

In Rio de Janeiro, the *Tribune* arranged for JTM to broadcast a report about his trip via a radio linkup to a coast-to-coast audience in America at 10 p.m. JTM recalled, "For 15 minutes, I covered the high spots of the last three weeks, and ended with a few words about the Zeppelin." Jackie listened in an outer office, Barr, age seven, was awakened by his grandmother to listen in Lake Forest, and Shaw "heard me from an automobile on a ranch in Wyoming."

Early on Saturday, August 17, 1935, they boarded the *Graf Zeppelin* at a field called Santa Cruz located fifty miles south of Rio de Janeiro. There were twenty passengers—sixteen men and four women. They followed the coast to Recife, where at 8 p.m. they "said good-bye to South America and headed out through the darkness over the Atlantic Ocean toward the westernmost bulge of Africa, about 2,000 miles away." When they crossed the equator, a steward sprayed them with an atomizer—"an equatorial baptism with essence of tannenbaum from the Black Forest," and they each received a certificate signifying membership in the Order of Zeppelin Equator Crossers. JTM sent dispatches daily with the help of the airship's radio operator, who "accepted my dispatches collect."[3]

By Tuesday they had crossed the Atlantic Ocean and cruised off the coast of Senegal. They passed over Morocco and up to Tangier, where they crossed the Straits of Gibraltar, then along the Spanish coast and across France, where the *Graf Zeppelin* had permission to fly only within a five-mile-wide lane or "she must immediately radio an explanation to the Air Ministry in Paris." They continued on to the Rhine River and eventually could see the city of Friedrichshafen—the home port of the *Graf Zeppelin*—in southern Germany.

After landing, they met Hugo Eckener in the hangar, a sturdy old man who spoke fair English and who "showed us through the new airship still under construction." The framework of the 750-foot long airship was only half covered. It would become famous for the wrong reason a few years later:

> This was the ill-fated *Hindenburg*. When she made her first round trip, Jackie went from Harvard University to Lakehurst [New Jersey] to greet her. On her second arrival in Lakehurst, she burst into flames.[4]

The McCutcheons spent the next six days visiting city zoos in Europe—including Munich, Berlin, Hamburg, and Paris—as part of JTM's role as president of the Chicago Zoological Society.

NOTES

1   John T. McCutcheon, *Drawn From Memory* (Indianapolis and New York: Bobbs-Merrill, Inc., 1949), 426–27.
2   Ibid., 429.
3   Ibid., 430.
4   Ibid., 438.

13

HARD TO BE LOST ON A STRAIGHT ROAD

McCutcheon offered some career and life advice in the closing pages of his autobiography, *Drawn From Memory,* which was published in 1950 after his death:

> In my albums I find many cartoons about jobs and opportunity. Real success, and it need not be financial, seems to depend pretty much on the efforts of the individual, regardless of his start in life, if he knows where he wants to go and bends every effort upon that one objective. When I spoke at Jackie's graduation from Milton, I asked several successful men of my acquaintance to give me a sentence to quote. Major General W. D. Connor, at that time superintendent of West Point, sent me this one:

> "In these get-rich-quick days, when so many are seeking short cuts to their desired goals, I feel that the saying of the wise Mogul Emperor Akbar can hardly be improved upon. Said Akbar the Emperor: 'I have lived a long time, but I have yet to see a man lost on a straight road.'"[1]

JTM held to a philosophical view about his own success:

> Sometimes success thrives on adverse conditions which sharpen the wits
> as well as the appetites. Sometimes one is led to believe the lucky breaks
> are essential. That I became an editorial cartoonist seems to have been
> as fortuitous as many other things that happened to me. When, thanks
> perhaps to the friendliness engendered by the little dog, I had got a fair
> start as a cartoonist, chance turned me into a foreign correspondent.
> Since I enjoyed the work tremendously, I might easily have made this
> my permanent career. Happily it turned out that I was enabled to com-
> bine my two lines, which doubtless helped to give variety both to me
> and to my work.[2]

As he looked back, JTM found "many inconsistencies in my life, many wide
and striking divergences from the code commonly prescribed for success":

> There are instances of glaring deficiency in the manners of my child-
> hood. Take the time Emma, the hired girl, came out to the Elston barn
> to call me for dinner—"Yonnie! Yonnie! Come!" There being no answer
> she stepped up the ladder toward my lofty retreat. On the third rung a
> brick fell on her head and knocked her flat. It was rigged for especial
> protection against Injun Joe, as I recall.[3]

He wondered whether his "qualities of ability" remained evident to readers
once they learned that when he was alone in a big city and "presumably
intent on serious pursuits, I used to blow myself to a cake of Lubin's helio-
trope soap whenever I was particularly flush." Or whether he demonstrated
"economy and self-restraint" when he was older "and undoubtedly wiser"
and would purchase cigars manufactured in Manila a thousand at a time
and smoke twenty a day.

> What may be got out of this biography of a cartoonist, I am not certain.
> Since there have been few disappointments in my life to act as a spur,
> the lion's share of any credit must go to chance, to the number of lucky
> breaks that have come my way.[4]

Dubbing his adventures "quite kaslosterous," JTM felt he could "look back with a smile, and trace hereditary tendencies in my sons," (even though he was) unable to explain why they are good at algebra. "Still it is handy always to have someone around who knows what x equals."

Not to mention the "warm feeling of pleasure" he enjoyed as he followed son "Jackie through his apprenticeship at the *City Press* and on to the *Tribune*."

Almost fifty years to day after JTM sailed from New Orleans with a cargo of mules for the Spanish Army in Havana, son "Barr sailed from the same port with a cargo of horses bound for Trieste as UNRRA [United Nations Relief and Rehabilitation Administration] aid." Barr called himself the "meadow-muffin magnate" and said his job was to "dump dung through the dung bung. Since the animals were seasick, it didn't much matter at which end he worked."[5]

JTM was equally proud of his son Shaw:

When I galloped into Elston with those sizable sums for Cad Bell, I wonder whether he felt the same way I did when I caught sight of Shawie at a most undependable age, paddling down the lagoon with $15,000 worth of newsreel equipment in the canoe, "so the man wouldn't have to carry it." Much later I was glad to co-operate with him when he borrowed the lionskin from my studio floor at Ragdale and draped it over a log down the lane near the Skokie [Lagoons]. Then, with a flashlight, he took a young lady for a walk. Presumably she retreated into his arms.[6]

All of JTM's sons attended Harvard, which seemed to the Purdue alumni to be "doubtless poetic justice." Ever faithful to his alma mater, JTM recalled his own reaction attending a football game with the hated Harvard Crimson team:

I must have crowed too loud back in 1927 when for the first time our hayseed football team was invited Down East, and Harvard spelled it P-E-R-D-U-E. They learned better, though, when we licked 'em 19 to 0, even though they may continue to associate us with the French spelling.[7]

JTM never missed an opportunity to wield his humble self-confidence through gentle humor. Like when he described a time after World War II when he and Evelyn gave a party to welcome their two new daughters-in-law:

> I didn't stand in the receiving line. Instead I played invalid in my den where, to my surprise, all the guests came to greet me. I never kissed so many ladies in my life, and I was glad to note that I had not lost the knack of it.[8]

Or how he was generous to a fault when trying to accommodate the many requests for his time:

> For nearly 40 years my regular job, when I was at home, had been to draw seven cartoons a week. Prompted by pats on the shoulder from old Anno Domini which couldn't be laughed off, these were gradually reduced to six and then to three. Outside demands kept pressing, too; charity programs, speeches, favors—the usual lot. Evelyn was stern with me: "Johnnie, you didn't accept?" "Well, I told him I didn't think so, that I was under doctor's orders and—No, no, Evelino, I think it's all right. I was almost firm."[9]

At last, JTM's hectic schedule and work pace began to ease in 1944, thanks to the "generosity of both Colonel McCormick and (contributions from *Chicago Tribune* cartoonist) Carey Orr—another evidence of kindness of which I have had so much":

> It was arranged for me to do only the Sunday cartoon. I could not have wished for a more satisfactory adjustment. It left me still one of the *Tribune* family, sharing its prosperity and its vicissitudes; but since the Sunday cartoon could be drawn well in advance, I could draw it wherever I happened to be. My health, to say nothing of the state of the world, encouraging fewer and fewer trips, it came about that we spent longer and longer winters in that part of the world abaft the Tropic of Cancer.[10]

In his seventies, JTM faced the unavoidable reality of the mortality of his own existence with a perspective that combined humor, old-fashioned wisdom, and a practical view of life's realities:

Now I have reached an age when I am frequently referred to as the dean of American cartoonists.[11] This simply means that I have managed to survive the various hazards of peace and war and that my aging contemporaries have either died or found a better way to spend their time. If one can look back such a long way, it suggests that one cannot look ahead so very far. Whenever I find myself lamenting that I am getting old—or older, as I prefer to call it—I also find myself unwilling to part with a single year of those I've lived. If I were asked to sacrifice the experiences of any five or 10 of them in order to be that much sprier now, I don't believe I would be able to give them up, even to be young and handsome.[12]

He noted that "many things have happened on this trip down the years from the 1870's of the last century to the seventies into which I have moved slowly and somewhat creakingly." He summed up the historic events he witnessed firsthand:

Since I left the banks of the Wabash to seek my fortune in the city, I have been on hand for the greatest boom, the greatest depression and the greatest wars the world has ever known, and the greatest period of scientific discovery. I have been on the reception committee to greet the arrival of electric light, the telephone, the automobile, the airplane, radio, television, and now atomic fission.[13]

His view of the state of mankind was shaped by four trips around the world and a collective work of observation and commentary that included ten thousand cartoons and sketches. At a banquet in his honor in 1940, he recalled: "I have been on the reception committee to greet the arrival of the telephone, the phonograph, the movie, the talkie, the radio, the automobile and the airplane, electric light, television and the X-ray, to mention only a few. I have been on hand for the Greatest War, the Greatest Panic, the Greatest Depression and I suppose the Greatest Political Landslide . . . And now we don't know where we're headed." [14] In a 1946 editorial announcing JTM's retirement, his *Tribune* colleagues marveled that "into his lifetime he has crowded more activities than most men dream about."[15] Yet, despite his wealth of experience, he seemed to hold to the notion that the more we know, the less we understand, as he wrote in his autobiography:

> Nowadays explorations no longer seem to be in remote places. They are close at hand in the fields of science, economy and sociology. All over the world men seem to be groping for new answers to old problems. Doubtless some of the old [nautical] charts and pilots that have stood the test of time can never be improved on, but we may be in a transition between one historic epoch and another, the nature of which only the perspective of years and experience can reveal and appraise. The world and I are engaged in overlapping serial dramas, each new installment of which has always left me with a feeling of suspense and unsatisfied curiosity. Just now the plot of the world's story seems unusually tangled, but I'm hoping for a happy ending. For my own too . . .[16]

At the end of his autobiography, JTM described the final day of a visit to his beloved island getaway, perhaps offering it as a metaphor to the closing of his career and the coming curtain call for his own life:

> And so I draw to a close—perhaps my most successful drawing. The end of our annual island visit is at hand. The bags are packed. All day we have wandered about in that aimless, nostalgic fashion, looking last long looks at the views, sitting for restless moments in each hammock, dipping— some of us—at each beach. Once more we walk down the alley between the casuarinas, each of whose needles is already tipped with its bead of dew, toward the last sunset. At bedtime [the constellation] Orion will have one foot in the sea and [the constellation] Scorpio will be halfway up. Josephas lowers the flag ceremoniously. Our favorite dishes are served at supper. The candlelight sheds a special luster on the yellow flowers of the table-cloth, on the blue Syrian honey jar with its fragrance of oleander blossoms.

> Into the deepening dusk along the porch comes the wait staff to join in the well-loved songs:

"My boss, you goin' to leave us, God Almighty goin' to bless you.

I hope you res' wid Jesus, For you is goin' home.

Shake you' han' in de good-by, God Almighty goin' to bless you.

Shake yo' han' in de good-by, For you is goin' home."

We always allow ourselves to think with gratitude and humility that there are worse places than a tropical island in which to try to forget, if only for a little while, the grim realities of depression days or world war clouds.

Tomorrow from the Pan American Clipper, I will watch the island fade, first its lizard length, then its crown of palms and last the tip of the watch tower gleaming in the afternoon sun. Over the rim of the world each will sink, to become a mirage that beckons us through another year. With real appreciation, I fall back on another old favorite hymn:

"Spare me one more year, O Lord.

Spare my one more year, O Lord.

Take me to Havana, feed me a banana.

Spare me one more year, O Lord!"[17]

NOTES

1   John T. McCutcheon, *Drawn From Memory* (Indianapolis and New York: Bobbs-Merrill, Inc., 1949), 453.

2   Ibid.

3   Ibid., 454.

4   Ibid.

5   Ibid., 455.

6   Ibid.

7   Ibid.

8   Ibid.

9   Ibid., 455–56.

10 Ibid., 456.

11 For one of the earliest examples of the use of this title, see the editorial, "A Sermon in Ridicule," *San Diego Union*, December 2, 1930, ProQuest Historical Newspapers.

12 McCutcheon, *Drawn From Memory*, 456.

13 Ibid., 457.

14 Tom Morrow, "J.T. McCutcheon Draws a Steady Job at *Tribune*: Thinks He'll Stay—After Forty Years," *Chicago Daily Tribune* (1923–1963), July 1, 1943, ProQuest Historical Newspapers.

15 "J.T. McCutcheon Lays Pen Aside for Retirement," *Chicago Daily Tribune* (1923–1963), April 28, 1946, ProQuest Historical Newspapers.

16 McCutcheon, *Drawn From Memory*, 457.

17 Ibid., 457–59.

Postscript: A City Mourns the Passing of Its Cartoonist

IN THE MID-1940s as he neared the end of his long and distinguished career, JTM's health gradually declined. He began to reduce his workload, drawing fewer and fewer cartoons as time went on. In a newspaper article published in 1961, colleague Carey Orr recalled the final phase of JTM's career for *Tribune* reporter Charles Collins:

> He was failing rapidly but he continued to deliver three cartoons a week. Colonel McCormick suggested he might decrease his output to one a week, but McCutcheon declined thinking it would diminish his salary. Then Orr wrote him a letter stating that the Colonel had said the new arrangement would not affect his salary and that he strongly advised him to accept. McCutcheon answered, "Dear Carey: Your prescription has been received and swallowed. I am feeling much better."[1]

Non-newspaper obligations also suffered due to his poor health. JTM was forced to step down as president of the Chicago Zoological Society in November 1948 after serving as the organization's president for twenty-seven years.[2] JTM continued to produce a front page cartoon for the *Sunday Tribune* until early 1946. But at age seventy-five, he was forced to put down his pen for good and retired from active duty at the *Tribune* in April 1946.

John Tinney McCutcheon, age seventy-nine, died in his sleep at 1:30 a.m.[3] on June 10, 1949, in his home in Lake Forest, a northern suburb of Chicago. He suffered from a number of ailments, but the immediate cause of death was listed as heart failure.[4] With him in his last hours were his wife, Evelyn, and their three sons, John T. Jr., Shaw, and George Barr McCutcheon.[5]

The *Tribune* eulogized his death on June 11:

> It's a great pity that men like John McCutcheon can't go on living and working forever, for the world never has had enough of them. John could not have been the cartoonist he was if he had not been a skillful and ready draftsman, the master of three or four matured styles. But this was only the beginning of his art. His special excellence lay in a combination of a highly developed sense of irony, a delight in the ridiculous, a small boy's curiosity, a big boy's delight in excitement and adventure, and an all-pervading warmth of personality. Our distress at his going is tempered by the knowledge that he lived a full and happy life, a life spent in the sunshine.[6]

In a 1975 retrospective looking back at two centuries of famous cartoonists, *New York Times* reporter John Russell noted that McCutcheon saw the cartoon as "a sort of pictorial breakfast food" that "has the cardinal asset of making the beginning of the day sunnier."[7] In their eulogy, *Tribune* editorial writers were even more direct: "He made the sunshine," they wrote.

Funeral services were held for JTM at 2 p.m. on Monday, June 13, at the Fourth Presbyterian Church (where they were married) at Michigan Avenue and Delaware Place in downtown Chicago. More than 1,200 people attended, including a who's-who of dignitaries that included Chicago Mayor Martin H. Kennelly, Colonel McCormick, and Arthur Sears Henning, emeritus chief of the *Tribune's* Washington Bureau.[8]

*A copy of McCutcheon's Certificate of Death obtained in December 2013
from the Lake County Clerk's Office, Waukegan, Illinois.*

Reverend Harrison Anderson presided over the service and read Bible passages from the 23rd Psalm and St. Paul's First Epistle to the Corinthians. Music filled the church in JTM's honor and according to the *New York Times*, he would have been pleased with the selections:

The McCutcheon gravestone with the inscriptions "John T. 1870–1949" and "Evelyn Shaw 1894–1977" in Graceland Cemetery, 4001 N. Clark St., Chicago. Photo by Tony Garel-Frantzen.

The Metropolitan Male Quartet sang Mr. McCutcheon's favorite Bahamian spirituals, including "When the Saints Go Marching Home," "Old Time Religion," "Down on Your Bendings" and "Shake Your head in the Good-Bye."[9]

Following the funeral services, family members attended a private service at Graceland Cemetery on north Clark Street in Chicago.

The genuine affection that readers held for JTM after welcoming him to their breakfast table each morning for decades came down to four simple words, according to his colleague Orr: "This man understands me," which to Orr was obvious throughout JTM's work:

McCutcheon's cartoon of the boy away from home at Christmas Time solaced many a homesick lad. The heart of the soldier who didn't get a letter was consoled by McCutcheon's cartoon. The nation, the whole nation, understands and loves "Injun Summer." It can be said there was more than art in McCutcheon's work; more than pen lines, composition, technique, and action to his cartoons, for in his work there breathed the spirit of kindliness and friendliness . . . it was the spirit of John T. McCutcheon.[10]

Those who knew him best recognized that spirit early on. Forty-six years earlier, a 141-word op-ed page announcement trumpeted the news that the *Tribune* had "secured the services of John T. McCutcheon as its regular cartoonist." In searching for the best written "appreciation" of JTM's talent, the *Tribune* turned to JTM's good friend, George Ade, whose words proved prescient:

> Those who have studied and admired Mr. McCutcheon's cartoons in the daily press doubtless have been favorably impressed by the two eminent characteristics of his intent. First, he cartoons public men without grossly insulting them. Second, he recognizes the large and important fact that politics does not fill the entire horizon of the American people. In (his) cartoons we admire the clever execution and the gentle humor which diffuse all of his work, but I dare say that more than all we admire him for his considerate treatment of public men and his blessed wisdom in getting away from the hackneyed political subjects and giving us a few pictures of that everyday life which is our real interest.[11]

Notes

1   Charles Collins, "Life in the Cartoonists' World," *Chicago Daily Tribune* (1923–1963), July 30, 1961, ProQuest Historical Newspapers.

2   "John Tinney McCutcheon. No Cartoon Character," *Chicago Zoological Society,* accessed November 29, 2013, www.brookfield zoo.org.

3   "McCutcheon Rites Will Be Held Monday," *Chicago Daily Tribune* (1923–1963), June 11, 1949, ProQuest Historical Newspapers.

4   State of Illinois Department of Public Health Division of Vital Statistics and Records, *Certificate of Death, John Tinney McCutcheon,* 1272 N. Green Bay Road, Lake Forest, IL., June 10, 1949.

5   "John McCutcheon, Noted Cartoonist," *New York Times* (1851–2010), June 11, 1949, ProQuest Historical Newspapers.

6   "John T. McCutcheon," *Chicago Daily Tribune* (1923–1963), June 11, 1949, ProQuest Historical Newspapers.

7   John Russell, "2 Centuries of Cartoonists' Thrusts Hit Home Again," *New York Times* (1923–Current File), December 3, 1975, ProQuest Historical Newspapers.

8   "1,200 At Chicago Rites for J.T. McCutcheon," *New York Times* (1923–Current File), June 14, 1949, ProQuest Historical Newspapers.

9   Ibid.

10 "John T. McCutcheon," *Chicago Daily Tribune* (1923–1963).

11 "McCutcheon Joins the *Tribune*," *Chicago Daily Tribune* (1872–1922), June 7, 1903, ProQuest Historical Newspapers.

Index